EDUCATION, EQUITY, AND THE STATES

WITHDRAWN

THE EDUCATIONAL INNOVATIONS SERIES

The Educational Innovations series explores a wide range of current school reform efforts. Individual volumes examine entrepreneurial efforts and unorthodox approaches, highlighting reforms that have met with success and strategies that have attracted widespread attention. The series aims to disrupt the status quo and inject new ideas into contemporary education debates.

Series edited by Frederick M. Hess

OTHER BOOKS IN THIS SERIES

EDUCATION, EQUITY, AND THE STATES

How Variations in State Governance Make or Break Reform

SARA E. DAHILL-BROWN

Harvard Education Press
Cambridge, Massachusetts

34

KH

Paperback ISBN 978-1-68253-272-0
Library Edition ISBN 978-1-68253-273-7

Library of Congress Cataloging-in-Publication Data

Names: Dahill-Brown, Sara E., author.
Title: Education, equity, and the states : how variations in state governance
   make or break reform / Sara E. Dahill-Brown.
Other titles: Educational innovations.
Description: Cambridge, Massachusetts : Harvard Education Press, [2019] |
   Series: The educational innovations series | Includes bibliographical
   references and index.
Identifiers: LCCN 2018049682| ISBN 9781682532720 (pbk.) | ISBN 9781682532737
   (library edition)
Subjects: LCSH: Education and state--United States. | Educational
   change--United States. | Education--Political aspects--United States. |
   Public schools--United States.
Classification: LCC LC89 .D35 2019 | DDC 379.73--dc23 LC record available
   at https://lccn.loc.gov/2018049682

Published by Harvard Education Press,
an imprint of the Harvard Education Publishing Group

Harvard Education Press
8 Story Street
Cambridge, MA 02138

Cover Design: Ciano Design
The typefaces used in this book are Minion Pro and Myriad Pro

10/3/19

Contents

In all likelihood, their efforts and resources would have ensured a positive experience regardless of the state where I attended school.

However, I also now see the distinctive and unmistakable imprint of my home state's particular challenges, politics, educational culture, and approach to K–12 governance. Too often in the last two decades of education reform, the singularity of these state-level educational ecosystems—in which history, culture, resources, and politics combine to shape a child's opportunities—has been little acknowledged.

As it turns out, for children in families with few economic resources or social advantages, these between-state differences are especially consequential. Failing to adequately attend to this reality is a significant factor presently undermining reform efforts. It has hindered the implementation of promising policies and invited political backlash from those who feel ignored, ultimately fostering a counterproductive volatility. Perhaps most of all, it has perpetuated a mismatch between policy solutions and the problems they seek to tackle. The structural underpinnings of educational inequality vary systematically, from state to state, and so policy responses must as well.

In this book, I aim to draw the attention of scholars, reformers, educators, parents, and college students back to state-level education governance, identify key aspects of state school systems, and set forth recommendations for how to approach reform with state context in mind. Though local school governance has been a more consistent area of focus for those who study educational policy and politics and will be a subject of much discussion in this book, local decision-making and inequalities are shaped heavily by state-level factors. Likewise, a federal government increasingly engaged with educational policy has—rightly—commanded the attention of many scholars and the public at large, but these analyses regularly sidestep the fact that states have tremendous power to dampen or amplify the impact of federal efforts. My own K–12 education offers a glimpse of the pervasive influence of state context.

SCHOOLING IN UTAH

Each morning as a young child I plodded, skipped, or pedaled to Canyon View Elementary, a traditional, neighborhood public school several blocks from my home. My classmates and I waited for the bell that signaled the start of the school day, at which point we would be ushered through a coatroom and into classrooms full of forty or so eager students. Utah was then and remains today the state with the largest proportion of its population below the age of eighteen (31 percent in 2013). As such, it has long been loath to place restrictions on class size. Large classes were the norm for me all the way through high school, and they continue to be a major challenge for public schools all over the state. In the fall of 2013, Utah persisted as the state with the largest overall ratio of students to teachers.[1] That same year, it was also the state claiming the dubious honor of spending the least per student, just as it had been in the fall of 1989 when I was in second grade ($6,546 and $2,577, respectively).[2]

Nearly all of the students at Canyon View shared my pale skin, another factor that remains largely consistent today. In 2010, the US Census estimated that just below 90 percent of the states' residents identified as white, a proportion out of sync with the national average. Given this relatively homogeneous student population, low levels of child poverty, and a dense network of social supports undergirded by the Church of Latter Day Saints, Utah's public school students have tended to perform relatively well on nationally normed assessments in spite of the large class sizes and low spending. Little in the way of sustained pressure has mounted to alter this state of affairs. Despite its low per-pupil spending, Utah is one of a handful of states that has not faced a major lawsuit regarding whether or not its school finance system provides adequate or equitable resources under the state's constitution.

Notably, a recent analysis suggests that Utah students' academic achievement, given the demographic and socioeconomic composition of its student body, is considerably less impressive than raw test scores would suggest. When these factors are accounted for and Utah students are compared to demographically similar students across the fifty states, the state's rank falls from twenty-fourth to forty-seventh.[3]

As a student, I had little frame of reference for class size or per-pupil spending, but my teachers, many of whom I saw often outside of school, felt quite strongly about these circumstances. As I got older, more than one let slip their frustration. The teacher union in the state organized a walkout in 1989, protesting large class sizes, low pay, and the Republican legislatures' staunch preference for tax cuts over increased funding for the state's public schools.[4] The Republican Party has held sizeable majorities in both houses of the Utah legislature since 1978 as well as the governorship since 1985. Teacher unions are weak organizations in comparison both to the party and to their counterparts in other states. While the union is not without influence, its legislative victories have often been limited.[5]

At Canyon View Elementary in the late 1980s and early 1990s, the teachers and their students were separated from other classrooms only by rolling barriers decorated in brightly colored butcher paper. The tallest students could see over the top of our classroom "walls," while the rest of us peeked through the gaps between each barrier. I confess that my mind sometimes meandered into other lessons. Schools in Utah, far from major hubs of educational research and innovation, tended to be slow adopting new reforms and had hopped onto the open-concept bandwagon just as other states and districts were abandoning it.[6] While some states are regularly cited as pioneers in education, Utah has more often lagged behind, either waiting to learn from innovators or resistant to their innovations.[7] Since there was little money in the budget to remake a building that was otherwise in good condition, and since bulging class sizes made movable walls functionally appealing, the school continued the experiment well into the 2000s.

The social conservatism that predisposed political leaders to regard new proposals with some skepticism also manifested in other ways. As an elementary school student, I began to notice that girls who raised their hands too often had fewer playmates during recess, and over time, I became deliberately quiet, sitting on my hands to prevent myself from speaking up too often. It seemed, too, that teachers more often chose boys to answer questions in math class and preferred them for demonstrations during our science hour, rare events in our cash-strapped school—I vividly recall my third-grade classmates crowding around two students as they dissected a single cow eye.

So, though I had tested in the ninety-eighth percentile for math as a fifth grader, on a different sort of exam that year I ranked my math abilities as "fair," the option right below "average," rather than marking the choices for "above average" or "excellent."[8] This self-assessment made its way into my permanent file, and when the time came, middle school administrators refused to place me in advanced math courses, explaining that my lack of self-confidence indicated that I should avoid algebra for at least another year. My mother, a former New Jersey educator, met with guidance counselors in protest, but to no avail. She argued that their reliance on a self-assessment was gender-biased and reflected disproven ideas about placement, but it wasn't until my father visited the school and made the same argument that they relented.

Educational economists have demonstrated that the state of Utah boasts some of the largest, gendered achievement gaps among the fifty states, favoring boys over girls in math and science, and conversely girls over boys in reading. They link this to particularly strong, traditional gender norms and show that weaker gender norms in other states are linked to greater gender parity in achievement.[9] Slowness to adopt new pedagogical innovations, too-full classrooms, and a cultural adherence to traditional gender norms very nearly conspired to keep me from enrolling in algebra on time, which would have left me in a far less favorable position when I began applying to college some five years later.

In retrospect, my experience is particularly illustrative of the way that social and economic inequalities can interact with the informal norms and cultural practices that subtly shape state governance regimes. While I was exposed to and internalized traditional gender norms around math, and while school counselors operating within that context employed biased exams as a way of allocating scarce spaces in an algebra class, my well-resourced and persistent parents were able to intervene when these elements of the educational system in Utah threatened my opportunity to learn.

In high school, the state of Utah's requirements for graduation sought to balance high expectations with an explicit commitment to local autonomy, leaving plenty of space in my transcript for engaging electives and allowing my teachers considerable freedom to innovate.[10] I took the standard slate of AP courses available to ambitious students (albeit with textbooks that were sometimes a decade old, less a problem for calculus than for biology), but also classes on world religions and "American Problems"—classes that had been proposed and designed locally by passionate, accomplished, experienced teachers. In the latter, teachers guided us through a series of performances and simulations designed to provide experiential learning opportunities. We visited nearby elementary schools, acting out the assembly meetings of ancient Athens and discussing the origins of democratic government with younger students; played a Risk-like game of global politics; and spent ten days simulating life under a fascist totalitarian regime.

At the same time, the state's halfhearted approach to funding schools created some challenges when I began planning for college. When I arrived at my counselor's office for the allotted fifteen minutes of college counseling in the fall of my senior year of high school, she scanned my transcript, determined that I was college-bound, and quietly ruled out Salt Lake Community College and Ricks College (at the time a two-year institution, now a four-year institution known as BYU-Idaho). She asked me whether I planned to attend Brigham Young University (BYU) or the University of Utah, the choices she

system of K–12 education governance—the institutions it comprises, the constituents who influence it, and the politics and policies they produce—come together to shape the opportunities that students, teachers, and parents encounter in K–12 schools, as well as the challenges and problems they must confront on a daily basis. Importantly, if the problems facing schools, the mechanisms by which those problems were created, and the institutional context in which those problems are embedded differ from state to state, it should follow that the solutions most likely to change opportunities for students will also need to be different.

Yet federal policy makers and education reformers have tended to underestimate or gloss over the differences between states' school systems and their approaches to governance, failing to consider historical patterns, disregarding the role of state variation in mediating the impact of a policy proposal, or actively seeking to promote policy congruence across the states. Joanne Weiss, who was responsible for administering the $4 billion Race to the Top grant competition, has written that the US Department of Education (ED) sought to promote "comprehensive and coherent" reforms. ED was intent on urging the states toward tightly coupled systems that were coherent not only internally, but also from a policy standpoint from state to state.[18] Many observers now casually refer to these efforts as the "one-size-fits-all" model of school reform.[19] All the while, state contexts make or break federal policy and programs and have an independent, dramatic impact on children in schools.

Further, state governance and policy regimes are increasingly distinct and determinant in arenas beyond educational policy. This is especially true of the social and antipoverty policies that affect children and families outside of schools and interact with schools to shape intergenerational social mobility. Research published in 2015 by the Stanford Center on Poverty and Inequality described considerable between-state variation in poverty, life expectancy, and health outcomes, emphasizing that a portion of these differences could be attributed to state-level policies.[20]

As with those trying to make and change policy, many researchers and analysts have too rarely focused on differences in states' education governance. Instead, in recent decades, more attention has been paid to the increasing activism of the federal government, and to broad trends in state governance: the convergence of policy agendas, particularly with regard to standards-based reforms and accountability; the general increase in state policy activity; and the growing integration of educational politics with general partisan politics, exemplified by governors and mayors who are more active and vocal on educational issues than they have been in the past.

The shortcomings of the last decade and the passage of the Every Student Succeeds Act (ESSA) in December 2015 require a shift for policy makers and reformers as well as for analysts and scholars. Though ESSA maintains a focus on standards and accountability, it also returns power and autonomy over many aspects of education policy to the states. It closes the door on No Child Left Behind (NCLB), Race to the Top (RTTT), and ED waivers. In doing so, it creates an opportunity to check assumptions about what works, to design programs and enact policies that more directly engage with the structure of inequality in each state's system.

Even as federal efforts to make over school systems in the United States have garnered headlines, states have become stronger political entities.[21] In the coming years, education reformers and policy makers will recenter their advocacy efforts on state-level policy change. State differences, always important even when they have been unacknowledged, will become even more determinant. Under ESSA state leaders now have greater freedom to design programs and policies that tackle the opportunity gaps most salient for their students.

If this new era of reform is to translate into real benefits for children in schools, policy makers and reformers must move beyond the one-size-fits-all approach to education policy, an approach that has raised the profile of schools on public agendas but simultaneously created many problems over the last two decades, leaving largely intact the achievement gaps it sought to close. If scholars, reformers, teachers, and a growing community of concerned students, parents, citizens, and pundits hope to understand, evaluate, and anticipate policy change, they will need to become more familiar with the dynamics of state-level education governance and politics. This book is my attempt to help make sense of an educational system that is often daunting in its complexity.

The first step toward navigating the American educational system requires recognizing that we are not confronting a single system but rather fifty state systems, each a product of a unique centuries-long historical process. Though an entire volume could be devoted to each one (and in some cases has been), this book focuses on three key dimensions along which state systems differ from one another: *fragmentation*, the extent to which they are institutionally broken up into many local school districts or consolidated into a smaller number of jurisdictions; *exceptionalism*, the degree to which educational policy processes and constituents are integrated into the state's political system or sequestered from it; and *local control*, the extent to which policies are committed to school and district autonomy and flexibility versus exercising state authority. These characteristics of state governance combine to influence every stage of the policy process, from agenda setting to implementation, and in so doing reshape socioeconomic and racial inequalities.

I investigate how states currently differ from one another, and how they have differed in the past. I also examine how these differences relate, and suggest that reformers and policy makers deliberately consider these aspects of state governance as one part of ensuring that schools around the country are able to make sustained improvements, rather than endure constant reforms. Governance is not just about government—it refers to something larger, a regime that is cocreated by governmental institutions in concert with stakeholders and citizens, and it can evolve not just through institutional reforms, but also through different strategic choices made by individuals and organizations about how to conduct their advocacy.

Though this book is critical of recent reform efforts, it is not an argument against policy change or against states learning from and adopting one another's policy innovations, nor is it an argument against a federal posture that pressures states to consider equity and remains vigilant to discrimination; on the contrary, such pressure is vital. This book is instead an exploration of how states differ from one another in the way they govern and administer their schools and how those differences impact policy processes and outcomes. Given that the states possess the greatest capacity and legitimacy to determine educational policy, such a study is needed. I do argue that accounting more carefully for those differences would yield more sustainable, effective reforms.

Next, I explain briefly why states have so often been afterthoughts for reformers and federal policy makers, and how this inattention fosters policy churn and ultimately interferes with sustainably improving schools. I then describe the backlash against one-size-fits-all reform efforts and assertive federal education policy, after which I preview the chapters of the book.

WHY STATES HAVE BECOME AFTERTHOUGHTS

The recent tendency among policy makers and reformers to overlook state governance, policy, and culture is part of a shift toward nationalized partisan politics that has impacted many policy arenas. But it is also grounded in a set of more specific rationales. Education reformers throughout the history of public schools in the US have had grand ambitions to improve the moral fiber and academic opportunities of as many children as possible. Often they have combined this ambition with a strong commitment to a specific, narrow set of reforms. High hopes, clarity of vision, and a desire to help vulnerable children naturally foster a palpable sense of urgency and frustration when confronted with incremental policy change—the little-by-little reforms that dominate America's sclerotic-by-design system of governance.[22]

Grand Ambitions and a Specific Reform Agenda

Given this combination of ambitions (to reach all children) and beliefs (that there is a best way through which to accomplish that end), reformers have often eschewed labor-intensive strategies that promise diverse reforms and a more uneven pace of change. Rather than navigating and coalition-building across fifty different political environments or thousands of local communities, to collaboratively identify a slate of reforms that best suit the needs of the students in each state, they have attempted to consolidate administrative units or to target a higher level of government whenever possible. They have focused on promoting a specific set of top-down reforms.[23] The reformers who have come to dominate in the twenty-first century, concerned about achievement gaps, committed to standards and accountability, and armed with technologies that speed communication, fit neatly into this historical pattern.

Even conservative policy makers and reformers, who have tended to oppose muscular federal policy and have steadfastly argued for state autonomy in other policy arenas, have often suspended their usual wariness of central authority and thrown their support behind federal initiatives that promise to advance standards-based reform, accountability, and school choice. The primary example of this is NCLB. Even efforts directed at state-level policy change have centered on advocating for a particular school choice or accountability policy, rather than on evaluating the assets and challenges of a state's school system and working to rally local and state stakeholders to develop proposals that would address the direst needs of that state's students and families or challenge that state's most dysfunctional institutions.

For example, the national education reform organizations 50CAN and StudentsFirst (now partners) have created state chapters across the country. While the groups' timing has clearly been strategic in terms of choosing states where legislatures may be particularly open to their agendas, the policy goals for each state's chapter are remarkably similar to one another. Both the National Alliance for Public Charter Schools and the pro–charter school Center for Education Reform have annually produced reports that rank states' charter school laws on a variety of dimensions and promote the adoption of a specific version of charter school legislation. Similarly, the American Legislative Exchange Council has drafted and disseminated model legislation for charter school laws, K–12 education tax credits, teacher evaluation, and parent trigger laws, among others. Michael Mintrom describes a similar phenomenon in his 2000 study of the spread of school choice across the states. Policy entrepreneurs, committed to the idea of school choice, worked to advance it—without evidence that it necessarily benefited students or was needed in the state.[24]

Distrust of State Governments on Matters of Equity

Beyond the smaller scale and more uneven pace that come with a more state-centered, differentiated approach to education reform, there is an additional set of reasons why reformers, on the political left in particular, might view such a strategy with skepticism. Liberal, progressive education policy makers and reformers of the last two decades have endorsed high academic standards and accountability as mechanisms for improving academic achievement and measuring inequality. However, ensuring equal opportunity for the nation's poor and nonwhite children has been what, at least ostensibly, drives them. That goal of equity has remained essential, even when the policies put forward are focused on standards and accountability, which take less direct aim at inequality than the more traditional civil rights campaigns like desegregation and funding. These reformers talk and write often about closing achievement gaps between privileged and less privileged groups of students, and they have often spoken of educational inequality as "the civil rights issue of our time."[25]

For progressive reformers in particular, the federal government's track record on issues of equity, especially regarding race and ethnicity, is much stronger than that of the states. In fact, the phrase "states' rights" provokes a visceral response among many students of American history. They simply do not trust states to fulfill their obligations to all children equally.[26] The tendency for advocates on the left to focus strategic efforts on federal policy is evident beyond the scope of educational policy and has translated into extraordinary Democratic losses in state legislatures over the last decade.

Distrust of state governments on matters of equity is also apparent in the design of educational policies. NCLB, for example, afforded states very little flexibility around reporting requirements and school accountability for economic and race-based achievement gaps. Under the law, schools had to report achievement based on race, ethnicity, and economic status, and states were legally required to intervene with sanctions if any group fell below the targeted proficiency rates. This is not to say that states universally pursued equity as an aim, but the law's provisions were more specific on this point compared to others.

Arguments in favor of states' rights—that is, of limiting federal authority and locating power at the state level—were deployed in defense of slavery, to resist the US Supreme Court's *Brown v. Board* ruling of 1954, and to protest the Civil Rights Act of 1965. Since the 1960s, campaign promises to uphold states' rights have regularly been used as coded appeals by candidates who on the one hand found the political climate hostile to open expressions of racial animus, but on the other hand wanted to signal solidarity with voters who still held such resentments. These voters were strongly opposed to federal policy interventions.[27]

The phrase and the strategy are therefore associated with violent suppression of black Americans and political resistance to granting them full equality under the law. Today, the phrase connotes a cynical willingness to leverage that legacy—to stoke racial animus among voters—if it might help to secure an electoral victory. When recommended as a strategy for change or referenced in critique of federal policy, the concept of states' rights is reasonably met with skepticism by those who are committed to racial equality.

If reformers' frustration with a slow pace of change is understandable, their wariness is also justified. Recent state policies on voting rights suggest that there remains in many state capitols, at a minimum, a willingness to disenfranchise black voters if it will secure a partisan victory. Multiple studies have also demonstrated a link between punitive state approaches to welfare reform and stronger attitudes of racial resentment.[28] Further, women, racial minorities, and ethnic minorities remain underrepresented in state legislatures.[29]

THE TROUBLE WITH IGNORING STATE DIFFERENCES

There are also perverse consequences associated with top-down federal mandates as a core strategy for promoting educational reform, however.

This is in part because policy-making does not end with the passing of a law. Once a policy has been enacted, it must be implemented—tests designed, standards written, textbooks edited, teachers trained, websites built—and there are myriad ways in which the implementation of a policy can depart from the ideal envisioned by lawmakers in Washington, DC. In education policy, federal programs and mandates are typically implemented by state and local actors who may differ both in the extent to which they believe in the reform (i.e., willingness) and in their ability to fully comply (i.e., capacity). Hence, a policy takes hold and appears effective in one state but ineffective in another.

Variable Implementation

This uneven implementation process was on display after NCLB was signed into law in 2002. On its face, the requirement that states adopt standards and administer reading and math tests to students in grades 3–8 seemed straightforward. Yet, in practice, implementation varied greatly; some states developed detailed standards, while others generated learning goals and objectives that were so broad as to be vague. Similarly, some states set the threshold for proficiency quite low, while others set it much higher.[30] States that had already implemented standards, testing, and accountability measures had more to build on than those that abstained from the reform wave of the 1990s.[31]

Even administrative decisions as seemingly unimportant as timing of the tests could alter the impact of the policy in a big way. If a state complied with NCLB by administering assessments in the fall of the school year versus the spring, it could substantially reduce the tests' impact on instruction. This particular adaptation may not have been a bad thing, given the extent to which NCLB's testing requirements more generally caused schools to narrow the scope of their instruction.[32]

Variable implementation is unavoidable in federal education policy. The federal government does not operate public schools, lacks constitutional authority over them, and provides only 10 percent of the funds that support public K–12 education.[33] Therefore, it must design policies and programs in ways that preserve flexibility for state and local leaders. Sometimes this flexibility allows state and local policy makers to adapt a program so that it better fits their local needs while maintaining fidelity to the core aims of its designers. Sometimes partial fidelity to implementation is anticipated by policy makers and accepted. Other times, this flexibility simply affords state and local policy makers adequate opportunity to subvert the intention of the law. In the latter case, precious resources—money, time, and creativity—are often spent on compliance rather than invested in something that might have a more direct, beneficial impact on students.[34] For its part, NCLB appears to have had no significant or substantial overall effect on race-based achievement gaps in the United States, though there are differentiated effects on achievement gaps across the states.[35]

Political Backlash

Even when reformers leverage their political clout to lobby for adoption of a program by state-level leadership, failure to adapt the policy to state contexts or efforts to bypass regular political channels in search of a quick victory can generate political resistance later in the policy process. This was the case with the Common Core State Standards (CCSS), in which reformers partnered with interstate organizations, chiefly the Council of Chief State School Officers (CCSSO); philanthropists, including the Bill & Melinda Gates Foundation; and ED. Together, they convinced and coerced legislatures and state boards of education to quickly adopt the common standards.[36] However, the often closed processes by which the standards were adopted in many states served to delegitimize them in the eyes of educators and parents. Difficulties, inconsistencies, and lack of resources to support implementation efforts further exacerbated public antipathy to the new standards and to the process by which they had been adopted, and many legislatures began to consider repealing them.[37]

In a number of states, legislators took their response a step further to redesign the institutional process by which content standards were adopted.[38] The standards themselves may be a sound foundation upon which to build a curriculum and design assessments, but their academic value is almost beside the point, given how they have been enacted, implemented thus far, and received by the increasingly politicized public. In 2015, 35 percent of the public and 50 percent of teachers expressed antipathy toward Common Core.[39]

Policy Mismatch

At the root of both the disappointing implementation of and the political resistance to reform efforts is often a mismatch between a new policy and the needs and capacities of the public schools in a particular state. The RTTT program of 2010, for example, demanded significant and specific policy commitments from states—raising academic standards, collecting better data on students, and using data to evaluate teachers and principals, among others—in exchange for federal funds. Signaling this mismatch, many states opted out of the RTTT process, including California and Texas, two of the largest states in terms of population and both states that serve a large percentage of the nation's Hispanic and Latino children. Because of the way the US population is distributed, undifferentiated reform efforts risk repeating this kind of exclusion.

Many of RTTT's policies may work well, under the right circumstances, given adequate time and resources. However, few states had in place the necessary infrastructure to leverage the full potential of these ideas. Ultimately, there was a great deal of legislative reform in response to RTTT, and grand promises were made, but the results of the $4 billion program—in terms of improved outcomes for students—were on the whole disappointing.[40]

In spite of resistance to RTTT, the policies it incentivized states to adopt were effectively mandated when Congress failed to reauthorize NCLB, and states found themselves having to apply for waivers to avoid the law's most stringent accountability requirements. By November 2015, forty-five states had applied for flexibility waivers, and forty-three states' plans had been approved.[41]

Volatility and Churn

All of these factors have translated into a kind of policy churn that presents real challenges for school leaders, educators, parents, and students. Too much reform can be as much of a problem as not enough.[42] In the last fifteen years, escalating federal and reform efforts have created an environment in which the critical tasks of school leaders and teachers—regarding what students are supposed to learn, how their learning should be assessed, how content should be taught, and how states will monitor educators and hold them accountable for those learning outcomes—are constantly being redefined and are frequently in conflict as a result.[43] The same policy turbulence that primarily affected urban districts in the 1990s is now an endemic problem.

The byproducts of a volatile policy environment have been well documented.[44] Teachers must learn and implement a new program every few years, rather than being allowed the opportunity to advance their expertise, and with each passing reform they find themselves increasingly skeptical of the next.[45] Good policies and programs are not granted the time they need to take effect. Programs that are beneficial to a specific group of students can be abandoned because they do not have broader impacts. New policies and programs crowd out other tasks.[46]

RESISTING REFORM

So policies have shifted dramatically and often, leaving district leaders, principals, teachers, parents, and even education researchers scrambling to keep up. It is no wonder that many of the people most closely engaged with schools are struggling to reconcile feelings of whiplash with a nagging sense of déjà vu as mandates change yet again. The widespread frustration over too-frequent reform has provoked a palpable shift in the political environment—both greater skepticism toward reform in general and a targeted effort to rein in the federal government.

These responses go beyond simple disavowal of the Common Core. When state legislatures in Indiana and Oklahoma reconsidered those standards, they also reconsidered other assessment and teacher evaluation policies in the process. Large majorities of parents now say there is too much emphasis on standardized testing in public schools.[47] And, according to *Education Next*'s 2014 and 2015 polls, the percent of those in favor of charter schools, tax credits for private school tuition, school vouchers, merit pay for teachers, and ending teacher tenure protections—all high-profile elements of the reform agenda—decreased across the board.[48]

Narratives of failed reform efforts seem to be ubiquitous, cautioning that there are no silver bullets when it comes to improving schools. In the aptly titled *So Much Reform, So Little Change*, Charles Payne argues that thirty years of reform efforts by both liberals and conservatives have failed to produce meaningful change in Chicago's schools, largely because they have little bearing on the daily challenges that educators and school leaders confront.[49] Sarah Reckhow writes about the pitfalls of philanthropic engagement with policy reform when it bypasses local stakeholders.[50] Dale Russakoff describes the failed efforts of Facebook CEO Mark Zuckerberg and then-Mayor Cory Booker to rehabilitate the Newark City Public Schools.[51] And, in *The Allure of Order*, Jal Mehta describes both the impulse to rationalize schools through top-down reforms and the ultimate failure of those efforts to achieve their aims.[52]

Applications to Teach for America have also fallen dramatically in recent years.[53] And the education reform movement—once a loose but surprisingly coherent alliance of Republicans and Democrats, liberals and conservatives—has begun to fracture. In May 2016, at the New Schools Venture Fund Summit in San Francisco, leading education reformers gathered to discuss the future of the movement. The opening plenary featured a conversation with a Teach for America executive who had been active in Black Lives Matter, and throughout the summit issues of racial identity and solidarity featured prominently in dialogues. Following the summit, bloggers from the Thomas B. Fordham Foundation, the Century Foundation, and the American Enterprise Institute, as well as the leader of the New York Campaign for Achievement Now, all described a growing split in the movement. Conservatives reported feeling alienated by a liberal orthodoxy that seemed to be moving beyond the singular focus of reformers on schools—the narrow agenda that had for so long facilitated collaboration across party lines. Liberal writers explained that they viewed a broader focus on antiracist and antipoverty actions as critical aspects of achieving lasting change in schools.[54]

WHEN REFORM WORKS

At the same time, prominent examples of improved academic outcomes can be found in places where reform efforts have been measured, steady and responsive to state and local governance, both in the process of pursuing policy change and in the design of policies themselves.[55]

In a 2013 letter to the *Boston Globe*, Thomas Payzant, former superintendent of the Boston Public Schools, and Elaine Weiss of the Broader, Bolder Approach to Education wrote that RTTT funds were well spent in Massachusetts, because the state's efforts at education reform had been ongoing for more than two decades and were guided throughout that period by a consistent vision. The grant funding supplemented efforts already under way and embraced by local and state leaders.[56] Their letter echoed one written by Payzant in 2005, explaining how political stability had facilitated reform and contributed to substantial academic gains in the Boston Public Schools.[57] Indeed, Massachusetts' academic gains between 1992 and 2011 rank among the highest in the nation, according to an analysis of the forty-two states that participated in the National Assessment of Education

Progress (NAEP) over the entire time period.[58] Notably, Massachusetts tops the list of states for its NAEP achievement, even when scores are adjusted to account for differences in the demographics of students across the states.[59]

Also ranked highly for its progress as measured by NAEP between 1992 and 2011 is Kentucky. In 1990, in the aftermath of a lawsuit brought against the state by superintendents of poorer school districts, the state legislature and a coalition of education and business leaders came together to support a sweeping package of reforms, the Kentucky Education Reform Act (KERA). Rewriting the state's school finance laws was a key element of KERA, but it included other provisions that altered the formal relationships between the state's commissioner and state board of education, encouraged community engagement, raised academic standards, introduced accountability testing, and allowed for grouping K–3 students by need and ability rather than simply by age.

These policies demanded massive change from school leaders, faculty, and parents, but the package of reforms was carefully negotiated; addressed a critical disparity in the state of Kentucky through a significant redistribution of resources to poorer districts; and—crucially—was backed by a coalition that remained engaged throughout the long implementation process. Since KERA's adoption, core education policies in Kentucky have largely remained true to the vision set forth in the law, even as some programs were added or amended. A recent analysis of the state's success in raising high school graduation rates named this slow, steady approach—a willingness to invest resources and allow time for reforms to take hold—as key to the state's success in improving K–12 outcomes.[60]

To be clear, measured and steady does not imply apolitical: schools are inherently political institutions, and conflict over their funding, organization, and operation is inevitable, and—arguably—healthy in a multicultural, multiethnic democracy like the US. Rather, it means that reforms are the product of negotiation, and are passed with the support of coalitions that include the educators and school leaders who will be charged with doing the work of implementation, as well as the businesses and parents who will need to encourage and monitor those efforts. As a result of this work, the goals and broad outlines of reforms stand a greater chance of being maintained and built upon rather than done, undone, and remade. The likelihood of implementation failures, political backlash, policy churn, and mismatch can be substantially lessened.

PLAN OF THE BOOK

This book offers a framework for making sense of complex but consequential systems. It is a structured inquiry into how school governance varies and how that variation matters, and as such it offers scholars of education governance and analysts a set of conceptual tools for understanding and navigating these different systems. It investigates how states differ at present and how they have differed in the past. This is also a book about how these differences have impacted policy, how they relate to one another, and how reformers and policy makers can engage with state differences in order to ensure that schools around the country are able to make sustained improvements, rather than endure constant reforms. Each of these aspects of a state's system shapes the policy process.

This framework requires assembling what we know about specific policies, actors, and institutions to consider states as systems. To accomplish that aim, I employ a mixed methodology, drawing on quantitative data collected from a variety of public sources as well as more qualitative data collected from administrative and legal records, gubernatorial public addresses, other public statements, and interviews with public officials.[61] This mix of data facilitates both big-picture and close-up analyses, allowing me to describe the aggregate characteristics and context for education governance in the United States and then to parse state differences and local dynamics.

The first three chapters examine the theoretical grounding and history of education governance in the United States. Chapter 1 presents an iconic episode of reform centered on the famed teacher unionist Albert Shanker and the passage of the first charter school law in Minnesota. This case study serves as a jumping-off point for exploring the concept of governance—what it includes and does not, and how it should be analyzed. Drawing on other writings in the field, I then present a simple schematic framework of governance and its components: government institutions, constituents and stakeholders, and the politics, processes, and practices that they coproduce. The framework highlights the larger context in which education governance is embedded and introduces terms and ideas that will recur throughout the book.

Chapter 2 explores the emergence of public school systems and describes key moments in the development of education governance in the United States through the middle of the twentieth century, with a particular focus on government institutions and how they have evolved. It introduces the core concepts explored at the state level in the second half of the book: fragmentation, exceptionalism (the inverse of integration), and commitments to local control. These have been the subjects of much writing in that they characterize American education governance in the aggregate, and distinguish it from the systems common in other countries. Chapter 3 builds on this early history by discussing more recent changes in education governance, starting with the civil rights movement and concluding with the adoption of ESSA. Though states in particular built up administrative capacity throughout this more recent history, the character of education governance was transformed most significantly by policies, practices, and an expanding circle of constituents, rather than the kinds of institutional upheavals that stand out in chapter 2. The chapter highlights concerns about equity and excellence, standards and accountability, and the shifting relationship between state and federal governments with regards to public education. Together chapters 2 and 3 comprise an investigation into historical factors that have shaped differences among the states and tensions among levels of government that persist today.

Chapters 4, 5, and 6 explore specific aspects of education governance among the states, with each chapter addressing a particular dimension and how it evolved, varies across the states, and impacts opportunities and outcomes for students. Chapter 4 focuses on institutional fragmentation. The school district is the foundational administrative unit of education governance. State school systems vary tremendously in the extent to which they are divided into these units. At one extreme, Hawaii's public school system is consolidated into a single district; at the other, more than one thousand regular local school districts were operating in Texas during the 2012–2013 school year.[62] The fragmentation or consolidation of a state's school system has important consequences for educational policy. Large numbers of districts create a coordination challenge for local school boards or superintendents who may want to influence a state's political process. They may present challenges for the state as well, in terms of providing consistent support, monitoring the implementation of programs, or rallying districts around a new initiative.

Understanding the impact of state approaches to education governance is, however, about more than discerning different patterns in policy-making and administration. Systems of governance can reinforce or create problems that lay at the root of divisive politics or inequality. Fragmented state systems can reinforce racial and economic segregation in the public school system, concentrating students who are wealthier, more educated, and white in one district and cutting them off from their poorer, black and brown neighbors. Large, urban districts can be—and often are—extraordinarily segregated. However, large numbers of small districts make it easier for families to self-segregate, and school district boundaries formalize these divisions, raising institutional barriers that keep states and localities from pursuing policies that might encourage integration or redistribution. A recent wave of school districts attempting to split from one another makes understanding these dynamics all the more pressing.

Chapter 5 continues exploring the institutional foundations of state education governance. Americans have long believed that major decisions about public schools ought to be apolitical—in other words, that partisan conflict has little place in education policy and that professional educators and administrators are best equipped to make decisions about public schools. The chapter explores the theory behind exceptional education governance, and the reality of low turnout and engagement. It describes the mechanisms at both the state and local levels that are intended to insulate educational politics from partisan politics, including off-cycle elections for local and state education leaders, nonpartisan electoral contests, and limits on fiscal authority.

While state systems have each at some point included at least one of these mechanisms, their particular configuration has always varied, with some states going further to sequester education governance than others. This chapter describes these differences at present and the relationship between local and state mechanisms that drive or prohibit exceptionalism. There is an unmistakable trend away from governing schools separately. Governors and legislatures have pursued institutional reforms that sync up educational elections with general elections, or they have attempted to eliminate these elected offices entirely in favor of appointed ones.[63] In recent decades, state legislatures have become more active, governors more vocal, and parties more proactive in endorsing nonpartisan candidates. Yet this trend has clearly not been embraced with equal fervor across the states. This means that in some states educational policy is debated in an increasingly mainstream, partisan political environment, whereas in others major policy decisions about public schools remain primarily the province of education leaders.

As with fragmentation, this chapter argues that these institutional mechanisms therefore make certain kinds of political conflict—between educational leadership and other state leaders, or between parties—more or less likely to arise.

Chapter 6 examines one of the most commonly studied aspects of education governance in the United States: local control. It illustrates how local control is a near-constant refrain for educators and school leaders throughout America, as well as among those who study educational policy and governance. In fact, drawing on both interviews with policy makers and analyses of their public statements, this chapter describes how most state-level policy makers believe they are committed to local control and operating within an educational system dominated by deference to the ideal of local autonomy. This belief is important, especially as it shapes legislative agendas and policy design. But what *is* local control? The term's ubiquity renders its meaning and consequences unclear.

With a few exceptions, when scholars identify local control as a salient feature of the American school system or write about the significant shift of power away from localities, they have generally neglected to consider how commitments to and conceptions of local control differ in important ways across state contexts.[64] Often, the fragmentation of a state's school system or the degree of exceptionalism—the aspects of state education governance discussed in chapters 4 and 5, respectively—are assumed to indicate levels of local control, yet the term implies something more than just the presence of many school districts. It suggests local autonomy over budgets, curricula, and personnel decisions.

In order to assess degrees of local control in a more nuanced fashion, this chapter suggests that one way to gauge local control could focus on the density of education policies a state has produced, the restrictions it has placed on the use of funding streams, and the limits imposed on state action. Examining substantive policies related to curricula, teacher certification, spending, and state takeover enables levels of local control to be traced over time and compared across states. Without question, local autonomy appears more constrained now than in the past. However, again there is variation across the states. Some states emerge from this analysis as active policy makers, where local autonomy is narrowly circumscribed by a dense regulatory environment, while others appear to be purposeful laggards, where state activity is restrained and preserves local autonomy. Even more notable is the extent to which some states in recent years have deliberately stepped back their regulatory efforts, reducing the number of exit exams and directing their efforts toward enhancing local capacity and expanding the scope of local decision-making. Of course, the impact of local autonomy on educational outcomes and opportunities depends on the nature of that autonomy, on the capacity of local districts, and on the inequalities that manifest between them. (The data used throughout the book and the empirical analyses underpinning chapters 4 and 6 are described in the appendix.)

The concluding chapter builds on these discussions in order to consider how the three aspects of state education governance interact with one another and how advocates and reformers might take stock of state-level education governance in their efforts to improve schools. Engaging these structures rather than circumventing them offers up the possibility of anticipating implementation pitfalls, increasing the public legitimacy of policies and programs, and allowing local and state priorities to drive the policy process, all of which combines to create more lasting, sustainable reform.

ROLLING BACK FEDERAL POLICY

The turn away from education reform, and this slight shift toward an alternative theory of change, is intertwined with the perception that there has been overreach on the part of the federal government. Some measure of this sentiment was apparent in 2009 when President Obama assumed office and announced his plans for the reauthorization of NCLB. The president sought to expand the federal government's efforts at turning around the lowest achieving schools, strengthen teacher evaluations by linking them to student assessments, broaden the use of merit pay, and reduce restrictions on the operations and growth of charter schools.[65] At the time, the law was already overdue for reauthorization by two years, but his opening gambit met with resistance from those who hoped for a reduced federal role in education. The Great Recession and the legislative battle over the Affordable Care Act further ensured there was little debate in Congress on the subject of NCLB's reauthorization. When the issue resurfaced in 2011 and 2013, prospective bills could not garner enough support to clear the Senate.[66]

Central to these debates over NCLB's reauthorization was the degree to which federal power over public schools would be rolled back. While

NCLB's reauthorization languished in Congress, schools and states struggled. Under NCLB's provisions, 100 percent of students in every school needed to achieve proficiency by the spring of 2014 in order to meet the federal government's Adequate Yearly Progress requirements (AYP). The goal was established when NCLB was adopted in 2002, with the expectation that the law would have been reauthorized well before 2014, and no school would actually be declared failing for its inability to reach that high benchmark. President Obama and Secretary of Education Arne Duncan leveraged the opportunity to take an extraordinarily active role first through RTTT and Common Core, and then by issuing states waivers from NCLB's AYP provisions under somewhat arbitrary conditions. Often waivers were withheld or delayed because states resisted implementing teacher evaluation systems that included student test scores.[67]

Opposition to a strong federal role coalesced in response to these efforts, as governors, chief state school officers, the National Conference of State Legislators, and many members of Congress demanded that the reauthorized law include greater autonomy for the states.[68] In December 2015, when ESSA managed to clear both houses, many regarded it as a law shaped very much by reactions against federal activism.[69] ESSA earned at least partial approval from the administration, both parties, teacher unions, and even civil rights groups. It is widely regarded as a bill that reduces federal power over schools. The secretary of education, for example, is prohibited from encouraging or requiring states to adopt a particular set of standards.

In the process of reducing federal influence, ESSA returns to the states considerable authority over the design of accountability systems and the nature of annual assessments. The law maintains a number of NCLB's provisions—including annual testing of students in grades 3–8 and once in high school, and reporting of test score data for schools by subgroups of students—but the flexibility it returns to states is substantial.

ESSA presents policy makers, reformers, scholars, and analysts with equal parts opportunity and challenge. With the federal government playing less of a role in determining the structure of accountability systems and assessments throughout the states, state and local leaders will have greater freedom to create policies and programs in concert with state and local stakeholders. Shifting the locus of control over education to state capitols also means that a more diverse array of individuals and organizations, including groups not able to maintain a presence in Washington, DC, will theoretically be able to participate in the policy process. There is a renewed imperative, then, to explore and understand state-level education governance and politics. It is my hope that this book will facilitate that exploration and in doing so better equip the many people who care about education to ensure that states more effectively use the authority granted by ESSA to achieve equitable and sustainable outcomes for students.

1

A Foundation and Framework for Understanding State Governance

On March 31, 1988, fabled teacher unionist Albert Shanker delivered a speech on education reform at the National Press Club (NPC) in Washington, DC.[1] By the end, the moderator was asking Shanker whether his proposals might throw public school districts into a state of anarchy. This was the beginning of the charter school movement.

The origin story of charter schools, described momentarily, is illustrative for several reasons. First, and perhaps most importantly for this discussion, although the charter school movement can trace its early history to Shanker's moment on a national stage, it was the combined efforts of advocates and policy makers at the state level—to reallocate funding, partner with new authorizers, and define the parameters of autonomy—that ushered charter schools into the world as active and durable policy. In Minnesota, the first state to enact a charter school law, the process of drafting the legislation was driven by state-level actors who fought and negotiated over a period of years before compromising on a plan that earned the support of a majority coalition in the legislature. Since then, states around the country have established charter school sectors, but evidence suggests that they are highly differentiated from one another, heavily shaped by the specific provisions of each state's law and preexisting circumstances (geographic dispersion of the population between rural and urban areas, diversity and segregation, poverty and inequality, etc.).

The story of the charter school movement is also important because charter schools constitute a substantial, ongoing attempt to remake the governance of public schools. Though the particular critiques have varied with time and place—too partisan or not partisan enough, too democratic or

not democratic enough—education reformers throughout American history, like charter advocates today, have cited the existing system of governance as a major reason for why schools fall short of collective aspirations.
Charter reform is one of the many cases in which reformers have sought to
improve educational quality and opportunity indirectly, *through* restructuring governance, by manipulating the configuration of power, the process for
making decisions, and the mechanisms of accountability. The most public
debates about charter schools may center on whether or not they improve
academic outcomes, increase racial or economic segregation, or overuse
punitive disciplinary practices—all important questions—but state charter laws do not directly speak to those issues. Nonetheless, both charter
advocates and vehement opponents believe that transforming how schools
are governed can significantly alter educational practices and outcomes.
Studying the history of the charter school movement reveals that questions
of governance, even when they are not named as such in public discourse,
are often central to proposed reforms.

Finally, as the idea to create new, innovative, independent public schools
diffused and evolved, it was actively engaged by many of the governmental
institutions and nongovernmental constituencies who contribute to school
governance throughout the United States. The emergence of charter schools
therefore highlights the intersection of several major threads of education
governance reform: an affinity for hyperlocal site- or school-based decision-
making; standards, testing, and accountability, which advance a vision of a
more streamlined hierarchy; and school choice, which relies on a vision of
market-like innovation, specialization, and competition. Today, these latter two threads arguably comprise the conventional wisdom of a great deal
of reform, with testing and accountability theoretically supplying the information that a market must rely on in order to function. The charter school
narrative thus offers a glimpse into the complexity of and conflicts around
education governance, and in so doing demonstrates the need for a framework to structure analyses of these many players and stakeholders.

While the story of charter schools' emergence serves well to illustrate
the centrality of governance to reform efforts, it is limited in its scope. One
could easily get lost interrogating the peculiarities of a small number of
reform efforts in a small number of places and lose sight of the big picture.
Recognizing that states are critical actors in education governance is one
step; starting to make sense of the many actors and institutions who collaborate on education governance is the next. To that end, later in this chapter

I present a conceptual framework that categorizes the key elements of governance and establishes a foundation for comparing states to one another and measuring changes in governance over time. I then examine the characteristics of good governance and identify reasons for the backlash against education reform, including critiques of charter reform.

INVENTING AND REIMAGINING CHARTER SCHOOLS: A GOVERNANCE STORY

At the time of his speech, Shanker was in the fifteenth of his nearly twenty-five-year tenure as president of the American Federation of Teachers (AFT), the smaller of the two major teacher unions. He authored a regular column for the *New York Times* and was well known to educators and policy makers alike. He was by then a prominent figure, what political scientists might call a *policy entrepreneur*—someone whose endorsement of an idea carried weight enough to catapult proposals into the national spotlight, and if the circumstances were right, onto the agendas of other leaders.[2]

Historical and Contemporary Contingency in Education Governance

Education governance is shaped by entrepreneurial individuals like Shanker, but also by the contingencies of history: the policies, problems, politics, and institutions that have come before and which in combination can create windows of opportunity during which reform is especially possible. Shanker began his address by reflecting on the recent past and the new policies that had been sweeping through schools all over the country. Just five years earlier, in 1983, a presidential commission had set off a moral panic when it published the *A Nation at Risk* report, declaring that American schools had fallen low and were mired in an epic crisis. According to the report, American students were lagging behind their international peers, endangering the country's economic future and ultimately compromising its security in the midst of the Cold War.[3]

Though many disputed the report's conclusions, pointing out that academic achievement was not in fact on a downward trajectory and underscoring the progress and tumult of recent decades (racial integration, the inclusion of students with disabilities, and more equitable funding systems), these critiques never earned as much attention as the initial report.[4] Concerns over the quality of education seemed to eclipse concerns over access and equity.

school districts and networks where this more bottom-up style of reform was under way, describing these efforts as a smaller but also more promising and innovative wave of reform.

Though he admired the efficient practices of private enterprise and expressed gratitude for business communities' renewed interest in schools, Shanker remained a proud socialist. He was careful to specify that there were some necessary conditions for successful reform. These included adequate public investment and physical infrastructure; some measure of political stability so that leaders might feel secure; strong collective bargaining rights that empowered teachers; trust between labor and management; and partnerships with key constituencies like universities or foundations who could help maintain momentum and bypass bureaucracies when necessary. In short, Shanker believed local reform could succeed, but only when local agencies possessed capacity and resources; when they were supported by political leaders, civil society, and the business community; and when relations between governmental and nongovernmental actors were positive. While labor relations might have been highly localized, the availability of adequate resources and the extent of collective bargaining rights were conditions largely in control of the states.

Having described models of bottom-up efforts and called on state and local leaders to establish baseline conditions for effective school reform, Shanker finally turned his remarks to a specific proposal developed by Ray Budde, a school administrator and professor of education in Massachusetts. Budde was a great believer in John Dewey's assertions that high-quality teachers were the critical element for any endeavor in education reform. As such, he had proposed a redesign of the traditional school district's four-part hierarchy with the school board at the top, superintendent as CEO, principal as manager, and teacher at the bottom.

In *Education by Charter* (1988), Budde recommended a flatter configuration in which groups of educators would petition school boards to obtain charters and form their own schools. He plotted a timeline for the stages of developing and monitoring chartered schools, even sketching a case study in which a hypothetical school district entirely reorganized itself over the course of ten years. Through the case study, Budde imagined the new system gradually but fundamentally altering the roles of nearly every actor within the school district. He suggested that such a system would change teachers' relationship with their work and encourage them to develop special expertise; draw parents and other members of the community into dialogue about educational practices; and weave research, learning, and collaboration into daily activities.[12]

A few months after his speech at the NPC, Shanker presented Budde's idea to the national convention of the AFT, earning the delegates' collective endorsement for the proposal. In his July 10th "Where We Stand" column for the *New York Times*, he wrote triumphantly about a "new course" for schools. Newspapers broadcasted Shanker's words around the country. In several states, serious conversations about the scheme began to take shape.

Charter Schools in the States

Members of a nonprofit, bipartisan organization in Minnesota were especially moved to study the potential of charter schools more closely. The Citizens League membership was influential and had been working to rethink public management and advance school choice in the state since the 1970s. They had failed to get a voucher law through the legislature in 1983, but in 1987 they successfully backed an open enrollment plan, which allowed students to attend any public school that had room, regardless of where they lived. The buzz Shanker created around charters offered these long-time activists an opportunity.[13] Through the summer and fall of 1988, they drafted a proposal, drawing heavily on their own earlier idea for cooperatively managed schools.[14] They believed that something like the charter school proposal was vital in order to realize the potential of open enrollment. For choices to have any cumulative systemic effect, schools needed to be demonstrably different from one another. Rather than remake entire districts as Budde had envisioned, however, the Citizens League ultimately recommended that innovative schools could be chartered by the state or a university as well as by a school board. By introducing multiple authorizers, the plan's authors deliberately carved out space for innovative schools to be established both outside and inside the traditional district system.

In October 1988, the Minneapolis Foundation brought Al Shanker to Minnesota for a seminar. After watching his presentation, two Democratic state legislators resolved to sponsor legislation that would create a firm legal framework for charter schools. At first, their efforts failed. The charter school provision progressed in the Senate but was rejected by the House in 1989 and again in 1990. Minnesota teacher unions aggressively fought the proposal, in particular the stipulation that would have empowered agencies other than local school boards to grant charters. As debates progressed, Shanker stayed conspicuously quiet.

Eventually, in 1991, charter advocates won out, and Minnesota became the first state to enact a charter school law, though only local boards and the state were empowered to serve as authorizers. The compromise had been necessary to secure the initial legislative victory, but it turned out to be a temporary détente. In response to persistent lobbying, the legislature amended the law in later years to expand the universe of charter authorizers.

Charter schools now are public schools that operate independently under a performance agreement with a school district or other authorizing agency. They are freed by state law from some of the regulations that apply to traditional public schools, and in some states can be operated by private management firms who bid for contracts. Charter schools can experiment with pedagogy, curriculum, discipline, and the structure of the school day, but state laws generally create only an opportunity for those innovations, not a mandate.

In the same year that Minnesota became the first state to enact a charter law, Bill Clinton endorsed the idea at the Democratic National Convention. In 1992 California passed the second charter law, also in the aftermath of a highly contentious debate over private school vouchers. Six more states followed suit in 1993. By the 2014–15 school year, 5.4 percent of all public school students in the United States attended a charter school, and as of March 2017, forty-three states and the District of Columbia had passed charter school legislation. Once passed and implemented, charter school laws have been revisited by state legislatures, but generally not repealed.[15]

Yet the popularity of charter schools varies wildly from state to state. Minnesota, where the phenomenon began in earnest, enrolled 5.6 percent of its public school students in the 2014–15 school year, roughly the same as the proportion of public school students enrolled nationally. Arizona, which passed its charter law in 1994, reported the highest rates of enrollment at 18.6 percent. Several states reported enrolling less than 1 percent of their public school students.[16] Average levels of academic performance vary tremendously from state to state as well. A 2013 study by Stanford's Center for Research on Education Outcomes estimated that charter school students in Rhode Island gained 86 days of reading and 108 days of math, relative to traditional public school students in that state. On the opposite end of the spectrum, charter school students in Nevada were estimated to have lost 108 days in reading and 137 days in math relative to students who attended traditional public schools.[17]

The geographic distribution of charter schools and the extent to which they are racially or economically segregated also varies. While the majority of charter school students throughout the United States are concentrated in urban areas, charter students in Hawaii, North Carolina, and Oregon are most likely to live in rural areas. Similarly, while Latino students are under-represented among charter school students in some states, they are overrepresented in others. Measures of racial segregation—*exposure*, the likelihood a member of one identity group will encounter a member of another, and *isolation*, the likelihood a member of one identity group will encounter only other members of their group—are also quite varied. These differences are partially explained by state environment; the exact same charter school law would be implemented differently given dissimilar geographies, racial and ethnic diversity, preexisting levels of residential segregation, and rates of poverty. However, those factors do not account for the entirety of the variance; the design of the state laws also has an impact.[18] For example, states generally require traditional public schools to provide free transportation for students, but many do not require the same of charter schools. Such provisions have consequences. Where transportation is not provided, a smaller proportion of children from low-income families are likely to choose charters.[19]

State legislatures possessed the ultimate authority to bring charter schools from the realm of the hypothetical to that of the real, and they demonstrated differing degrees of willingness to use that power. Although some quickly pursued charter reform, others took a great deal of time to deliberate. Each state negotiated critical details and wrote laws that made charter schools fundamentally different entities from state to state. Funding sources, authorizers, and the amount of time schools have to meet their achievement targets all vary tremendously. A handful of states have resisted charter schools entirely.[20]

ANALYZING MANY STORIES IN EDUCATION REFORM: A GOVERNANCE FRAMEWORK

In almost any story of education reform, from the birth of the charter school movement to the proliferation of zero-tolerance discipline, states emerge as critical for comprehending school governance and policy. Policy entrepreneurs like Albert Shanker may propose big ideas on a national stage, and local leaders deserve credit for well-run districts and schools, but it is state governments that are constitutionally empowered as key decision makers in education. State laws shape every aspect of the policy process in education, from school board elections to funding arrangements. State leaders decide whether or not a new proposal will be debated seriously on the state floor, and establish the details of implementation for new and old programs alike. Focusing on state governance can help to surface patterns of reform, conflict and collaboration, and success and failure.

At the same time, the inception of the charter school movement demonstrates that within states there are complex dynamics at play. The actors and organizations engaged with governance are numerous and diverse, and governance is constantly in flux, altered intentionally as well as incidentally. Given that intricacy, how might one classify and sort these actors to better understand the roles they play, and which aspects of states' education governance merit the closest attention? If the process of policy adoption is this varied across the states for charter school reform, how can students, parents, teachers, analysts, and advocates build and then leverage a more robust understanding of whole systems to enrich their engagement and advocacy?

A framework can help make sense of the many important stories in education governance. Frameworks are useful for confronting complex systems, because they offer up simplified models of reality built around a few clearly defined critical concepts. They help to separate signal from noise. Drawing from research and writing on governance in education and beyond, in this section I define governance, explain how it differs from government, and describe major changes in governance in recent years. I then outline a multidimensional framework describing the actors, activities, and outcomes education governance comprises and articulate why states are a particularly important level of analysis.

What Is Governance?

Governance is defined by purpose and power

Succinct definitions of governance are elusive, because governance is a response to the many challenges that arise when people live in community. How can a group of people with distinct interests and ideas work and live peaceably with one another? By what means can they make decisions together, resolve individual or group-based conflicts, and coordinate their actions to labor toward common goals?

Governance encompasses the systems and processes devised to address these questions: rules that allocate power within a community, including who can and cannot participate in debates, vote, or hold positions of leadership; procedures that define the legitimate exercise of that authority; boundaries that demarcate what is and is not up for negotiation; guidelines that are created for resolving disputes and determining a course of action; and mechanisms for enforcing laws and implementing collective decisions.[21] Governance is therefore many parts linked by the functions they perform for a society, and by the way they combine to organize power and authority, though both may remain diffuse, wielded formally and informally, and contested and shared by many actors.

Schools are vital institutions within any system because they function as both subjects and agents of governance. In other words, they are targeted by laws and regulations, but are also a vehicle through which power and authority are expressed. While education is recognized in the United States as a human right—vital for enabling the individual pursuit of happiness—an educated citizenry has also been deemed critical to the functioning of private enterprise, community social life, and the larger democratic system. So schools exist not simply to provide opportunities for personal and academic development, but also to sustain a common civic culture and build a labor force for the future. Leaders must continually reconcile collective aspirations—visions of community that vary widely and change over time—with individual aims and group-based differences rooted in wealth and poverty as well as religious, racial, and cultural identities.[22] Certainly, the intensity of these conflicts was on display in Minnesota during the 1980s and 1990s. To have power and authority over curriculum, pedagogy, discipline, and funding is also to possess the ability to reshape a community on a grander scale.

The elements that compose any system of governance are never neutral. All systems empower only a select few as decision makers, create advantages for some groups over others (intentionally or unintentionally), and even militate for or against certain kinds of policy change.[23] In a community as politically, racially, culturally, and economically stratified as the United States, governance can disrupt or maintain inequalities and disparities.

Governance continues beyond policy adoption and is bigger than government

The complexity, diversity, and importance of governance has long been a subject of study, but recent years have witnessed a veritable avalanche of scholarship. In 2016, the Social Sciences and the Arts and Humanities Citation Indices registered more than 5,800 articles in which governance was a topic (versus just 19 articles published in 1980, 33 in 1990, and 601 in 2000). These works come from academics and practitioners trained in diverse disciplines and located in countries and communities around the world. They reflect a growing interest in governance and a tremendous array of perspectives.[24]

Though originating from many different places, the recent proliferation of scholarship has emphasized a need for broad, inclusive frameworks that look beyond elected decision makers to understand the scope of governance.[25] In part, the embrace of an inclusive model of governance is a matter of changing perception, a growing recognition that implementing agencies possess a great deal of discretion in the administration of a regulation or the management of a program. Governance therefore evolves throughout the policy process since public managers and street-level bureaucrats exercise real power even after a law has been enacted.[26]

NCLB, enacted by Congress in 2001, offers a prime example. State agencies charged with implementing the law adapted—and, in many instances, subverted—its spirit by manipulating standards and proficiency levels so that these new benchmarks would have only the most minimal impact on instruction.[27] Local leaders managed a similar feat by diverting children with challenging needs into alternative learning centers, ensuring their impact on graduation statistics and accountability might be concentrated in a few schools.[28] Likewise, agencies authorized by a state to vet and supervise charter schools have often had considerable latitude in how they deploy this authority.

The growing attention to governance also stems from a desire to better understand how nongovernmental actors contribute to governance. Public goods and services have long been managed, provided, and shaped through formal and informal partnerships with nongovernmental actors.[29] Many schools, for instance, rely on close relationships with community organizations, nongovernmental organizations, and private businesses. Charter schools today are often operated by private businesses or nonprofits.

Nongovernmental actors can also wield power earlier in the policy process. The Citizens League and the teacher unions are part of Minnesota's education governance regime. As mentioned earlier, the idea of charter schools earned a place on the Minnesota legislature's agenda as a result of a seminar organized by the Citizens League, and the original charter school proposals in Minnesota were drafted by its members, who had become influential players in the state's policy process over time. Along similar lines, the teacher unions who organized against the original charter school law were informally but consistently powerful actors in state politics. They failed to stop the proposal entirely, but were able to slow its advancement and win concessions in the process.

Government's role in governance is changing

The explosion of interest in governance and the demand for a broader definition are born also of changing practices, not just an expanded field of vision. The widespread crisis of faith in government, the organizing efforts of business interests, and an evolving consensus among public administrators have helped drive real changes in how governance operates. Charter schools are just one instance of this phenomenon.[30] Governments increasingly rely on, operate in partnership with, and are challenged by actors from civil society and private industry, outsourcing or surrendering what might have been regarded as key government responsibilities just decades ago. To develop and implement public policy, these collaborations often rely on networks comprising actors linked together by some interdependency as well as market-like mechanisms that rely on competition and iterative provider–customer transactions.

These collaborations and market modalities both are likely to be less stable than a hierarchically organized bureaucracy—a good thing or a major problem depending on one's vantage point. Those who support the expanded use of contracting, networks, market-like processes, and the measurement of outcomes emphasize the flexibility of these mechanisms: the way they use information, their ability to adapt quickly, and the potential for gains in efficiency. They suggest, for example, that state education agencies ought to concentrate on coordinating and planning rather than doing.[31] Those who view these changes with concern point to the expanded roles of private, for-profit firms in providing public services and of nonelected actors in making major public policy decisions. They ask how these shifts will affect democratic accountability and whether or not such changes will magnify the impact of social and economic inequalities on governance.[32]

Somewhat paradoxically, the rise of new governance has been accompanied by the growth of an increasingly professionalized, independent, and active bureaucracy. State and federal agencies in particular possess greater capacity to initiate and advocate for policies; they often exercise broad authority and discretion when implementing complex programs; and they have had to develop sophisticated mechanisms of oversight for managing the providers with whom they contract and the networks with which they coordinate.[33] These shifting practices of governance appear in some ways at odds with one another. One ostensibly disrupts government authority (e.g., charters and choice), while the other appears to concentrate it (e.g., standards and accountability).

Part of the explanation for the simultaneous rise of these seemingly contradictory reforms lies in the fact that the collective tasks and challenges of governing have become demonstrably more intricate. For one thing, the modern world increasingly recognizes the distinctive needs of many groups as legitimate. Polities—the communities of people who claim membership in a nation or other political entity—are larger and more diverse, both through migration and the hard-won, woefully incomplete inclusion of groups who were once excluded from participation (chiefly ethnoracial, linguistic, gender, and religious minorities).[34] In addition, social movements, political moods, financial crises, and environmental calamities move rapidly and show little regard for jurisdictional boundaries. These circumstances present quandaries that in some instances require more technically sophisticated governance and in others call for negotiation and collaboration among coequal governments and powerful nongovernmental actors.[35]

These collective challenges can be readily identified in US education governance. School systems face more complex challenges than they have historically. They now educate the most diverse group of young people—in terms of racial and ethnic identity, country of origin, native language, religious identity, gender identity, and disability—in the country's history. Students are also mobile, more often switching schools and moving to new cities, states, or even countries. Schools confront globalization and technological change on many different fronts. At the same time, the academic skills students need to be successful after high school have also advanced significantly.

Nongovernmental constituencies that have always played an important role in supporting schools throughout the United States find federal, state, and local governments seeking to formalize those relationships or expand existing collaborations. High-profile philanthropists have sought to magnify their political influence in service of furthering various reforms.[36] Competitive or market-like processes—from teacher merit pay to private school vouchers to school choice—increasingly structure educational systems, and horizontally ordered, intergovernmental associations collaborate on new policy projects (e.g., Common Core State Standards).

Elements of Governance: A Conceptual Framework

The inclusive definition of governance that has come to be widely accepted among scholars and writers provides a strong foundation for studying education governance. Government is recognized as playing a critical role, while the role of nongovernmental actors, so prominent in recent decades, is also underlined. A broad definition of governance reinforces the importance of agency and the idea that systems of governance are dynamic, shaped by what individuals and organizations actually do and how they interact with, change, challenge, or reify structures and institutions. In other words, policies and practices constantly remake both institutions and constituencies.[37] The many actors and dynamic relationships of cooperation and accountability that make up this governance framework are laid out in figure 1.1 and discussed in the following subsections.

Institutions

Public sector governance revolves around formal institutions in which public officials reside and authority is vested, from decision makers in legislative bodies to street-level bureaucrats like teachers in schools, police officers in precincts, and social workers in welfare agencies. Constitutional and legal arrangements as well as informal norms shape how institutions relate to one another, the scope of their authority, and the political or administrative

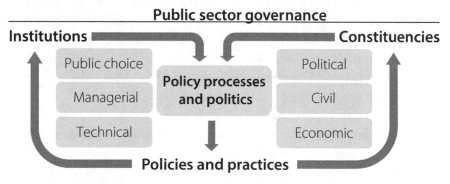

FIGURE 1.1   A public sector governance framework

mechanisms by which leaders are held accountable. This category of actors is large and diverse. As of 2012, in addition to the federal government and the fifty state governments, there were more than ninety thousand autonomous or semiautonomous local governments in the United States—so many that the Census Bureau tallies them every five years.[38]

The many institutions in government can be sorted in at least two ways. One is hierarchical (as depicted in figure 1.1).[39] This way of categorizing government institutions places public choice entities at the top. Public choice bodies possess broad powers to propose, enact, or review laws and new policies. They include legislatures, courts, and governors, which serve as sites for political contests and representation of constituents. The primary accountability for individuals leading public choice institutions is through elections. Just below public choice institutions lie the managerial levels— the bureaucracy—where strategies are detailed, regulations written, and programs designed. Formal oversight of these bureaucrats might be the responsibility of those in the public choice level, and less formally of the constituencies they serve. Below the public choice and managerial levels lie technical institutions, where policies are executed, services are delivered, and regulations are enforced. These are formally accountable primarily to the institutions farther up in the hierarchy and less formally to the constituent groups they serve directly.

While both traditional public schools and charter schools clearly inhabit a position at the bottom of the hierarchy, the scheme points to one reason why school governance is challenging to understand. School governance institutions often do not fall neatly into one category or another. Chief state school officers (CSSOs) and state boards of education (SBEs), for instance, occupy the top state positions in education governance, but they manifest characteristics of both public choice and managerial institutions—part politician, part bureaucrat. Even in states where these leaders are elected and constitutionally endowed with authority over the school system, their power will be more narrowly circumscribed than a legislature's, and they do not possess authority over the critical element of funding.

The hierarchical approach to classifying governmental institutions mirrors distinctions found elsewhere in studies of law and governance. Kenneth Meier and Laurence O'Toole emphasize that "governance systems cover three basic functions: the aggregation of preferences, decisions on policy options, and the implementation of policies."[40] They distinguish between "governing institutions" that primarily perform the first two functions and "implementing institutions" that translate policies into concrete programs and services, though they acknowledge that many institutions (local school boards, for instance) perform overlapping functions.

Another approach to categorizing governments focuses on substantive areas of authority and responsibility—that is, which institutions are empowered to decide what.[41] In multilevel governments, like that of the United States, these distinctions can be helpful in the sense that agencies often have specialized responsibilities. The North Carolina Textbook Commission, which is appointed by the governor, has a very clear mandate to vet and approve textbooks. Likewise, school boards are "single-purpose" governments. However, even where these specialized institutions exist, authority is shared.[42] Power over academic standards might reside with the state agency, while the ability to raise and collect taxes might be shared between the state legislatures and the local school board.

Constituencies

The constituencies and stakeholders who regularly interact with formal institutions also contribute to governance, both in the process of policy-making and during implementation. These groups may be political parties, civil society groups, or even private business interests, and their engagement may also be formally regulated or informally encouraged and expected. The extent of their power may be less neatly articulated than that of government institutions, but nongovernmental actors nonetheless possess power and authority.

The power of nongovernmental actors may derive from the size of the population they represent, resources they control, social prestige, personal relationships, or specific expertise or experience in a particular policy area. The Citizens League of Minnesota leveraged many of these factors to influence reform. Charter laws in other states subsequently elevated the influence of for-profit and nonprofit actors within K–12 education by designating them as authorizers, meaning that not only are they in a position to supervise or operate a school, but they are also likely to be consulted when changes are being considered for the law.

In the context of education, teachers are one of the most important constituencies, the people who translate policy into classroom practices. In some instances, teachers, or at least their membership organizations, possess some formal legal authority at both the state and local levels. Their inclusion in governance is statutorily prescribed. In Arkansas, for example, the CSSO is required to have ten years of teaching experience and to hold a current teaching license. In Michigan and North Carolina, the states' teachers of the year occupy seats on the SBE, though in neither instance are they full, voting members. At the local level, in states where collective bargaining remains intact, teacher unions can and often do exercise considerable control over policy issues like the structure of the school day.[43]

However, formal, legal authority is not necessary for constituent groups to exert influence. Teachers are so intrinsically important to education that their experience, expertise, and the organizations that represent them (unions and professional associations) ensure a measure of informal authority. For instance, academic standards could be designed and adopted without sustained consultation with educators, but such a process risks being seen as illegitimate. This illegitimacy would make the standards vulnerable to the extent that teachers could resist teaching them, waging a quiet war of attrition throughout the implementation process and effectively enforcing a slow death upon the new requirements. They might also take a more direct approach, marshaling their political organizations and rhetorically leveraging their position as classroom experts to challenge the standards openly.

Policy processes and politics

Together, governmental institutions and nongovernmental constituents drive and structure policy processes and politics, from elections to agenda setting to implementation to policy evaluation. Such processes may be contentious or harmonious, partisan or not, inclusive or exclusive, competitive or collaborative, efficient or sluggish. They should always be understood as political processes in which power is at work, even when actors rhetorically frame procedures and processes as inherently commonsensical.[44] Returning to the standards example, the inclusion or exclusion during a policy process of a key constituency—teachers—could shape the likelihood that a policy is viewed as legitimate, implemented faithfully, maintained, altered, or even abandoned.

Policy and practice

From these processes emerge policies and a repertoire of common practices, which can be symbolic as well as concrete. *Policy* in general refers to the specific programs, initiatives, regulations, and budgets produced in the traditional manner, through legislative action.[45] However, a governance lens attends to the fact that policies are often initiated outside of government, established through inaction, deferred to elected executives, and delegated to nongovernmental actors.[46]

While some scholars view policy as distinct from governance, an output rather than a key element within the system, I include it in this framework. The line between policy and governance is a fluid one; it does not run strictly in one direction, with governments and constituents simply producing policy outputs. The arrow also points in the reverse. Policy can, and often does directly, formally alter institutional arrangements.[47] Charter school policies are, at their core, legal arrangements that expand the universe of who is legally authorized to start and run a publicly funded school.

Policy also remakes governance in more subtle ways, especially when viewed over the course of many years. As charters expand, they empower new constituents and gradually remake the institutional environment in which education governance takes place. State policies that establish minimum standards for teacher certification may not be intended to diminish local district autonomy, but in practice they could have this effect, slightly tilting the balance of power away from the local district and toward the state. With time, each new law governing the process of teacher credentialing would further constrain the choices available to a local district. Whether or not such policies lead to an improvement in student outcomes and school quality is a separate question; the policy limits the choices available to the local agency and therefore has an impact on the system of governance.

That said, policy made at one level or by one institution does not necessarily diminish the power and authority of others; in other words, power is not a strictly zero-sum resource. A new state or federal program might force a local district to build greater capacity and incidentally expand the scope of its policy activity.[48] Changes in the scope and scale of policy can also shift expectations about responsibility and perceptions of legitimacy. Thus, policy can impact both the formal and informal aspects of governance.

Policy is the most tangible manifestation of governance, especially when considered in the context of other policies and viewed over time. Patterns can be discerned in a corpus of policies that indicate something important about governance, surfacing influential logics like neoliberalism or pervasive racial, gender, and class biases.[49] Support for charter schools is driven partly by a market-like commitment to competition and differentiation; the pervasive influence of this idea is far more obvious when charters are examined as just one policy among many. Policies and the practices employed in their delivery should be understood as direct expressions of power and authority, particularly when they are viewed in context, as part of the "regimes of laws, rules, judicial decisions, and administrative practices that constrain, prescribe, and enable the provision of publicly supported goods and services," rather than evaluated in isolation.[50] Jeffrey Henig writes that policies together can indicate "broad changes . . . in how collective decisions are made about what schools should do and how schooling should be organized, funded, and evaluated."[51] Policy is therefore key for understanding the ways in which governance varies from place to place and over time.[52]

Levels of analysis

Even with a framework in hand that identifies the particular classes of actors, activities, and outputs that comprise governance, analysts also need to consider the level at which they intend to focus their studies: whether they wish to conduct an exploration at the level of the forest or the trees, or perhaps concentrate on an organizing unit of analysis somewhere in the middle (groves, perhaps). In this modification of an old analogy, these represent the macro, micro, or meso levels of analysis, respectively.

Many researchers, when facing this question of how to delimit their inquiry into a system, draw on the idea of a *holon*, something that "is a whole system at one level [but] is part of a system at another level."[53] Holons operate within larger systems, but simultaneously constitute systems unto themselves; they display persistence over time, consistency of character, and distinctiveness from other entities at the same level.[54] Schools, for example, could constitute holons, as would districts nested within states, or states nested within a nation. Each merits inquiry on its own terms, though it would be reasonable to consider relationships with the levels above and below. To focus on one level is not to ignore the existence of the others, but it does mean analyzing them in somewhat less detail.

There are at least two reasons for carefully considering how level of analysis is treated. The concepts and measures useful for describing a process or characterizing a system at one level may or may not be appropriate when applied to another. Second, systems function as more than the sum of their parts, and patterns or relationships present at one level may not hold true for the composite elements. For example, it would be reasonable to state that education governance in the United States is shaped by an antipathy toward top-down policy, yet that truism does not hold in all states. Drawing such a conclusions from one level of analysis to the next is what social scientists refer to as an *ecological fallacy*.

COMPETING CHARACTERIZATIONS OF GOOD GOVERNANCE

Beyond identifying and understanding the components that constitute the framework of education governance, it is equally crucial to explore how those elements (institutions, constituents, policies, etc.) combine to foster "good" or "bad" governance. As with the concept of governance itself, there are conflicting ideas about what is most important: process or outcome. This section examines the factors that foster or threaten good governance from both points of view, and describes examples in which each perspective is highlighted.

Democratic Governance and Legitimacy in Education Reform

For those who focus primarily on process, good governance means democratic governance, wherein the authority and *legitimacy* of decision makers is granted by the citizenry. Legitimacy is necessary for establishing a stable foundation upon which policies can be made—and will be accepted. When governments or policies are not perceived to be legitimate, citizens and organizations will be more inclined to challenge them, the foundation upon which a stable system of governance resides will be jeopardized, and even smart policy may fail.[55]

Legitimacy is a product of time and rests on process. Robust *participation* by citizens and key stakeholders, both in the selection of governmental leaders and throughout the policy-making process, is considered key to a good governance regime. Participation should be *representative, accessible,* and *equitable.* Good democratic governance calls for policies and practices that are *responsive* to citizens' needs and preferences. Decision-making and implementation processes should be *transparent,* to facilitate participation and *accountability.* Decision makers, and other key actors in a system of democratic governance, should be politically accountable.[56]

Good governance from this vantage point is threatened by corruption, but also by policies and practices that weaken or subvert democratic control and limit engagement. Those who define good governance primarily along these lines might regard both trends highlighted earlier—the movement toward governance through networks and market modalities for making decisions or delivering services—with some skepticism, in that they seem to attenuate citizen control over policy-making and public programs and create room for wealthier and better-connected citizens to exert disproportionate influence over public programs and institutions.

Consider the charter school movement once more. On the one hand, charter school laws have been debated and shaped by recognized constituent groups. State by state, over a period of more than two decades, these laws have mostly passed through the gauntlet of established political processes. Negotiations have been contentious at times, but they also served to legitimize the end result for both the public and core constituencies. The legal framework that supports charters' existence has proven remarkably durable. In California, an effort to repeal the state's 1992 charter legislation has gained little traction, and in Washington, a state court decision that seemed to declare charter schools incompatible with the state constitution appears now to be just a temporary setback.[57] But despite their durability, charter school laws passed through traditional processes do often set schools outside the direct control of locally elected leaders. As they grow in number, enroll more students, and earn an increasingly prominent place in public debates, their advocates will increasingly be faced with questions about democratic control, legitimacy, and process.

One of the most recent episodes in the charter school movement unfolded in New Orleans. There, charter schools grew by circumventing regular political processes, and the lack of democratic control over an entire local school system provoked an increasingly angry public outcry.

In the aftermath of Hurricane Katrina, the governor and the state legislature of Louisiana collaborated to allow the majority of New Orleans public schools to be taken over by the state's Recovery School District (RSD). The takeover, which displaced the elected Orleans Parish School Board (OPSB), occurred with little public comment. The governor also suspended the provision in the state's charter school law that would have required the legislature to consult parents, teachers, and staff before converting a local public school to a charter. At the time, citizens of New Orleans were struggling to navigate FEMA bureaucracies and meet their most basic needs, and it seemed to many that the governor and legislature took advantage of the situation to advance their policy goals. The few schools left under the elected school board's supervision were higher performing schools, which also happened to be those that served most of the district's wealthier and whiter students. Local democratic control was effectively suspended for poorer, blacker communities, and left in place for wealthier, whiter communities.[58]

As the RSD turned the daily operations of each school it supervised over to charter school operators, it brought the city's school system into close alignment with Budde and Shanker's original vision: an entire district of charter schools. Education reformers and experts from all over the country descended on the city. Thousands of experienced New Orleans teachers were summarily fired, predominantly black women who had formed the backbone of the black middle class before the hurricane. Many did not return to teach anywhere in Louisiana.[59] The teachers who took up positions in the new charter schools were whiter, younger, and far more likely to have come from outside New Orleans.[60] Unsurprisingly, citizens of New Orleans did not view this new regime as legitimate.[61] Layered on top of the federal government's catastrophically slow response to the disaster and the racism that permeated news coverage of Katrina, black residents of New Orleans described feeling as though reforms happened "to them" rather than being designed and implemented "with them." In the decade after the hurricane, public pressure mounted in favor of returning control of the schools to the locally elected OPSB.[62] In 2016, the Louisiana legislature passed a law to begin that process, though the final bill included provisions that required schools' charter status be preserved under district leadership.[63]

Questions of legitimacy affect the entire ecosystem of education governance. In the United States at present, the legitimacy of the federal government has reached historic lows. On most surveys, fewer than 20 percent of Americans report that they believe government in Washington, DC, can be trusted do the right thing.[64] Though there is some variation, this pattern of decline holds for different branches of government and across political parties. Confidence in other major institutions and actors, including the US public schools, has also plummeted in recent decades.[65] This crisis of legitimacy has been articulated by both conservative and liberal opponents of the CCSS, who shared a critique rooted at least partly in process.[66] In a 2016 op-ed for the conservative *Washington Examiner*, Lance Izumi wrote "the process that gave us Common Core is a perfect example of a rigged system." He continued:

> The NGA [National Governor's Association] and the CCSSO [Council of Chief State School Officers] formed committees of education insiders and technocrats to do the work. While there were 60 members on these various committees, only a small handful actually created the standards. Despite the fact that their work would affect every child in America, deliberations took place behind closed doors. . . . Common Core was the brainchild of political, education and business elites—and continues to benefit them.[67]

Izumi's comments lined up in part with those offered by Stan Karp in *Rethinking Schools*, a progressive magazine devoted to education reform, equity, and social justice. Karp also emphasized the exclusionary nature of the process, though his critique added that the standards would fall most heavily on nonwhite, urban communities even as they were excluded of the process of policy design:

> Too many standards projects have been efforts to move decisions about teaching and learning away from educators and schools, and put them in the hands of distant bureaucracies and politicians. Standards have often codified sanitized versions of history, politics, and culture that reinforce official myths while leaving out the voices and concerns of our students and communities. Whatever potentially positive role standards might play in truly collaborative conversations about what schools should teach and children should learn has repeatedly been undermined by bad process, suspect political agendas, and commercial interests.[68]

Notably, though trust in state and local governments has declined along with faith in other institutions, it remains relatively high, with 62 percent and 71 percent of Americans, respectively, stating that they have high levels of trust in those institutions.[69] There are many reasons for these patterns, but legitimacy is about acquiescence, trust, faith, and confidence. These attitudes shape how policies are received by the public (i.e., whether or not there is likely to be resistance—a backlash—to them) and how they will be implemented by street-level bureaucrats (i.e., whether faithfully or in name only). Indeed, in his essay, Karp called on readers to resist the CCSS by pushing back against implementation timelines and deemphasizing assessments.

Rational Governance and Outcomes in Education Reform

Of course, good democratic governance does not ensure that policies, programs, and public goods will always be administered *effectively* and *efficiently*—though many hope that this will prove true. This is the other side of good governance: *outcomes*, or whether or not a particular system is able to provide public goods and achieve collective goals.[70] Those focused more on outcomes are likely to advocate for the adoption of high-quality, consistent, evidence-based, *rational* practices—specific policy instruments. This perspective can contribute to a narrow focus on the most measurable aims and preclude engaging with the value differences that lie at the heart of political disagreements.

Those who view good governance as rooted in outcomes rather than process may prefer to locate power in professionalized, technocratic, independent bureaucracies that will be better equipped than democratically controlled bodies to collaborate with knowledgeable constituencies, trade short-term costs for long-term gains, or impose costs on a powerful few in the name of the greater good. Indeed, obfuscation of responsibility or displacement of authority is paradoxically one way that representative bodies can contrive to prioritize the public good, rather than representing only the narrow interests of their constituents.[71] Those who view good governance in this way may also emphasize the use of market mechanisms as a way of providing lower-cost public services or *flexibility* in response to changing public preferences. From their vantage point, good governance is threatened most acutely by gridlock, factionalism, and the inscrutable whims that sometimes seem to win the day in political contests.

Along these lines, defenders of the CCSS often dismissed resistance by describing it pejoratively as political, positioning themselves as neutral guardians of children's best interests. They emphasized over and over again to the public and to educators that the standards were academically rigorous, internationally competitive, clearly articulated, and just all-around more *rational* and *equitable* than the standards that had previously differentiated academic requirements across the fifty states.[72] In March 2014, the *Los Angeles Times* Editorial Board published an op-ed endorsing the CCSS, emphasizing that they were simply better than the state's previous content standards: "What gets lost amid the political and administrative squabbling is the issue that ought to matter most: whether the Common Core standards are a solid improvement on what most states, including California, had before. And with a few caveats, they are."[73]

Thus, education reformers and stakeholders bring to public debates conflicting ideals about how education governance is failing (or not) and should be reformed (or not). Some make a strong argument that democratic process values should be centered in design, while others argue that questions of efficacy—in particular academic success—should be considered more prominently.

Of course, while these visions of good governance may differ and come into conflict, most people can recognize the importance of both process and outcome to a sustainable reform effort. In New Orleans, many charter school reformers persistently downplayed concerns about democratic accountability and exclusionary processes, citing dire circumstances in the school district prior to Katrina. The high school graduation rate for New Orleans schools was 56 percent, and test scores ranked the system sixty-seventh among sixty-eight parishes in the state. The OPSB was also regarded as a dysfunctional institution; voter turnout for elections was low, eight superintendents were hired and left between 1998 and 2005, and the FBI indicted district employees for serious financial mismanagement.[74] By 2016, the graduation rate had increased to 72 percent, and reformers declared the RSD and its charter schools to be a success, sidestepping in their evaluation the frustrations of New Orleanians, the displacement of black teachers, and the struggles to gain access experienced by special needs students.[75] Yet some of the most prominent charter school advocates were aligned behind returning control over the schools to a locally elected board, albeit with limits that prevented the board from dissembling the charter system. They recognized the importance of legitimacy and process.[76]

This chapter has introduced the concept of governance and laid out a simple framework for navigating the complexity of public sector education governance. It has also outlined a major conflict between competing conceptions of good governance, a philosophical difference that clearly animates political disagreements today. These ideas establish a broad context and vocabulary for the remainder of this book. Next, chapter 2 describes the institutional foundations of education governance throughout the United States, and the political processes those institutions were intended to foster, while chapter 3 explores changes in governance wrought by increasingly mobilized, diverse constituents, and their evolving ideas about what outcomes schools needed to achieve.

2

Early Roots of Education Governance in the United States

To grasp why states are such a critical level of analysis for making sense of the institutions, constituents, politics, policies, and practices that education governance comprises, and how it is that governance at this level interacts with inequality in the United States, it is helpful to zoom out, examine the larger context in which states are embedded, and identify the patterns and relationships that characterize the system as a whole.

The number of governmental institutions responsible for funding, administering, monitoring, and regulating public education today is staggering. In the 2013–14 school year, the National Center for Education Statistics counted 13,491 regular local school districts. *Regular* means that number excludes charter school districts, regional administrative and service centers, and special school districts like those that serve children with special needs or the children of active-duty military officers.[1] As emphasized in the previous chapter, institutional structures do not entirely determine governance, but their configuration is of profound import, especially given that constituents and stakeholders shape their organizations and activities in response to these structures. In addition to these thousands of local agencies, federal and state governments also house K–12 policy makers and bureaucrats located in three different branches of government at the public choice, managerial, and technical levels. This means there are three vertically nested, internally divided levels of active, legitimate institutional authorities involved in American school governance.

At the local level, there are thousands of different governments responsible for providing educational opportunities, most of which are single-issue agencies focused only on schools in a specific geographic jurisdiction. The majority of these are regular or traditional local school districts, though a growing number are new entities like charter school districts. Most regular local school districts are *independent* from other local governments, though a substantial minority are classified as *dependent*, directly accountable in some fashion to, or integrated with, other local leaders—city councils, mayors, or county governments—often for budget approval or revenue. In most instances, whether formally implicated or not, these general-purpose governments maintain an interest in K–12 education and strive to partner or cooperate with local districts, especially given that schools can be an important site for coordinating social services.

At the state level, there are fifty state governments (fifty-one including Washington, DC), each of which is divided into legislative, executive, and judicial branches responsible for the full gamut of state policies, including the decision-making, execution, and review of educational programs and policies. These general-purpose institutions are ubiquitously complemented by a bureaucratic agency, the state education agency (SEA). SEAs are led or supervised by elected or appointed leaders—state boards of education (SBEs) and chief state school offices (CSSOs), which are focused entirely on education.

At the federal level is a central authority that is also divided into three branches, each responsible not just for education but for the full range of national policies. The federal court system, in particular, maintains a visible presence all around the country. And located squarely within the executive is a cabinet-level bureaucratic agency, the US Department of Education (ED), headed up by a political appointee.

At all three levels are elected leaders (Congress, state legislatures, SBEs, and local school boards) who might be held accountable for the policies they make through traditional electoral processes, though the specific way in which local elections are organized varies both within and between states. These leaders are also accountable—more or less—to one another: localities to states, states to the federal government, SEAs to various other state and federal institutions. At each level there are also bureaucrats who implement, reshape, and even propose policy. In theory these bureaucrats are directly accountable to elected leadership and to supervisors for school operations and student outcomes, and are often tasked with evaluating the performance of other agencies. At all three levels are leaders who engage in goal-setting, monitoring, finance, curriculum, and teacher training, and can therefore claim substantial influence over what happens in classrooms.

Coordinating, monitoring, implementing, and making sense of policy across such a landscape is a mammoth task. Determining who is responsible for what with any consistency is likewise daunting. It seems unlikely that anyone would purposefully design such a complex system. So how did such a tangled web of institutions come to be? Why are there so many thousands of school districts and so many overlapping lines of authority? The answers to these questions lie in the past. Education governance in the United States today and attitudes about legitimate institutional arrangements for it echo patterns and conflicts that emerged in colonial America and have evolved over the last two hundred years, yielding the complex power-sharing arrangements we now confront.

In this chapter and the next, I discuss several key aspects of education governance that will serve as a foundation for the subsequent chapters in the book. First, in the aggregate, and particularly in comparison to other nations, education governance in the United States has been and remains extraordinarily *decentralized*, meaning that power and decision-making authority are widely dispersed across a large number of institutions and constituents who are generally closer to the action on the ground, versus being concentrated in a central governmental authority among an elite few. That decentralization is manifested in several ways: through institutional fragmentation, through the formal and informal mechanisms of political and administrative exceptionalism, and through legal and rhetorical commitments to local control.

Second, over time, education governance has become progressively, measurably more centralized; this is a long-term trend, not a sudden development. School districts have merged with one another, and federal and state governments have assumed more authority through revenue and policy, sometimes incrementally and at other times in rapid, decisive bursts. The pattern is clear: power over schools has shifted away from local communities over time. Yet education governance, especially the institutional configuration of public school systems, bears the imprint of its origins, creating this array of overlapping authorities and a system that is both more centralized than it once was and yet still decentralized.

These are important lessons. The fragmented nature of political authority in the United States can make it difficult for reformers of any stripe to provoke a significant, sustained break with past programs.[2] Nowhere is this insight more apt than in the arena of education governance, where decisions made by earlier generations of elected leaders and advocates have fashioned a system that frustrates efforts to pursue sustainable reform.

However, these aggregate characteristics and patterns do not hold uniformly when one considers the state systems. States do influence and learn from one another; reform movements and policies do diffuse from state to state; and yet there is and has always been tremendous and consequential variation in many aspects of states' education governance. In some states, education governance has long been centralized and well integrated with general-purpose government and partisan politics. Likewise, other states have been openly more reticent than others to assume greater control over the schools within their borders, preferring instead to defer to localities. The federal government's lack of constitutional authority, stacked against the states' unambiguous constitutional authority, means this variation is likely to persist.

Finally, governance reform, in particular the tug of war between centralized and decentralized authority, is about power and politics. Even governance reform aimed at efficacy has implications for the distribution of power over schools, and even projects rhetorically dedicated to equity and access have often been undergirded by a logic of social control. Conflicts over education governance are associated time and again with attempts to expand or contract the universe of people who are welcome in schools—and who can have influence over them. In short, variations in education governance are shaped by political contests, especially those that center on the racial and economic inequalities most salient in a given place and time (a topic that is touched on here but will receive further attention in chapter 3).

This chapter investigates these issues and other historical factors that have influenced the current system of education governance, with a particular focus on governing institutions and how they have developed. The historical narrative presented here, although not comprehensive, traces the evolution of US education from its prerevolutionary roots through the Progressive Era, exploring early aspects of decentralization and pivotal moments that have informed the role of states in education governance today.

THE FRAGMENTED EMERGENCE OF SCHOOL SYSTEMS IN EARLY AMERICAN HISTORY

The origins of fragmentation, local control, and even exceptionalism can be traced all the way back to the prerevolutionary United States, as can some of the persistent regional and state-level differences that will be explored more thoroughly in later chapters. Yet, even in early America, where schools were established on an almost hyperlocal level, state and federal governments played a significant role in supporting their expansion. This is worth reiterating: schools developed locally, and differences between states are partly a result of cultural differences intersecting with geographic boundaries, but the establishment of local school systems was often encouraged and supported in critical ways by state and federal governments. There is a tendency to frame the more recent decades of state policy activity as a dramatic break from the past, and certainly the state and federal governments are more overtly powerful than they once were, but their concern for the schooling of their citizens is long-standing and part of a pattern of growing engagement.

Community Resources Shape Schools in the Prerevolutionary United States

Prerevolutionary American communities were not ruled by a coherent central authority, and possessed a deep skepticism toward centralized governments. There was no state-sponsored system of public education. Instead, socioeconomic status, race, religious affiliation, community beneficence, and geography determined whether or not a child received informal tutoring at home, was educated by a private tutor, attended a formal academy, enrolled in a school for paupers, traveled to Europe to attend a prestigious boarding school, entered into an apprenticeship, or grew into adulthood illiterate.[3]

Whereas systems of education in Europe typically arose as a result of governmental actions, the first schools that evolved in the United States could be credited more to the interventions of civil society.[4] Geography was therefore particularly important in the colonial period, insofar as it was related to wealth, parental education, religious denomination, and cultural heritage.

The immigrants who populated the northeastern colonies—what are now Massachusetts, Maine, Connecticut, Rhode Island, and New Hampshire— were by and large religious, intellectual, and literate. The Puritans' regard for literacy and their commitment to intellectualism contributed to the formation of basic reading and writing schools throughout New England. Primary schooling quickly became a community undertaking throughout the region (with the exception of Rhode Island), one backed in part by legislative commitments from colonial legislatures.[5] The New England colonies and later New York were some of the first polities in the world to enshrine public education legally, requiring communities to levy property taxes and parents to secure some training for their children.[6] Enforcement was limited, however, and local preferences ultimately dominated both the decision to establish schools and the decision of what to teach in them. Nonetheless, these laws represent the earliest state commitments to public schooling and created an environment conducive to the rapid expansion of schooling in the region.

Most education historians regard the Northeast as the birthplace of the modern American school system, and institutional structures, norms, and specific policies have often diffused from these states to others.[7] Just before the American Revolution, white adult male literacy in New England was nearly universal. Though not praiseworthy by today's standards, this fact placed education levels in this region far ahead of other regions.

In the middle colonies—what are now New York, New Jersey, Pennsylvania, and Delaware—schooling was not a consistently established community responsibility, though there were charity schools for the education of indigent and Native American children. Immigration to the area was extremely diverse in terms of both original nationality and religious beliefs. Immigrants from the Netherlands, Germany, England, Scotland, Sweden, and Norway, for example, tended to establish private schools where they could safeguard their religious, linguistic, and cultural traditions. In these middle colonies, on the eve of the American Revolution, sectarian differences remained salient, and an acceptance of a pluralistic approach to education had developed; secular schools were growing more common only in the most densely populated cities.[8]

Circumstances in the Chesapeake and southern colonies—now Virginia, Maryland, the Carolinas, and Georgia—differed vastly from the colonies to the north. Immigrants to the southern colonies had belonged to a lesser social class than those in the northern colonies, with one text describing them as illiterate "beggars and vagabonds."[9] Because a majority of early immigrants to the lower colonies arrived as unskilled, indentured servants (or in the case of Georgia, debtors who had been imprisoned in England), fewer of the families who arrived were equipped to provide their children with instruction. As in the middle and northern colonies, religion and cultural heritage were still significant factors affecting community preferences for and ability to provide public schooling, but fewer communities opted to establish schools. The effects of social class, language, and religion were further magnified by other conditions of life in the lower colonies—namely, the agricultural basis of the economy and slavery.

Education Rises and Falls Before a New Federal Government

When the Revolution began, some of the divisions between ethnic and religious groups had weakened, but access to education was still highly variable and tied closely to families' socioeconomic and cultural circumstances. Nonetheless, it was during the Revolution that education emerged as a major concern on the national agenda. Early leaders, including Benjamin Rush of Pennsylvania and Thomas Jefferson of Virginia, worried that the young nation might devolve into anarchy, absent some government-led initiative to foster the development of "intelligence, wisdom and virtue amongst the people."[10] They pressed for the establishment of a public school system. Yet the majority of delegates at the constitutional convention remained skeptical toward central government, and they sought to limit the scope and scale of activities that it could conduct. Education was widely regarded as important, but those who viewed it as a public matter lost out to those who insisted that it was a personal and local one, arguing that the definition and cultivation of virtue and intelligence were best addressed by local leaders, clergy, and families.

Public schooling was therefore considered, debated, and deliberately excluded from the United States Constitution.[11] Article I, Section 8, which specified the explicit powers granted to Congress, made no mention of education. The Tenth Amendment effectively codified America's skepticism by reserving powers not granted to the federal government "to the States respectively, or to the people." Thus, an informal but strongly held cultural norm—ingrained wariness of strong centralized power—fostered the adoption of express constitutional limits on the authority of the federal government over public schools.

The First School Districts and Boards Emerge in the Early Republic

In spite of the failure to establish a nationally supported system of a schools, momentum built locally in favor of public education. As with the timing and character of the first community schools, there were pronounced variations in terms of how and when the public school systems emerged.

In the northern states, more and more localities assumed responsibility for creating and maintaining public schools. They were often open for only a few weeks per year, but by 1825, most rural communities in the Northeast and Midwest—Maine, Vermont, New Hampshire, Rhode Island, Connecticut, New York, Ohio, and Illinois—had established schools controlled by localities and funded through property taxes (and to a much lesser extent, state aids).[12] Historians have referred to this system, in which schools served and were monitored by very small communities, as the district system, though these were much smaller than today's US school districts; one particular town at this time would likely have encompassed many districts.

Specialized governing bodies were a component of the district system. In early nineteenth-century Massachusetts, as population growth led to a dramatic increase in the responsibilities of local government, special committees were established for the purpose of governing schools in the district system.[13] These committees, one for each school, controlled the selection of teachers and curriculum and influenced the formation of similar governance institutions throughout the Midwest and Northeast.[14] These were the early forerunners of modern school boards and presaged exceptionalism, the separation of education from general governance.

Urban communities in the North supported a more divided and varied system of education compared to rural areas.[15] Schools were not so uniformly publicly supported, but rather comprised a hodgepodge of independent schools and academies, selective boarding schools for the wealthy, and "dame" schools operated by women out of their homes. Church schools and charity schools also emerged to discipline and indoctrinate a growing population of urban poor.[16] While the district system in rural areas functioned to maintain linkages between communities, family values, and schools, in urban areas charity schools were often intended to supplant community and family values that were deemed lacking by philanthropic elites. Charity schools, eventually open to most children, became the dominant feature of the urban school system in the North.

In the southern states the development of educational systems tended to continue both more slowly and in a more stratified fashion. Whereas enrollments of primary-age male children in New York grew from 37 percent in 1800 to 60 percent in 1825, enrollments in the South stagnated at around 16 percent between 1800 and 1839.[17] The more aristocratic class system and slavery—salient features of southern life in both urban and rural areas—militated against the formation of both a district-style school system and the broadly subscribed charity schools that had achieved popularity in the North. Instead, children received such education as their parents could pay for. This ranged from private tutors to apprenticeships in useful trades to pauper schools to brief sessions with itinerate schoolmasters.[18]

State and Federal Governments Promote the Expansion of Education

Clearly, local preferences were a dominant force in all school systems during this time period, yet even this earliest history of school governance complicates the traditional American affection for and narrative of local control. Rather than being embedded in a grassroots dialogue and stemming from a preference for participatory democracy, local control existed and was defended in the northern states primarily to reinforce cultural values, or to impose them. Moreover, the district system of local governance emerged first in states with explicit statutory commitments to maintaining a school system. In the southern states, more than an active tradition of local democratic participation and control, an effort to maintain class divisions fueled resistance and outright hostility toward state or any other governmental intervention.[19]

The federal government was also actively encouraging the expansion of education, despite its limited authority. Much like today, it leveraged resources to induce states to establish their own education funds—specifically, by offering land grants. In 1787 the Northwest Ordinance authorized the sale of publicly owned land for the support of education, and by 1896, the federal government had granted more than 77 million acres to western and southern states.[20] In this manner, it was able to influence state and local priorities for development at a time when those governments' resources were particularly scarce.[21]

Early state aspirations for public education were also evidenced in state constitutions.[22] During the early years of the Republic, even though responsibility and decision-making for primary education remained with families, communities, and religious authorities, most states made the deliberate choice to include mention of public education in their founding constitutions. Many began chartering state universities. Despite the many forces arrayed against state intervention, most of the forty-five state constitutions written and adopted between 1792 and 1912 included provisions for state oversight, leadership, or funding of a public school system.[23] These leadership positions and oversight bodies included state superintendents, state boards, and county superintendents.

Once enshrined in state constitutions, state boards and superintendents became entrenched, institutionally legitimized advocates for public schooling.[24] Yet decisive state policy action was slow to arrive. As in earlier periods, this was partly a result of informal cultural norms. Though in favor of establishing public schools, most state governors and legislators were loath to intrude on local decisions. So they limited their demands—for instance, requiring that localities establish schools but only for two to three months per year, or simply making funds available to support teacher training. Many legislators themselves had been educated in private academies and believed schooling to be a family or community responsibility.[25] Adding to this reticence on the part of early state-level policy makers, local leaders often resisted outright state efforts to regulate schools.[26]

States' limited involvement was not simply because they tended to lack the legitimacy of a mandate from the public; it was partly a practical choice. State government in the early nineteenth century lacked capacity. Tax revenues were low compared to present day, both in absolute terms and as a percent of gross state product. State education agencies, the bureaucratic organizations that today are charged with the quotidian oversight of state school systems, had little capacity to establish, support, or monitor schools. As late as 1890, the median number of staff at an SEA was just two; the entire agency regularly made up of only a superintendent and a secretary.[27]

Many states focused what resources they had on higher education. This avoided conflict over local control while still supporting schools. College and university systems trained teachers and provided opportunities to students who had exhausted opportunities at the local level.

THE COMMON SCHOOL MOVEMENT AND THE EXPANSION OF PUBLIC EDUCATION

Starting in the 1830s, *common school* advocates pursued the expansion of public systems of education, and the tug of war between centralizing authority and protecting local autonomy became a more clearly articulated, persistent part of public debates in education. Once again, these reform efforts and their impacts were initially concentrated in the Northeast and the Midwest, eventually moving outward to the rest of the country.

Horace Mann, dubbed the father of the common school movement, is perhaps the most famous of these reformers. A legislator and the first superintendent of schools in Massachusetts, Mann advocated for a broadly inclusive, nonsectarian, free system of education with a longer school year, well-trained teachers, no corporal punishment, and broader availability of secondary schools.[28] To achieve these goals, Mann worked to end the district system in favor of a more centralized organization of schools. The common school model proposed placing one elementary school in a community, with a tier of secondary schools drawing students from across multiple communities. More formal and centralized governing boards that oversaw multiple schools were a centerpiece of his proposals.

Common school advocates saw significant problems with a decentralized curriculum, a short school year, dilapidated schoolhouses, and poorly trained teachers and hoped to solve these problems in part by reallocating policy-making authority. They believed that dissolving the district system in favor of more centrally administered town schools, guaranteeing more consistent public funding, and carving out a role for state governments in the training and certification of teachers would improve the quality of education.[29]

There was a distinct egalitarian tenor to reformers' arguments. They insisted it was the government's responsibility to provide citizens with opportunities to better themselves. At the same time, support for the common schools, especially in the northeastern states, was driven by the growing demand for a disciplined, literate labor force and by elite anxieties about the moral character of a new wave of European immigrants.[30] Leaders of the movement were white Protestant men intent on imposing their values and cultural ideals on an increasingly diverse, urbanized public.[31] During the 1850s, the Boston School Committee, speaking of recently immigrated Irish, described its mission as "taking children at random from a great city, undisciplined, uninstructed, often with inveterate forwardness and obstinacy, and with the inherited stupidity of centuries of ignorant ancestors; forming them from animals into intellectual beings."[32] For differing reasons, then, members of both major political parties (Whigs and Democrats) and members of different social classes supported the expansion and centralization of public schooling.[33]

Expansion of the Common School Movement

Though it originated and was most readily adopted in the Northeast, the common school movement influenced the administration of schools around the country. Mann's counterparts and colleagues, known at the time as *educationists*, worked toward similar ends in other states. They established systems of local elementary schools, proactively supported teacher training, and started to more consistently allocate public funding for local schools.

Henry Barnard advanced the cause of public education in Connecticut as a state legislator, in Rhode Island as an advisor to the governor, and later on a national scale as the first Commissioner of Education. John Pierce served as the first superintendent of state schools and promoted common schools in Michigan. Calvin Stowe, husband of Harriet Beecher Stowe, was instrumental in founding a teachers college in Cincinnati and, like Mann, urged his state to adopt a state system of schooling after touring schools in Prussia.

There were also commercial forces interested in promoting more homogeneous schooling. Schools around the country increasingly used the same curricular materials. The first widely disseminated textbook was the New England Primer, popular between 1760 and 1843. Next came the McGuffey Readers, a sequenced set of six textbooks, the first of which were published in 1836. Historians estimate that more than 120 million copies of the McGuffey Readers sold between 1836 and 1960.[34]

In North Carolina, the General Assembly enacted common school law in 1839, first at the discretion of the counties. By 1846, every county had established at least one common school. In the first decade after the law passed, funding was irregular, and the schools were not regarded as effective. Toward the end of the reform period, Calvin Wiley, the first superintendent of the North Carolina schools, brought some stability to the state's common school system, advocating tirelessly for funding. The state is often cited as an exception to the rule when it comes to regional differences in the governance and spread of public schooling—in part due to Wiley's efforts.[35]

Resistance to Common Schools

As with most great reform efforts, there was often a back-and-forth, stutter-step quality to policy change in this period. In Massachusetts, the legislature passed a statute encouraging the voluntary abolition of the district system in 1853. Six years later it enacted a law mandating the abolition of the district system, but then repealed the law less than a year later. The mandate passed again in 1869, then was repealed inside of a year, finally passing for good in 1883, thirty years after the original legislation.[36]

Many of the common school movement's most visible leaders were openly enamored of the centralized Prussian system of schooling. This may have galvanized opposition, given the skepticism with which many Americans viewed centralized government, for which Prussia was notorious. Conservative citizens fought for the maintenance of the neighborhood district system, though in comparison to the common school reformers, they were a disparate group, sometimes united by their shared opposition to centralized government, but more often divided by class, religion, and cultural heritage.[37]

Centralizing reform efforts did achieve some measure of success, making substantial progress in institutionalizing public school systems. The district systems in the Northeast and Midwest were eventually replaced with school systems that served entire towns. Enrollments had been trending upward prior to the introduction of common school reforms, and the common school movement streamlined governance and management, secured more consistent funding, and ultimately ensured schools would be able to enroll the growing number of school-age children.[38] Frequent, if fragmented, opposition nonetheless ensured that reforms could only be incremental, and authority over schooling was consolidated a little at a time.

PUBLIC SCHOOLS AND RECONSTRUCTION IN THE SOUTHERN STATES

With the exception of North Carolina, southern state legislatures generally dismissed the proposals put forward by common school leaders. Educationists made loud and frequent arguments in favor of publicly supported schools, and some communities did establish locally run common school systems. But for the most part, advocates found themselves outnumbered in the South—just as the opposition found itself outnumbered in the North.[39]

Southern resistance to public education continued to be fueled by a stronger tradition of localism, sharper class distinctions, slavery, a thinly spread population, a series of economic calamities, and the absence of dramatic industrialization and urbanization—trends that were rapidly changing the demographics, educational needs, and cultural environment in the Northeast.[40] As a result of immigration, the northeastern states had confronted more linguistic, religious, and cultural diversity. These factors motivated citizens and businesses to acquiesce to taxation for education more readily. It was hoped that schools would promote a more consistent civic culture and a productive economy. The white southern population was more culturally homogeneous and therefore less concerned with assimilation in the years prior to the Civil War than the white population of the North.

Instead of adopting a common school system, by 1860, over twenty-four hundred private academies opened in the South just prior to the breakout of the Civil War.[41] A number of southern states were making policy changes in the direction of expanded public schooling before the war halted their efforts. Common school reformers in Virginia were especially relentless, establishing community-supported common school systems in ten counties and four cities by 1855, though they were stymied in most parts of the state.[42]

Georgia, despite constitutional provisions dating back to 1777 that supported public schooling, never provided more than a minuscule amount of aid to pauper schools and private academies during the antebellum years. As in the North, the politics of public schooling were contentious in the state. A common schooling law was passed in 1837 but repealed in 1840. Eventually, the state legislature passed a bill that empowered counties and localities to tax for schools, but did not mandate participation.[43]

Public Education and Slavery

The growth of public schooling in the southern states was stunted by slavery. The egalitarian, democratic ideals that had resonated with communities in the North held less sway in the public discourse of a place where rigid caste distinctions were more readily embraced. In fact, such rhetoric threatened the status quo, especially as the practices of slaveholders became increasingly brutal.[44] Further, there was little need for a common civic culture when force was an accepted way to maintain the social order.

During the early years of the Republic, a number of integrated academies and schools for black children were established in the South, but in the aftermath of Nat Turner's slave revolt in 1831, state legislatures throughout the region criminalized the education of enslaved and even free black people.[45] Virginia and Georgia passed laws in 1831, Alabama in 1832, South Carolina in 1834, and North Carolina in 1835. At least two states—Mississippi in 1823 and Louisiana in 1830—enacted policies criminalizing the education of slaves and free black people prior to the revolt.[46] Maryland and Kentucky were the only southern states in which there were no sanctions for providing instruction to slaves or free black people.[47]

Southern states were therefore resistant, in varying degrees, to expanding educational access and institutionalizing a school system. Instead, they actively passed legislation to limit the population who could legally learn to read and write.

Reconstruction and the Centralization of Southern School Governance

Changes to the structure of education in the southern states began immediately after the conclusion of the Civil War with the establishment of the Freedmen's Bureau. While its activities in other policy arenas have been criticized as ineffective, the Bureau achieved real success in building educational infrastructure. It supervised and organized the activities of relief societies and missionaries to establish and support more than forty-three hundred schools by the time it shut down in 1870. Many of these schools were independently initiated by freed slaves.[48] Education was so widely regarded as important that from the moment the war began, Union military, abolitionists, religious groups, and freed slaves worked to educate newly liberated peoples.

During Reconstruction, state-sponsored public school systems became a fixture of the southern educational landscape. The Union demanded that southern states build educational capacity and assume authority for public school systems. It required Confederate states to adopt constitutional provisions establishing and maintaining schools at the public expense as a condition of readmission to the Union.[49] In this way, many southern states leapfrogged northeastern and midwestern states, centralizing authority over schools quickly and decisively.

One of the most contentious issues of this period involved whether or not southern states would be required to guarantee that public schools be integrated. The debate occurred frequently in Congress, but no formal legislation was enacted, and for the most part, decisions were made on a state-by-state basis. Louisiana and South Carolina both adopted new constitutions in 1868 guaranteeing that all schools would be open to students of any race. Alabama, Arkansas, Georgia, Florida, and North Carolina included equality provisions in their constitutions, but no language guaranteeing that children of different races would have access to the same schools. Texas, Mississippi, and Virginia enacted legislation to guarantee educational access for all children, but avoided language related to either equality or race.[50]

About a century after Thomas Jefferson, Benjamin Rush, and other revolutionary leaders pushed for the development of tax-funded education systems, they were finally implemented in the South. The magnitude and significance of the institutional change that took place during this period cannot be underestimated. Educational infrastructure and legal authority could have been accurately described as anemic in the period leading up to the Civil War. Afterward, public education became an entrenched component of southern state governments. In fact, many of the post–Civil War constitutions endowed the southern state governments with considerably more authority than their northern counterparts.

Since school governance did not evolve in the South as it had in the North—in a community-specific fashion, independent from the boundaries of other governments—southern states relied more heavily upon existing municipal and county borders in the creation of school districts and local boards.[51] They therefore not only created state institutions with more explicitly authorized powers, but also ensured that school governance would be better integrated with other components of state and local government than was the case in the North.

Backlash Against State and Federal Leadership

As with the common schools movement in the North, the establishment of public schools in the South constituted a major shift, and yet did not represent a final political victory. Fundamental disagreements over the public or private nature of education, and the proper relationship between the states and the federal government, surfaced during Reconstruction and were only temporarily resolved in favor of expanded support for public schools and greater access to education for children of all racial backgrounds.

These resolutions were short-lived. On the one hand, the federal government lacked both the capacity and the will to enforce them over the long term. On the other hand, communities and leaders throughout the South had not been convinced of the necessity and importance of public schooling, and had not made the autonomous decision to allocate local funds toward that end. State legislatures had not passed laws supporting common school systems, and white citizens in particular had not been convinced that black citizens deserved full inclusion in schools or politics.

While the common school movement entrenched debates over local autonomy and state authority in the northern politics of education, Reconstruction crystallized those same dilemmas and brought another to the fore in the South: state autonomy versus federal authority. When the Freedmen's Bureau closed its doors and the federal government withdrew the last of its troops from the South in 1877, old exclusionary patterns once again emerged and local resistance to state and federal intrusion and to taxation for education mediated the impacts of these changes.

Between 1888 and 1908, ten of eleven southern states adopted new constitutions. These new documents preserved state commitments to education for the most part, but included clauses aimed at preventing black citizens from voting, as well as provisions mandating that schools be segregated by race.[52] After two failed referenda in 2004 and 2012, Alabama's constitution still declares that "separate schools shall be provided for white and colored children, and no child of either race shall be permitted to attend a school of the other race."[53]

None of this is to suggest that black Americans in the North were welcomed and treated fairly in public schools. Most often they were not. In fact, at least twelve states outside of the South—in the West, Midwest, and Northeast—enacted laws during or after Reconstruction that required or encouraged the racial segregation of public school systems. In twelve states, these statutes went so far as to criminalize the operation of an integrated school.

THE PROGRESSIVES: PROFESSIONALIZATION AND EXCEPTIONALISM

If institutional fragmentation has its roots in the emergence of public school systems, political and administrative exceptionalism can be traced most directly to the Progressive Era. In the decades following Reconstruction, American society and government changed dramatically and rapidly. These changes affected what took place in schools and how governments related to one another in their administration of school systems. They represented the "beginning of a codified, organized, and hierarchical collection of educational institutions."[54] State and local governments, confronted with the myriad disruptions presented by industrialization and urbanization, worked to standardize practices within public school systems as a means of achieving more "rational" organizational structures for school regulation and divorcing educational policies from traditional partisan politics—the cornerstone of exceptionalism. These reforms are critical to understand, because the structures established by Progressives remain largely intact today.

Centralizing and Professionalizing Urban School Governance

At the turn of the nineteenth century, industrialization, which had begun in the Northeast and upper Midwest, accelerated and expanded its reach across the country.[55] The size and complexity of production were greater, and industries developed even in rural areas. Urbanization also intensified. Between 1860 and 1900, the proportion of the population living in cities doubled from approximately 20 to 40 percent. By 1930, more than 55 percent of Americans were living in urban areas.[56] While many of these new city dwellers were immigrants, a large portion of migration to the cities involved people coming from rural areas in search of greater economic opportunity. These developments coincided with the emergence of monopolies, glaring inequality between a class of ostentatious super-rich and a destitute urban poor, the rise of organized labor, and the dominance of corrupt political machines.

The Progressive movement rose to prominence amidst this turbulence. Liberal Progressives sought to promote social justice. They fought for increased citizen control of the political system across many states, advocating for grassroots powers, including the ability to propose referenda and to recall corrupt officials. This strand of Progressive thought produced the labor movement, and in the educational arena worked to promote child-centered, holistic pedagogical strategies. However, there was also a more conservative strain of Progressive thought. Drawing heavily from theories about modern industry, these Progressives sought to establish social order by reorganizing institutions into independent bureaucracies that delegated tasks of governance to trained experts who would make decisions based on the principles of rational management.

This second group of Progressives was extremely influential, reshaping the way that schools were organized and governed.[57] They advocated for the adoption of "scientific" techniques to bring schools into harmony with the needs of a growing, modern, industrializing society. These included age grouping of students, uniform curricula focused on easily sequenced and testable subjects, the creation of junior high schools, better training for teachers, and new school buildings, among others.[58] To maximize the efficacy of these modernizing reforms, they also pursued the consolidation of smaller schools into larger ones. As the average school district during the 1920s comprised only two schools on average, merging schools typically resulted in merging school districts.[59]

In their pursuit of efficiency, the Progressives also effected a reordering of the institutions of governance in school districts. The combination of increasing demands on school systems and reform efforts led to the development of a centralized bureaucracy. Progressives advocated a transition away from large membership boards that oversaw a single school and toward smaller boards that oversaw multiple schools, and the adoption of a corporate model in which board members no longer had influence over the day-to-day activities of schools, instead delegating managerial responsibilities to a superintendent.[60]

In this model, a superintendent of schools acted as a clerk: monitoring principals, compiling data, buying supplies, and making reports to a board or committee that oversaw the district. Often superintendents lacked the skill to do more than manage a district, but a significant component of Progressive reforms involved shifting greater authority to these supposedly less political actors. As they assumed responsibility for decisions previously made by large, heavily involved school boards, superintendents became increasingly professionalized and powerful.[61] A number of notable constituent organizations formed during this period of professionalization persist as major players in educational policy today. These include the National Education Association, the American Federation of Teachers, the Educational Testing Service, and the American Education Research Association.

Reformers pursued this corporate governance model not just to increase efficiency and effectiveness, but also to combat corruption. They charged that school-specific boards, which held authority over hiring, firing, building construction, and curriculum, were corrupt, ineffective, and beholden to neighborhood interests. By and large, historical evidence supports these charges.[62] Opponents of centralizing reforms argued, as do today's opponents of centralization, that decision-making was too far removed from the citizenry, that the democratic process was being subverted, and that the relevance and quality of education were likely to suffer. Indeed, these reforms enabled urban business elites to dominate local school boards. Upper-class citizens were represented, while working-class citizens were not.[63]

Progressive reforms had significant effects not only in the cities of the Northeast and Midwest, but also in the South. Southern political leadership began to abandon its laissez-faire approach to governing on economic and social issues. Industrialization, corruption, and urbanization were challenges affecting communities around the country.[64]

But while Progressives in the South ultimately pursued many of the same reforms, fewer school boards in these newer systems had reached a size considered ungainly, and many districts already shared borders with the municipality or country, so there were fewer opportunities for institutional consolidation and separation throughout the region.[65] Progressive reform in the South differed from the movement in the North on another dimension as well. The systematic disenfranchisement of black people through Jim Crow laws was in large part a product of laws proposed and passed by Progressive governors and legislators.

Excising Politics from Education

In addition to centralizing control over school systems and professionalizing their administration, Progressives took an additional step in an attempt to insulate school governance institutions. Local school boards had already evolved apart from general governance institutions in most places, but were treated in many cities as an integral component of the partisan spoils system. Coordinating with one another through organizations like the National Municipal League, Progressives fought to remove politics from education by establishing school board elections as nonpartisan in both the nomination and the election processes. They also sought to alter the timing of municipal and school board elections so that they would take place off-cycle, out of sync with major state and federal contests in which partisanship was likely to play a significant role.[66]

A parallel process of exceptionalism occurred at the state level, with states creating or augmenting statewide boards of education and state superintendent positions. Boards and chief state school officers were either independently elected in nonpartisan contests, or were insulated from the state executive branch in other ways, such as through staggered appointments, which limited gubernatorial control. Politics was a dirty, corrupt business, and in the eyes of Progressive reformers, schools required rational, apolitical management and oversight. In large part, these institutional arrangements persist today.

Stepping Up State and Federal Policy Activity

The changes that took place during this period were not exclusively alterations of the extant institutional structure. State legislatures asserted a more muscular authority over public education. One major state initiative was the enactment of compulsory attendance laws, requiring children of a specific age to attend school for a minimum number of days per year. These laws reflected a confluence of both the conservative and the liberal elements of Progressive thought. The first to enact these statutes were states in the Northeast, alongside California. By 1890, twenty-seven states required children of a certain age to attend school, and by 1918, all forty-eight states then in the Union had mandated public education.[67] Georgia and Mississippi were the last states to enact the law until Alaska joined the Union.

To a significant extent, the passage of these laws was motivated by desires to keep the unsupervised children of industrial workers off the streets, to provide them some protection from factory work at an early age, and to keep children from undercutting unionized adult laborers—so partially but not entirely as a result of concern for educational quality or having an informed citizenry.[68] In keeping with earlier efforts to expand public schooling, attendance laws were initially viewed as unenforceable in the Western states and were treated as little more than words on paper until later in the 1920s and 1930s.[69] Once enforced, however, these laws resulted in dramatically increased enrollments and considerably higher rates of literacy among the population.

During these years, the federal government also built capacity, establishing itself as the singular authority over currency, citizenship, and the military draft, and for the first time engaging in direct taxation.[70] In the realm of education, it began to more actively monitor the use and sale of federal lands for educational purposes and encouraged the expansion of higher education (primarily agricultural and engineering sciences) through the Morrill Acts of 1862 and 1890. The 1862 law granted lands only to states that had not seceded from the Union, thus exacerbating extant gaps in the infrastructure between the South and the rest of the nation. State incompetence in administering these early grants was later used to justify increased federal monitoring and supervision.

DISTRICT CONSOLIDATION AND GROWING STATE CAPACITY

In 1930, despite the substantial reorganization already implemented as a result of Progressive reform efforts, there were still over 120,000 school districts spread out across the country and approximately 200,000 schools in operation. The contentious process of school and district consolidation, at the end of the Progressive Era, was an unfinished task. States lacked the technical capacity to support, monitor, and liaise with this massive number of school districts, not to mention elected school board members. States were also missing the financial leverage to justifiably compel or constrain local school systems. Localities were responsible for more than 80 percent of school revenues.

In part, consolidation resulted from the efforts of reformers who sought to impose their ideas about scientific management on backward, inefficient rural communities.[71] But consolidation was also born of state governmental imperatives. In the wake of the Great Depression, many schools closed; some districts lost large portions of their revenues and could no longer continue educating students.

Schools and districts in rural areas were particularly hard hit. After the crash, farm failures decimated property taxes, the primary source of local school revenues. School closures, in combination with higher birth rates than in urban areas, led to increased demands on the remaining underresourced schools.[72] State governments around the country began assuming a larger portion of the responsibility for funding to offset the impacts of the revenues lost.[73] Between 1919 and 1929, there was virtually no change in the percentage of educational revenues for which state governments were responsible. Between 1929 and 1939, the local share of revenues dropped from over 82 to below 68 percent, and the state share rose from less than 17 to greater than 30 percent (see figure 2.1).

Administering aid to such a large number of districts was a challenge for states. Most state education agencies still possessed little in the way of

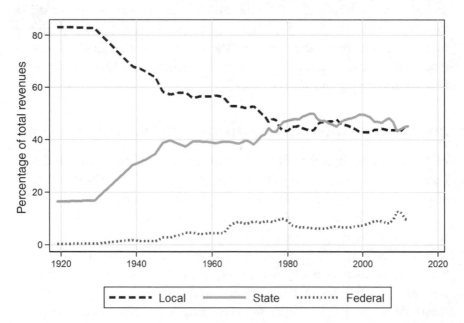

FIGURE 2.1   Public elementary and secondary education revenues by source: 1919–2012

staffing capacity or funding. States with many districts struggled to improve educational quality. They could not effectively regulate and monitor school accreditation, teacher certification, and curriculum in such densely populated institutional environments, so they forced small schools and districts to merge.[74]

Average state revenue authority continued to increase at the same time that district consolidation was under way, even after the US economy recovered. SEAs began to build considerable capacity during this time period. As the complexity of the requirements for educating students in this new, modern economy increased, so did the costs of educating students, further spurring state investments in the educational system. In the 1940s and 1950s, southern states, in which property taxes were simply not sufficient to support local schools, enacted what are now known as *minimum foundation plans*, which guaranteed districts a certain level of funding per student.[75] Throughout the country, as baby boomers entered the school system and the costs of education rose, states increased their financial support to help local districts cope with the influx of new students.[76]

In rural communities, where schools were often the most important neighborhood institution, consolidation raised the prospect of a significant disruption.[77] In particularly heterogeneous regions, it threatened integration of disparate religious, cultural, or ethnic groups and marginalization for whichever group was in the minority. Accordingly, consolidation met with fierce resistance in many rural communities, and often slowed.[78] In response to the threat of state-mandated consolidation, a few districts and schools merged preemptively, hoping to avoid the need for more drastic changes and to preserve some measure of local autonomy by voluntarily adopting incremental plans to make moderate changes.

States responded to resistance with a variety of strategies—sometimes direct mandates that involved the unilateral redrawing of district maps, and sometimes financial incentives.[79] Though the number of school districts declined steadily at the national level (as shown in figure 2.2), these disparate strategies and geographic constraints yielded varying trajectories of decline.

To describe these different approaches to consolidation, I compiled data from multiple historical sources, including retired and present-day federal surveys, in order to ascertain the number of regular school districts in each state between 1931 and 2012.[80] Examples of school district consolidation are displayed in figure 2.3. Many states exhibited trajectories similar to that of Illinois, where thousands of districts were shed rapidly between 1931 and

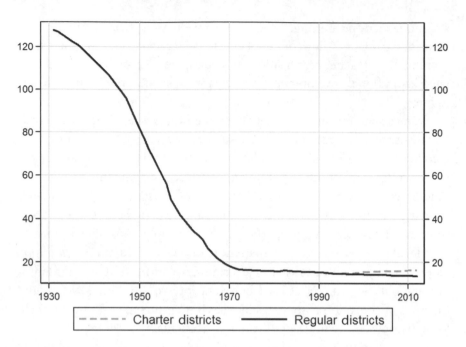

FIGURE 2.2   Number (1,000s) of regular public districts in the United States: 1931–2012

1971, and then the pace of consolidation leveled off, though the number of school districts in the state remained rather high. In Illinois and other states that conform to this pattern, there appears to have been little effort to bring school districts into alignment with the jurisdictions of general-purpose municipal or county governments. In 1971, there remained over fifteen hundred school districts in the state. At present, there are roughly eight hundred.

Arizona illustrates a more gradual process of consolidation, having started with a comparably smaller number of districts, five hundred, in 1931. Several states, including Kentucky and Georgia, followed this more gradual rate of decline. In California, three thousand districts declined little by little over forty years—largely because the legislature repeatedly failed to agree on a firm consolidation policy.

Over the same time period, between 1931 and 1970, there were no changes in a handful of states, including Maryland, West Virginia, and Florida, all of which had earlier established school systems that mapped onto county boundaries. Florida had sixty-seven districts at the beginning of the period,

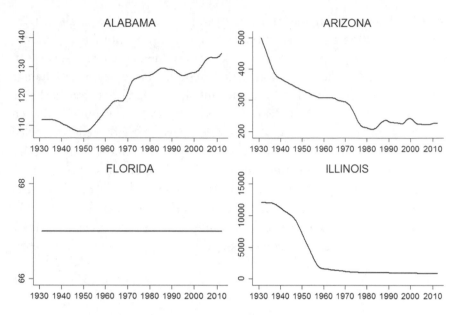

FIGURE 2.3   Trajectories of school district consolidation: 1931–2012

and the same number at the end. States that adopted county (e.g., Nevada) or county-municipal (e.g., Mississippi) modes of organizing school districts demonstrated a rapid, abrupt decline in the number of school districts but achieved a relative stasis, typically by the early 1970s. In Nevada, 177 districts became 17 in the span of only two years. These states are characteristic of three patterns of consolidation: rapid change, steady decline, or little to no change.[81]

By 1970, there were approximately 20,000 regular school districts and 100,000 operating schools, and states had assumed responsibility for 40 percent of school revenues nationally.[82] Most states found themselves with a more legible, manageable landscape of school districts and greater financial leverage with which to engage them. The pace of consolidation has proceeded much more slowly in the decades since. There was, however, a great deal of variation, both in the number of districts present in a given state and in the state's apparent financial commitments to those schools.

This is particularly evident when one considers a fourth group of states. Between 1931 and 2012, the number of regular school districts increased rather than decreased in Connecticut, New Jersey, Vermont, Virginia, Louisiana, Alabama, and Utah. For the most part, these increases were small and arose during the last twenty years. For example, a single district was added in the state of Utah in 2009 (bringing the total number of districts to forty-one), the only shift for the state during the entire eighty-two-year period covered by the series. In the cases of both New Jersey and Alabama, however, gains are somewhat more substantial and steady. Between 1931 and 2012, the number of school districts in New Jersey grew from 552 to over 600. In Alabama and Virginia, where districts have been either county or city led, a growing number of cities have opted to split from counties, driving the increase in the number of school districts. The increasing fragmentation of these states, and the slowing down of district consolidation, can be linked in part to efforts to avoid the integration orders that began with *Brown v. Board* in 1954—the landmark case that opens the next chapter's continued exploration of the historical context for education governance in the states.

3

Recent Federal Initiatives and the Changing Role of the States

During the second half of the twentieth century and into the twenty-first, reforms that had been somewhat common when public school systems were first being established, and which were explicitly intended to transform education governance, became less frequent (for instance, redrafting constitutions, creating new leadership arrangements, establishing new agencies, and dissolving districts). In this more recent history, transforming education governance was less a central goal than a side effect of pivotal federal and state policy projects aimed at shaping the core activities of teaching and learning and at expanding access for children who had historically been excluded from public schools (ethnic and racial minorities, the economically disadvantaged, and those with disabilities). This chapter discusses a number of these federal and state policy milestones, starting with the expansion of federal power during the 1950s and 1960s; moving through the emergence of federal and state policy regimes concerning finance, standards, and accountability; and concluding with the fight to roll back federal involvement, which resulted in the Every Student Succeeds Act. These episodes of policy change not only mark significant transformations of education governance, but also illustrate the nature of ongoing conflicts over where the legitimate authority to govern schools lies. They also document the shifting relationship between state and federal governments as their capacity to shape public education expands. These instances further highlight the role played by key constituencies and organizations in driving policy change and transforming governance. Throughout this period, differing constellations of actors and institutions at the state level mediated the impact of federal policy efforts and produced major policy innovations.

ESCALATING FEDERAL ENGAGEMENT: DESEGREGATION, EXCELLENCE, AND EQUITY

While the Great Depression spurred states to take a more proactive role in funding schools and encouraging district consolidation, it was the civil rights movement and the Cold War that drew the federal government into deeper engagement with public schools. In the process, it developed a new relationship with states, and also provoked changes in the relationships between state governments and the local school districts they supervise and support.

Brown v. Board of Education of 1954: Framing the Debate

Brown v. Board of Education, the 1954 case in which the Supreme Court ruled to strike down the doctrine of "separate but equal" and ordered the integration of public schools—and all public spaces—had profound effects on the civil rights movement, public discourse, and federal-state relations. In its decision, the court delivered a major blow to a long-standing legal regime that had forced black Americans to accept poorly funded schooling.[1] The *Brown* ruling brought an end to *de jure* segregation in public life more broadly, and it animated the civil rights movement in the late 1950s and early 1960s.[2] Along with the Voting Rights Act, it embedded equity in discussions of federal policy.

Nevertheless, the end of legal separation and the beginning of real integration were rather different things. Though many organizations had waged a campaign against segregation at every level of government for decades before the *Brown* decision was handed down, the agenda of desegregation was divisive within the community of civil rights activists. Ending segregation, while desirable in the long term, was not a first priority for many who felt it would threaten what economic security and prestige they had managed to achieve within the segregated system. This was a particularly acute fear for black teachers, many of whom held advanced degrees and constituted a large segment of the black middle class.

Indeed, the federal government's capacity and willingness to fully enforce the Supreme Court's mandate was limited. Large numbers of black teachers in the South lost their teaching positions or were forced out in spite of relationships between many black educators and teacher unions.[3] In a handful of southern cities during the 1940s and early 1950s, black educators had joined the American Federation of Teachers (AFT), which even filed an amicus curiae brief in *Brown*. The National Education Association (NEA) chartered black educator associations after *Brown* and supported wrongful termination suits along with the NAACP. Yet the attitudes of the union leadership were not necessarily the attitudes of white teachers, who often made working conditions for black educators unbearable.[4]

Brown inspired strong opposition among many southern whites. Michael Klarman and Charles Payne suggest that racial politics in nearly every southern state shifted toward the right in the aftermath of *Brown*, contributing over time to the broader realignment of partisan politics.[5] The decision "crystallized southern resistance to racial change."[6] Many southern legislatures enacted unconstitutional segregationist laws in deliberate defiance of the order to integrate. At the local level, fear of integration contributed to the slowing down of school district consolidation, to white flight, and in some cases to the splitting of existing school districts. School systems could not be legally segregated, but new school systems could be carved from existing borders.

This resistance inadvertently set the stage for later, more expansive federal education policy. The refusal of state governments to acknowledge the highest court in the land could not be tolerated, and the executive branch was drawn into the conflict to assert federal superiority. In so doing it established a precedent for dramatic federal intervention in local and state school systems. Further, as the energized white resistance in the South adopted repressive, brutal measures in an attempt to preserve Jim Crow laws and segregation, their actions yielded disturbing images of peaceful protestors repeatedly subjected to violent abuse. These images, broadcast nationally, converted many northern whites from passive observers of the civil rights movement to active supporters of its agenda. Over time, this public support was one of the components that facilitated a more active congressional role in education.[7]

National Defense Education Act of 1958: Establishing a Precedent

At the same time that equity emerged as a central concern of the federal government, a backlash against the holistic educational strategies associated with the liberal Progressives was also gaining momentum, though it would not dominate public agendas until the 1980s. The need for appropriately educated citizens, a feature of public school reform and policy throughout American history, reached a new prominence in national politics as the economy changed after World War II, and the United States entered into the Cold War.[8] A desire to improve the overall quality of schooling and to safeguard future economic competitiveness motivated state efforts to promote district consolidation and drove increases in educational spending from all three levels of government. This emergent concern for quality, and the growing consensus that certain subjects and skills ought to be commonly taught, reinforced the fight for equity. Not only were better schools an issue of fairness, but equal opportunity was key to ensuring that talented students everywhere could become economically successful adults.

Fewer and fewer jobs were available to those with a high school education or less, more and more formal training was required in the labor force, and the geographic mobility of the population was on the upswing.[9] Which subjects should be emphasized, how they should be taught, and who should be teaching them were debates that increasingly took place beyond the local level. The concern for quality contributed to growing state and federal activity in the form of state-regulated teacher certifications, state textbook adoption (which could also help to keep costs down for localities), and incentives for the provision of specialized courses.[10]

By far, the most significant event for reshaping public expectations and federal involvement in what schools could and should accomplish was the 1957 Soviet launch of *Sputnik*, just a month after the Little Rock Nine were escorted into Central High School. Critics of American public schools had argued for years that expectations of students were too low, that John Dewey's child-centered theories of education were failing to challenge the brightest students.[11] Regardless of the real discrepancies between the Soviet and American educational systems, *Sputnik* fueled the belief that the more advanced space technology reflected Russia's superior educational system.[12]

Framing the debate as a shift to a more academically oriented school system in the name of quality and international competitiveness gave congressional legislators the motivation and legitimacy they needed to try reshaping educational priorities. In 1958, the National Defense of Education Act (NDEA) was passed, part of a slate of science programs adopted under President Eisenhower.

Yet, in spite of its growing concern for equity and academic rigor, the federal government still lacked the constitutional authority of the states. NDEA could not be a mandate; instead, it attempted to incentivize state and local investments by providing aid to support science, foreign languages, and math at all levels of education. Participation in NDEA programs was voluntary, and in response to concerns about local autonomy, officials in the

Office of Education were expressly prohibited from attempting to exercise any control over local classroom curricula.

Republican Senator Barry Goldwater of Arizona, an ideologue committed to small government, and Democratic Senator Strom Thurmond of South Carolina, a committed segregationist, were specifically concerned about the precedent NDEA might set. They worried that the law would confer upon the federal government a new legitimacy in the realm of education, thus ensuring it would eventually have enough power to force states to integrate their school systems. Goldwater would later become the first Republican presidential candidate to win electoral votes throughout the South, running on a platform of states' rights. Speaking against NDEA, Goldwater famously warned: "'If the camel once gets his nose in the tent, his body will follow.' If adopted, the legislation will mark the inception of aid, supervision, and ultimately control of education in this country by federal authorities."[13]

The amount of money allocated through NDEA programming was not substantial in today's terms; in fact, the federal share of education revenues hardly budged in response. But in a sense, Goldwater was correct. The law stands out as the first real federal effort to shape K–12 education. It set a precedent for targeted federal assistance, spurred matching investments from local and state communities, presaged the outcome of the 1964 congressional debate over general versus categorical aid, included provisions that supported the expansion of testing to identify gifted students, and raised concerns about curriculum and standards more broadly.[14]

The mode of thinking about education policy that was manifest in NDEA—focused on academic achievement and rigor in specific areas of study—was subsumed on the public agenda by the civil rights movement, the war on poverty, and questions about basic access and skills. These ideas, however, helped shape the window of opportunity for the Elementary and Secondary Education Act, persisted in influencing state reform during the 1970s, and resurfaced with gusto in the 1980s, when the *A Nation at Risk* report was published.[15]

Elementary and Secondary Education Act of 1965: Building Capacity

Brown and NDEA effected broad shifts in the US political environment, without which the Elementary and Secondary Education Act (ESEA) might not have made it through Congress in 1965. Advocates for expanded federal funding of schools were repeatedly thwarted in the twenty years running up to ESEA's adoption.[16] Bills to expand federal aid died over and over again in Congress. Legislators believed that federal money would come with strings attached, and worried that federal influence would grow as schools and districts came to rely on those funds. Resistant members of Congress were especially opposed to efforts tying federal aid with enforcement of desegregation, such as those from Representative Adam Clayton Powell, a Democrat and the first black member of Congress from New York, who repeatedly put forward an amendment stipulating that federal funds could not be channeled to segregated districts. Others put forward the amendment in a deliberate effort to sink the bills, since it united conservative Republicans and Southern Democrats in opposition.[17] As the civil rights movement strengthened, this conflict was resolved through the Civil Rights Act of 1964, which prohibited schools and districts that practiced discrimination from receiving federal aid. Later that year, the balance of power in Congress shifted as elections brought forty-eight new Democratic representatives into the House (all of whom eventually voted for ESEA).

Federal aid to schools became more and more possible as pressure mounted to provide greater opportunities for the disadvantaged and resistance to desegregation began to give way. Social scientists and policy makers believed that providing higher-quality educational opportunities would be effective in eradicating poverty and promoting equality. Improving public schools seemed more politically feasible than other redistributive policies. American policy makers saw improving public schools as a way to "mitigate the social outcomes of the market, without directly intervening in the operations of the marketplace."[18]

Another conflict over ESEA highlights how the law was shaped by the institutions and norms that had bounded school governance to that point. At the time of the bill's introduction, Congress was torn between those who wanted to provide *general* aid to all school districts and those who preferred *targeted* assistance for poor students. President Johnson's "War on Poverty" and national public opinion encouraged the latter. Yet many House representatives were loath to vote for a bill that included no benefits for their constituents. Thus, the debate shifted to a discussion over the technical details of the funding formula. Eventually, members of Congress agreed to provide categorical grants to districts based on the density of economically disadvantaged students, but designed the formula to ensure that almost every school district in the country qualified for at least some federal dollars.

ESEA was signed into law in April 1965. Federal funding for education nearly doubled, from 4 percent of revenues nationally to 8 percent. The stated purpose of Title I, the bill's most prominent and well-funded section, was to provide educational aid to districts teaching disadvantaged students, but in the first years after the law's passage, a lack of oversight combined with a watered-down funding formula allowed many districts to spend the additional funds as general aid.[19]

A New Federal Role in Education Governance

The mandate from the Supreme Court in *Brown* eventually forced President Eisenhower to intervene in state and local education, raised the profile of educational inequality at the national level, and cultivated a role for the federal government to play: ensuring some measure of equitable outcomes and challenging local tyrannies when called upon to do so. The ruling also enrolled the federal court system in the direct supervision of integration efforts, a project that lasted for decades. At the same time, the decision helped crystallize resistance to federal involvement by linking it more definitively to the cause of racial justice.

NDEA set a critical precedent for programmatic support, and ESEA built directly on *Brown*, exemplifying a new federal willingness to set priorities for and offer incentives to states in the administration of their public school systems. ESEA began funneling substantial sums of money to poor districts through the states and in so doing subsidized dramatic growth in the capacity of state education agencies.[20] Title V of ESEA, for example, included funding that served to build up SEA capacity.[21] With larger staffs and expertise, SEAs could be more proactive in policy-making, taking on research projects, engaging in outreach to legislatures, and leveraging their expanded administrative capacity to more closely monitor local districts.[22]

At the same time, ESEA funneled the bulk of aid not to states, but to school districts, reinforcing the existing infrastructure of school governance. National policies have built on and around this first major federal education law, and state movements pursuing parallel ends were bolstered by federal action.

Brown, NDEA, and ESEA represent a significant shift in education governance in the United States. The character of this change is as much worth noting as the fact of it. Rather than the explicit institutional reforms of the earlier periods, governance itself changed, because an existing institutional actor successfully expanded the scope of its policy activity. In so doing, it normalized engagement of the federal government, in particular the courts and Congress; established superior authority in civil rights matters; expanded funding, a key avenue of influence; inadvertently galvanized the growth of capacity among state-level institutions; and redrew lines of conflict.

The decades following ESEA continued these patterns, advancing the federal role in guaranteeing access and developing its capacity to monitor and protect the rights of oft-marginalized students. Congress reauthorized and expanded ESEA and adopted the landmark Education for All Handicapped Children Act (EHA) of 1975. The courts continued to wade into battles over integration. Drawing on support from educators, who had heavily backed his presidential campaign, President Jimmy Carter convinced Congress in 1979 to grant cabinet-level status to education as a means of managing the growing number and size of federal education programs. His backers, who saw the federal government as an important political ally, included the NEA, the National School Boards Association, the Council of Great City Schools, the American Association of School Administrators, and associations of state education leaders including the Council of Chief State School Officers and the National Association of State Boards of Education.[23]

NEW POLICY REGIMES: GROWING STATE AND FEDERAL INFLUENCE

School Finance Litigation and Reform: The Limits of Federal Influence

Beginning in the late 1960s and building throughout the 1970s, activist networks composed of nonprofit groups, educators, parents, and civil rights activists—sometimes supported by philanthropic foundations—launched a series of court cases challenging the constitutionality of states' school finance formulas.[24] In the previous decades, the federal government had begun to provide supplemental aid to economically disadvantaged districts, ameliorating some between-state and between-district inequalities. Many states had likewise assumed a larger role in gathering and distributing revenues. However, between-district inequalities remained dramatic and highly visible in most states. Districts with high property values easily outspent their neighbors, sometimes multiplying several times over what was spent per pupil in the poorest districts. These disparities persisted in spite of the fact that poorer communities often taxed themselves at higher rates.

Two early lawsuits had a substantial impact on efforts to secure more equitable funding. The first came out of California. A group of Los Angeles parents sued the state in 1968, alleging that its school finance system violated the equal protection clause of the US Constitution as well as the California Constitution, in which precedent had established the existence of a right to a free public education. The case was decided in 1971 as *Serrano v. Priest*, and the court found in favor of the plaintiffs, declaring that the existing school finance system violated both constitutions.[25]

Also in 1968, an analogous case, *San Antonio ISD v. Rodriguez*, was brought by a group of parents in the Edgewood Independent School District (ISD) of San Antonio, Texas. They alleged similarly that education was a fundamental right and that the state of Texas's school finance system violated the equal protection clause by institutionalizing discrimination against the poor in favor of the wealthy. Though wealth and racial differences were correlated in the San Antonio area, advocates chose deliberately to focus on the economic disparities in their complaints. These parents brought their case through the federal courts, and initially judges found in their favor. The state appealed, and in 1973 the US Supreme Court narrowly overturned the earlier finding. The court's decision emphasized that the US Constitution included neither an implicit nor an explicit right to an education, and further that economic status was not a suspect class to which strict scrutiny could be applied.[26]

The decision in *San Antonio* forced the California Supreme Court to revisit *Serrano*. However, since the case had been decided on the grounds of the state and federal constitutions, the original finding was upheld in *Serrano II*. Subsequent cases brought by parents and advocates in other states focused on challenging the constitutionality of school finance systems under state constitutions, in the arena of state courts.[27] For example, eleven years after *Rodriguez*, Texas advocates brought another suit against the state, *Edgewood ISD v. Kirby*. In 1990 the Texas Supreme Court declared the state's finance system unconstitutional, ordering the legislature to devise a more equitable alternative. Since *Rodriguez*, more than seventy-six lawsuits alleging unconstitutional inequity have been brought in thirty-eight other states. Several states have undergone multiple challenges. Arizona's and New York's finance systems have been challenged six and seven times, respectively. The Texas finance system has been challenged on equity grounds four times.[28]

In part, when courts have decided against plaintiffs it has been due to a lack of constitutional language expressly guaranteeing access to an equal education. Plaintiffs in later rounds of finance litigation learned from early losses and challenged school finance systems based instead on *adequacy*, charging that the state constitution contained some provision explicitly or implicitly guaranteeing a certain baseline quality of education and that the state had failed to live up to this obligation.[29]

Though it cannot be directly correlated with the outcomes of lawsuits, the strength of such language varies from state to state—and over time. The Oklahoma Constitution, for example, requires the legislature to "establish and maintain a system of free public schools," a minimal guarantee. The New Jersey Constitution theoretically establishes a slightly stronger claim, requiring the state to provide for "a thorough and efficient" education. Until 1998, the Florida Constitution specified that "adequate provision shall be made for a uniform system of free public schools." Thereafter, it was amended to call for an "efficient, safe, secure, and high quality system," establishing a strong constitutional guarantee for children in the state and a clear obligation for the state legislature to provide the needed funds.[30] Through 2016 ninety-two cases had been brought in thirty-seven states. While a number were dismissed, often due to state supreme courts' reticence to intervene in a legislative activity—determining a threshold amount for funding public schools—half were decided in favor of the plaintiffs.[31] School finance systems have been struck down on equity or adequacy grounds thirty-two times in seventeen states.

The decisions in these cases have had varied effects, contingent largely on the popular and legislative responses to them. In both California and Texas, a public resistance to rising property taxes mounted in the aftermath of a finance decision. In California, the state's voters amended the state constitution with Proposition 13 in 1978, permanently limiting property taxes to 1 percent of assessed value, capping the rate at which assessed values could increase, and sparking a decline in the state's spending on public schools.[32] In Texas, after the legislature enacted a "Robin Hood plan" requiring wealthy districts to share their property tax revenues with poor districts, the better-off districts brought their own lawsuit, eventually overturning the plan in 2005.

In many instances, though, the very fact of a lawsuit was sufficient to motivate the state legislature to reevaluate the school finance formula, though modifications to it were often minor. Decisions in favor of plaintiffs, averaged across all of the states, reduced inequality, though they did not always yield the transformative changes envisioned by advocates. Often overall spending levels remained flat, or fell off as in the case of California.[33]

Throughout this process, most states have begun to exercise more control over many elements of educational finance, though each has chosen a different combination of policy tools.[34] Common approaches include placing limits on local abilities to raise funds, assuming greater responsibility for providing educational revenues, and exercising more authority in determining how those dollars would be spent—providing additional funds through categorical mechanisms (e.g., program-specific dollars).[35]

Scholars have struggled to evaluate the impact of these shifts in spending on student outcomes, with many emphasizing that an influx of funds does not constitute a sufficient condition for increased student achievement, emphasizing that *how* money is spent is a much more significant determinant.[36] However, recent evaluations of this wave of litigation and reform are able to take advantage of large datasets and more sophisticated statistical tools. They suggest that when education finance reforms led to increased spending on low-income children, those children experienced a variety of positive impacts. Kirabo Jackson and colleagues, studying students born between 1955 and 1985, estimate that an increase of 10 percent in per-pupil spending led to an increase in the number of years of school completed, an increase in annual adult earnings of nearly 10 percent, and a 6 percent decrease in the likelihood of living in poverty as an adult. The researchers found that when spending increased, teacher salaries increased, school years lengthened, and student/teacher ratios declined, suggesting these may have been the primary mechanisms by which higher spending levels affected students.[37]

Ultimately, funding effort (proportion of income) and levels between states continue to vary dramatically, as does inequality between districts within states and even between schools within districts.[38] Lawsuits challenging state finance formulas have continued to proliferate, in many instances invigorated by state standards and accountability policies, which have ensured that legal advocates have state-endorsed documents explicitly defining what constitutes an adequate or proficient education, as well as an accompanying mountain of data demonstrating that disadvantaged and minority children are not being provided the resources and support they need to achieve at that level.

From Minimum Competency Testing to the Governors' Summit: State Policies in a National Spotlight

In addition to the focus on finance reform during the 1970s, state education agencies and many governors turned their attention increasingly toward teaching and learning. Ostensibly concerned about both equity and inefficiency, they began to use their expanding capacities and fiscal leverage to advocate for the establishment of a program of assessments. These early efforts to assess educational outcomes on a widespread basis focused on the adoption of *minimum competency exams* (MCEs) for high school students. The exams were intended to evaluate the most basic skills a student might need in order to function as an adult in society and earn a diploma.[39]

MCEs were most popular in southern states, adopted almost universally across the region by 1986, though a few other states were also early adopters. Florida and New Jersey were the first states to pass a law requiring such an exam. North Carolina, Nevada, New York, and Maryland followed suit in 1977, and Virginia and Hawaii in 1978. Alabama, Tennessee, Mississippi, South Carolina, Texas, Georgia, Louisiana, and New Mexico also adopted MCEs in the 1980s. In the southern states where they were most popular, the exams served as a facially race-blind means by which access to higher education (and therefore teaching positions) could be limited for black students, even during federally supervised K–12 integration.[40]

Just as state efforts to evaluate academic outcomes gathered steam, the federal government withdrew, cutting taxes and spending on programs. President Ronald Reagan was at the forefront of these efforts. During his first term in office, ESEA was reauthorized as the Educational Consolidation Improvement Act, funding was cut substantially, and many of the law's categorical programs were consolidated into block grants. The block grants allowed the states more autonomy in how they chose to spend federal dollars; the autonomy was cited as justification for lowered funding levels. Between the 1979–80 and 1989–90 school years, federal spending fell from 9.8 to 6.1 percent of total spending on education.[41]

In the midst of federal retrenchment, President Reagan's blue ribbon commission published the *A Nation at Risk* report declaring American schools to be in crisis. The "open letter to the American people" played on already percolating public sentiments: weariness with the struggle for integration, frustration that increased education spending had not yielded faster results, and fear about America's changing place in the world.[42] It suggested that the previous decades' focus on access and equity had come at the expense of academic achievement, and it prescribed rigorous standardized testing as a key element of fixing broken state and local systems.[43] The report echoed and amplified the sentiments of those who advocated for MCEs, even emphasizing the necessity of reforms at the local and state level. Its high profile and urgent tone helped to align broader political constituencies behind the standards and accountability movement, which had been primarily confined to SEAs and a few governors during the 1970s. An interest in academic achievement and accountability effectively displaced concerns about equity and opportunity for poor and minority children. It was during this decade that the federal government invested in expanding the National Assessment of Educational Progress (NAEP) program of testing.

Throughout the 1980s, state legislatures, SEAs, and SBEs voted to increase graduation requirements, expand assessment regimes, and introduce additional regulations for teacher certification. It was a flurry of primarily top-down reform that expanded state authority over public schools in a significant way, broadening the acceptable scope of policy activity in what is now described as merely the first of many successive waves of standards-based reforms.[44]

Federal deference to state and local governments, and the focus on accountability, nonetheless continued under Reagan's successor. Early in his term, President George H. W. Bush declared his intention to be an "education president" but did so by convening a summit of the states' governors to discuss national education goals. He emphasized at the summit that his intent was to be a supporting partner who would allow state and local policy makers to lead the way.[45] The summit produced a set of deliberately ambitious goals, including a 90 percent high school graduation rate by the year 2000.[46] Bush followed up the summit in 1991 with a series of proposals that included the development of national standards, expanded testing, and federally supported school vouchers.[47]

Standards, school choice, systemic reform, and opportunity to learn were all policy ideas that moved into federal dialogue largely as a result of their increasing prominence at the state level. Advocates believed that measuring academic outcomes and increasing transparency for them was key to establishing accountability in a fragmented federal system.[48] President Bush's efforts did raise the profile of standards-based reform, and managed to set the stage for a more assertive federal posture with regards to the nation's public schools. Federal funding for K–12 education and for ED also increased substantially during his tenure. Both the substantive dialogue sparked by President Bush's proposals and the increased funding devoted to schools laid the groundwork for President Bill Clinton's somewhat more assertive education initiatives.

Advancing Standards-Based Accountability Reforms: The Expansion of Federal Authority

As the governor of Arkansas, Clinton had implemented standards-based reforms and been a key figure in the summit hosted by President Bush. When he came to office as president, his policy commitments were largely similar to those of the prior administration. He hoped to align federal policy with the efforts of the states that had already adopted standards-based reforms, and to incentivize a policy change in the states that had not embraced the standards and accountability agenda.[49] Clinton's first major legislative proposal, Goals 2000, was enacted in February 1994. It created a grant program for states to develop their own standards, a compromise for those who opposed Clinton's preferred approach—national standards. There were no guidelines regarding subject areas, no targeted student groups, and little in the way of quality control.[50] Many states initially resisted the funds, fearing an increase in federal intervention, but only Oklahoma and Montana persisted in their refusal. Upon accepting the funds, states named their initiatives to communicate to local constituents that these were state, not federal, endeavors. Other states dragged their feet or delayed implementation.

Goals 2000 was not President Clinton's only education initiative. During his tenure in office, ESEA was also reauthorized as the Improving America's Schools Act (IASA). During his 1992 campaign, Clinton had depicted himself as a "New Democrat," one committed to active government but also to efficiency and reduced regulation.[51] He promised to take a stronger federal stance in support of the nation's schoolchildren but also to cut through what he viewed as unnecessary red tape. IASA built off of Goals 2000, requiring states that accepted federal aid to develop content and performance standards for all students, specifying also that economically disadvantaged students could not be explicitly held to lower standards.[52] In keeping with the principles of the New Democrats and with the changes to ESEA under Reagan, IASA further reduced the number of process-based regulations, which had required districts to document how they were using supplemental funds. IASA also increased the targeting of federal Title I funds toward poor districts, strengthening the law's focus on equity. All told, the new law demanded more of states than had previous versions of ESEA, strengthening the federal government's hand. Yet it did not significantly augment the resources it provided states to accomplish the goals of improved academic achievement and higher graduation rates.[53]

By the time President George W. Bush took office in 2001, ESEA was due for reauthorization, and IASA had been implemented, albeit unevenly. Thirty states had fully embraced the project of standards-based reform, administering tests and adopting consequential accountability systems throughout the 1990s. Illinois, Wisconsin, and Texas were particularly early adopters, beginning implementation before 1995. Only four states, however—Florida, Delaware, Michigan, and New Mexico—used the data collected from schools to analyze achievement gaps between groups of students.[54] As with MCEs, testing and accountability systems were most popular among southern states. They administered the largest number of tests—each year, an average of twenty-two during K–12, compared with an average of just ten among northeastern states. Mississippi was the only southern state that failed to get with the program.[55]

Almost every state had by that point completely drafted its content standards, though many were finished well behind schedule. But only half of the states had received approval from ED for their performance standards. Several states appeared to be especially determined to lag behind with the accountability project—Nebraska at that point was administering only three exams during K–12, all of which focused on English language arts.

No Child Left Behind: Strong Federal Authority, Failed Process, and Backlash

The No Child Left Behind Act (NCLB) in 2001 was influenced significantly by the belief that prior iterations of ESEA, including IASA, had failed to seriously make over classroom practices.[56] The traditional reticence to take a prescriptive stance, which had previously characterized the federal program, waned and a stronger stance was endorsed by a robust coalition of Republicans and Democrats. NCLB was hailed at the time of its passing as "the broadest rewriting of federal education policy in decades," and a dramatic step toward high-stakes accountability.[57] To continue receiving federal funds, states were forced to comply with specific, complex provisions.

The law required states to create more detailed content and performance standards for each grade in reading, math, science, and social studies. It stipulated that states must test students in reading and math annually from grades 3 through 8 and once in high school, reporting the percentage of students who were proficient by subject, grade level, and demographic categories at both the school and district levels. While achievement gaps between poor and wealthy and black and white students had long been present and measurable in the aggregate, this provision in NCLB ensured that disparities would be visible within and between schools, districts, and states.

Schools and districts were then evaluated based on whether or not the percentage of students who were at least proficient matched up against annual performance benchmarks known as Adequate Yearly Progress (AYP). Those that fell short of AYP for a given year—or neglected to administer assessments to at least 95 percent of students across every grade level, subject area, and demographic subgroup—were identified as failing and began an improvement process that carried escalating consequences. The law required that AYP increase to 100 percent by the 2013–14 school year. Any school that did not ensure that every single student was proficient across all grade levels and subjects would be flagged as failing to meet expectations.

Most of NCLB's authors did not seriously expect that this ultimate requirement would actually be implemented. ESEA was scheduled for reauthorization in 2007. While reauthorization had not always occurred right on schedule, perfect proficiency seemed safely distant on the day that President Bush signed NCLB into law.

For the thirty states that had already enacted some form of accountability, the law meant augmenting a preexisting testing and accountability regime. Often it meant reconciling more nuanced evaluations of school performance with AYP's up or down measure. For states that had been more reluctant to adopt test-based accountability systems, the law required more dramatic change. Even states that had embraced standards and accountability balked; in some instances, governors and indignant legislators threatened to forgo millions of dollars in funding rather than cede control over the design of their accountability systems to the federal government. Ultimately, none could afford to carry through on their threats. Federal funds supported the most vulnerable of students and some of the students who were most expensive to educate—children living in poverty, children who were homeless, and English language learners.

The testing provisions of NCLB created a set of incentives that inadvertently extended federal influence into the most minute aspects of classroom teaching, student learning, and district operations. Reports highlighted an increasing focus on preparation for multiple-choice tests and less time spent on untested subjects.[58] Though initially NCLB's implementation carried only limited consequences, with each passing year a growing number of schools in each state were rated as failing, and began to face more significant sanctions.

Many states responded by lowering thresholds for proficiency. The strategy might have proven effective if reauthorization of ESEA had occurred on time. As it turned out, this fix was only temporary, forestalling the moment when almost every school would be legally designated as failing to meet expectations and in need of intervention.[59] As the reauthorization of ESEA became increasingly delayed, frustrations mounted at every level. However, Congress could not, or would not, find space on its agenda to revisit the law. The financial crisis and the Great Recession dominated the end of President Bush's term and the beginning of President Barack Obama's. The debate over the Affordable Healthcare Act crowded out other major policy initiatives.

Race to the Top and Waivers from NCLB

With the reauthorization of NCLB stalled, the Obama administration pursued its educational policy aims via other avenues. In 2009, Secretary of Education Arne Duncan announced an unprecedented competitive grant program, Race to the Top (RTTT). The available prize, to be split among winning states, was $4 billion to assist with implementing state reform proposals. RTTT's policy agenda had a great deal in common with NCLB, but stepped beyond it, offering an even more prescriptive set of reforms. Whereas NCLB afforded states flexibility in terms of how they implemented its many provisions, particularly those around content-based standards, achievement targets, and teacher quality, RTTT put forth more specific guidelines. States were prohibited from competing unless state laws and regulations allowed linking student and teacher data for the purposes of professional evaluation.[60] As with NCLB, the prescriptiveness of these requirements contrasted with the broad goals of the program. The Obama administration and Secretary Duncan did not seek to reward just any credible plan for achieving the end goals of improved achievement, attainment, and reduced inequity, but rather a particular vision of the mechanisms through which these objectives were to be accomplished.

In theory, such strict expectations were legitimate given that the competition was voluntary. However, RTTT arrived as part of the federal stimulus at a particularly vulnerable moment for state school systems. It was therefore met with a clamor that might not otherwise have been so substantial. During two rounds of competition in 2010, ED reviewed comprehensive education reform proposals from forty-six states and the District of Columbia, and nineteen states ultimately won awards. However, stakeholders were frustrated, and as implementation progressed, the program drew critique. Organizations on both the left and the right challenged the substantive policies enshrined in the program as well as the manner in which the administration was attempting to advance its priorities.[61]

RTTT allowed the Obama administration to promote its agenda in spite of the delayed reauthorization of NCLB, but it could not address the larger, mounting problems with the law's accountability provisions. The closer states got to the 2013–14 school year, the larger the number of schools they were forced to identify as failing within the narrow confines of AYP provisions. Nor did RTTT address the growing frustration among parents and teachers with what they increasingly viewed as excessive amounts of standardized testing. Thus, as frustrations with RTTT were percolating, the administration was compelled to search for a means by which to provide state school systems with relief.

In September 2011, President Obama announced that ED would encourage states to apply for waivers from key provisions of NCLB's accountability requirements. In order to be granted a waiver by Secretary Duncan, states needed to fulfill many of the conditions that had been controversial under RTTT—using student growth to evaluate schools and districts, for example.[62] Waivering as a mode of governance was technically legal, but drew more ire from states and stakeholders, again partly because of disagreements with the specific policies that were advanced, but also because the waivers were traditionally used more modestly and in this instance were viewed as circumventing the appropriate legislative processes.[63] Republicans, especially, viewed the waivering process as an example of executive overreach, but some Democrats thought the administration did not go far enough to intervene on behalf of vulnerable students.

NCLB's Effect on Student Academic Outcomes

NCLB and RTTT clearly created a lot of political friction, but how have they—and the policy regime of which they are a part—affected student academic outcomes? On the one hand, there has been a dramatic increase in state and local capacity to track students over time. The testing and reporting requirements under NCLB forced even states that had already adopted standards-based reforms to look closely not just at their average outcomes, but at the outcomes of all groups of students, including the most disadvantaged. This raised awareness of achievement gaps and inequality within the school system.[64]

On the other hand, a major motivation for NCLB, and the central justification for federal engagement, is and has been equity—closing achievement gaps between students who are poor and those who are not, and between white students and historically marginalized racial and ethnic minorities. By and large, this aim has not been realized. At least one early evaluation suggested that there may have been some improvement in the outcomes of minority students, concentrated in states where there had been no consequential accountability in place prior to NCLB.[65] However, research on state-level accountability systems has demonstrated that in the early phase of implementing testing and accountability regimes, there are often gains in test scores, which flatten as students and teachers becoming accustomed to standardized testing. In other words, initial gains do not always indicate real improvements in learning. When accountability policies have positively impacted academic outcomes, they often fail to reduce inequalities.[66] According to NAEP, colloquially known as the nation's report card, achievement gaps remain substantial and significant.[67]

Several recent studies have shed further light on the effects of NCLB. First, the achievement gaps between wealthy and poor students, rather than shrinking, have actually widened in recent years. Evidence suggests that this is connected to increasing wealth and income gaps in the US population at large, and that these economic differences are increasingly reflected in parental investments in education, which have provided children of wealthier families a growing academic advantage.[68] Second, racial achievement gaps have been closing, but very slowly, and not aided consistently by NCLB. Sean Reardon and colleagues estimate that at the current pace at which achievement gaps are closing in the aggregate, disparities between black and white students will take more than 100 years to disappear, and disparities between Hispanic and white students will persist for another 50 years. They find NCLB's impacts on achievement gaps have varied by state, yielding little in the way of an average. In some states achievement gaps between white and minority students grew under NCLB, whereas in other states they shrank, mediated in part by the level of segregation in the state and the size of the population identifying with that particular minority group. In states where minority groups were smaller, gaps grew on average. In states where they were larger, gaps appeared to decrease at a faster rate. The study found no clear relationship between having adopted accountability prior to NCLB and the pace at which achievement gaps closed.[69]

RETURNING POWER TO THE STATES, ENCOURAGING STAKEHOLDER ENGAGEMENT

The Every Student Succeeds Act (ESSA) was drafted and debated in an environment where members of both parties found themselves and their constituents extraordinarily frustrated by NCLB's testing and accountability as well as the manner in which the Obama administration had leveraged NCLB's slow demise to coerce reforms. The stage was set for Congress to relinquish authority to the states.

The Every Student Succeeds Act: A Gridlocked Congress and Mixed Reception

The 2014 midterm elections seemed to offer up a window of opportunity. The Republican Party won control of the Senate, giving it unified control of Congress and placing Senator Lamar Alexander at the head of the Education Committee. The senator had previously served as the governor of Tennessee in the 1980s, leading early efforts to implement standards-based reforms, and then as secretary of education under George H. W. Bush in the early 1990s. Alexander had displayed open frustration with RTTT and with the use of waivers, particularly to compel states to adopt a particular approach to teacher evaluation.

The senator spoke often about excessive testing. Many observers in Washington, DC, believed that his version of a replacement law might do away with federally mandated annual testing altogether, a position that placed him in an unusual alignment with teacher unions, who had long protested overtesting under NCLB but have traditionally supported Democratic candidates during election season. Senator Alexander's antipathy toward federally mandated testing put him at odds, however, with many Democrats and civil rights advocates who believed that federal pressure was vital to maintain transparency and accountability for the outcomes of poor, minority, and disabled students. Indeed, the first draft of the bill that was released by Alexander's office in early 2015 included a plan that would have allowed states to continue with NCLB-era annual testing or to branch out and develop their own more holistic plans for assessment.[70]

The legislative process initially looked as though it might unfold in a partisan manner, with Senator Alexander and Republican leadership drafting the bill and moving it through committee on their own terms and bringing Democrats to the negotiating table only at the last minute. However, an unexpected partnership was forged out of mutual frustration with the status quo, shared concern for schools, and the fact that President Obama and Senate Democrats maintained enough power to hold up any final version of the bill they disliked strongly enough.[71]

There may have been an additional reason why bringing Democrats on board was an important strategic decision. Political scientists have long observed that the two parties have different levels of credibility in specific policy areas—that is, ownership over particular issues. To radically simplify the insights of a complex field of study: while the public is more likely to trust a Republican leader on matters of defense, it is more likely to trust a Democratic leader on issues concerning education.[72] Issue ownership is not static; it can shift and change, but such shifts are quite difficult and often are short-lived, and polling indicates that the Democratic Party has maintained a sustained reputational advantage over the Republican Party in education, in spite of the mounting frustration during President Obama's tenure.[73] From that perspective, partnering with a Democrat and producing a bipartisan bill would serve to legitimize a law that would ultimately depend on buy-in from states, localities, and stakeholders during implementation. Senator Patty Murray, a Democrat from Washington State, sought to become part of the process. In February 2015, she and Senator Alexander announced that they would work together to draft a bill. Though Murray did not speak out against the Obama administration as vociferously as Alexander, her state had publicly lost out on an ED waiver over a dispute regarding teacher evaluations and testing.

Negotiating between Democrats and Republicans, teacher unions and civil rights groups, the House and the Senate, Congress and the president, went on for months throughout the spring and summer of 2015. Senator Alexander and the more conservative members of his party sought to include vouchers or Title I portability in the law; Democrats were opposed. Murray was unshakeable in her commitment to expanded funding for early childhood education; Republicans were uninterested in increasing the scope of programming or spending in ESEA. President Obama wanted to build in a requirement that states intervene in the lowest performing 5 percent of schools—a required element of proposals in RTTT. Others viewed such a specific provision as a continuation of federal overreach. Civil rights groups wanted to ensure that states would still be required to report achievement outcomes based on student groups. Teacher unions wanted the finer details of accountability systems to be left up to state and local stakeholders. Parent groups wanted to be able to opt their children out of standardized testing, while advocates for children with special needs emphasized that maintaining NCLB's 95 percent testing requirement was vital; they feared schools and districts might simply send home children whom they expected to perform poorly when testing day arrived.

The House version of ESSA, adopted in July 2015, was passed along strictly partisan lines and included conservative provisions that President Obama promised to veto if they made it through the conference process.[74] So the Senate moved forward with its version of the bill, planning to resolve the differences between the two bills in conference committee. It passed just days after the House version, receiving broad bipartisan support.[75] Negotiation between the two versions of the bill went on throughout the fall months, with a conference bill agreed upon in November. The negotiating parties were motivated to move quickly to avoid getting derailed by the politics of the coming 2016 presidential election, though education is only rarely a major issue in presidential elections. When ESSA passed and was signed into law, Senator Alexander declared proudly that it would unleash a wave of innovation in the states, and later, when the last of the NCLB waivers expired, he declared happily that the era of "Mother, may I?" in education was at long last over.

Senator Alexander was not the only person to greet the final version of ESSA with a sense of excitement. Secretary of Education Duncan emphasized that in contrast to NCLB, which "prescribed a top-down, one-size-fits-all approach to struggling schools," ESSA offered "the flexibility to find the best local solutions—while also ensuring that students are making progress."[76] President Obama declared that the bill upheld "the core value that animated the original Elementary and Secondary Education Act signed by President Lyndon Johnson, the value that says education, the key to economic opportunity, is a civil right."[77] Major associations representing governors, state boards of education, chief state school officers, and local superintendents, as well as the NEA and the AFT, similarly applauded the law.[78]

Civil rights groups, disability advocates, groups representing English language learners, and some scholars greeted the bill with a little more trepidation. They worried there were not enough protections built in to the design of the accountability plan for vulnerable student populations.[79] Along those lines, Arnold Shober argued that ESSA could actually be interpreted as a continuation of federal retreat from classrooms, not a sudden break with the recent past. He pointed out that early versions of ESEA exhibited a deep skepticism toward state and local governments, and for that reason it had required that federal dollars be spent to serve particular groups of students and that documentation of service delivery be provided as evidence of compliance. Subsequent iterations of ESEA, including NCLB, relied less on accountability for process, instead directing federal efforts toward measuring and monitoring inequalities in outcome, with the expectation that the pressure would lead to *some* kind of change in classroom practices or even resource distribution.[80]

Key Provisions in ESSA

Whether ESSA's apparent refutation of the enhanced federal role was met with celebration or apprehension, key provisions of the law have in fact preserved many priorities of past federal policy. A brief inspection of ESSA's standards, testing, and accountability provisions suggests that a considerable amount of NCLB and several of President Obama's priorities remained intact through the legislative process, though states have won greater leeway in the design of their accountability systems.[81]

Standards

To continue receiving federal Title I funding, states are required to adopt content standards in math, English language arts, and science. As with IASA and NCLB, these standards must apply to all students, without making distinctions based on demographics. The state must specify at least three levels of achievement, and standards must be aligned with the demands of higher education at in-state universities and any relevant standards for career and technical education. This latter requirement constitutes a new addition to ESEA and continues a trend of encouraging closer linkages between K–12 and higher education.[82] How states will demonstrate alignment with higher education, and which institutions they will align standards to—community colleges or four-year colleges—are questions that will be answered with time.

Testing

As under NCLB, states must continue testing students in English language arts and math in grades 3 through 8, and once in high school, supplementing those assessments with three science exams. States are granted some leeway with high school exams; ESSA allows for nationally recognized tests like the SAT and the ACT to be substituted for other assessments, provided these align with the state's content standards. To promote innovation in the kinds of tests states use, the secretary of education is empowered to establish a pilot program for states that wish to develop new methods of assessment. To support reduction in testing, some funds are to be set aside to encourage states and districts to weed out repetitive and uninformative tests.

School accountability

The accountability provisions in ESSA make space for states to develop nuanced alternatives to AYP, while maintaining some very specific guidelines about what accountability systems must encompass. For example, states must describe what will happen in the event that fewer than 95 percent of all students, or students in a tested group, do not complete an assessment. Even if participation falls below that rate, a school's proficiency rate is calculated as though at least 95 percent of students had participated, meaning that a lot of zeros will be averaged into the school's proficiency score. At the same time, ESSA explicitly recognizes parental rights to opt children out of standardized testing.

States must establish long-term goals for the percentage of students who will be expected to meet state standards for proficiency in reading and math, as well as target rates for graduation. These long-term goals must be equivalent across all groups of students, but annual growth targets may vary so that for student groups who are further from those targets, markers of progress will be expected to advance more quickly. Schools must be evaluated based on overall performance against these interim and long-term goals, and will continue to report and be held accountable for all subgroups at the school. ESSA requires that schools be held accountable for consistent underperformance of any group.

Schools are also to be evaluated based on some combination of:

- academic achievement as measured by rates of proficiency or, at the high school level, growth;
- some additional indicator of academic achievement (graduation rates at high schools, and possibly growth at elementary and middle schools);
- English language proficiency; and

- some other valid and reliable indicator of school quality that may be academic or nonacademic.

The opportunity to include multiple academic indicators and nonacademic indicators in accountability systems is another intentional repudiation of NCLB, aimed at affirming a broader way of measuring school quality without neglecting the central importance of academics. States have latitude in deciding how to weigh each of these factors, though the first three must carry more weight than the last.

Support for struggling schools and students

Based on these measures, the law also provides for three different categories of schools that should receive support for improvement. The lowest performing 5 percent of Title I schools, and every high school with fewer than 67 percent of its students graduating, will be identified for comprehensive support and improvement. Districts will generate plans for these schools, which will in turn be reviewed by the state. Schools where one or more groups of students are consistently underperforming will be identified for targeted support and must similarly implement an improvement plan established by the district. Finally, schools in which one or more groups of students score so poorly on state assessments that their performance matches up with the lowest performing 5 percent of Title I schools will also be identified for targeted support. For this latter group of schools, resource inequities must be directly addressed in improvement plans.

Public reporting

As with NCLB, public reporting is a central component of ESSA, one that provides the public with even more data than will necessarily inform school accountability measures. States are expected to oversee the production of statewide, district, and school report cards. These must identify when schools have been selected for extra supports; provide results for each of the indicators in the accountability system, overall and disaggregated by student groups; and display assessment participation rates for all of those groups.

In addition, report cards must now include information that states have long been gathering for civil rights data collection. These indicators include the availability of advanced coursework; rates of suspension, expulsion, and absenteeism; and educator credentials and quality. Districts are explicitly required to calculate and report comparisons on all of these metrics between their schools. These requirements go beyond those for NCLB, especially in that they require districts to calculate and present comparisons between high- and low-poverty schools. It remains to be seen, however, what the impact of these report cards will be.

English language learners

In ESSA, English language learners (ELLs), a population growing in number, receive a great deal of attention. States must demonstrate they have established English language proficiency standards and that these standards align with general academic standards. They must assess ELL students annually to determine whether or not students are making progress toward English proficiency. ELL students will be excused from other statewide tests only for the first year in which they attend schools in the United States; thereafter, they must take all other requisite state exams (though reading and language arts assessments may be administered in their native language).

Students with special needs

Students with special needs also receive some specific attention in ESSA. Conflicts often arose under NCLB between its requirements and the rights guaranteed to students under the Individuals with Disabilities Education Act (IDEA). ESSA allows states to develop alternative standards for the most cognitively limited students, provided that the standards are rigorous enough to prepare students for postsecondary education or employment, align with the state's broader academic standards, and promote access to inclusive settings. States may utilize alternative assessments, aligned with the alternative standards, but these may be given to no more than 1 percent of students statewide, a number that theoretically captures the students with the most significant cognitive disabilities.

Planning and stakeholder engagement

While ESSA carries through many of NCLB's requirements and mechanisms, and even some of the policies advanced by President Obama and ED through waivers, it nonetheless represents a significant change for many states. Even the forty-two states that had been awarded waivers at the time of ESSA's adoption—and thus had already designed and proposed some amendments to their accountability plans—have had to go back to the drawing board to design new accountability systems and put together plans that adequately address all of the aforementioned elements. Once ESSA was signed into law, ED began the process of drafting regulations, laying out a timeline for implementation, and eventually publishing application documents for states to submit the details of their plans. States could then submit their applications for review by ED.

In June 2016, Secretary of Education John King issued a Dear Colleague letter regarding the proposed regulations for ESSA and offering specific guidance for including stakeholders in the planning process, explaining that states were expected to document that they had consulted with stakeholders in the process of drafting their plans.[83] The federal government seemed poised to take a lesser role in education governance, but was simultaneously attempting to ensure that policy processes as they unfolded at the state and local levels would be deliberately crafted in an inclusive manner.

ESSA actually includes an unusual number of references to stakeholders. The word *stakeholder* appears in the law itself thirteen times; by contrast, it appeared just one time in the text of NCLB, and only three times in the text of IASA. ESSA indicates that states should consult with "teachers, principals, other school leaders, parents, and other stakeholders" when determining the smallest number of students who must be present in order for publicly reported data to be disaggregated and when evaluating assessment systems. Later it suggests that local school districts should partner with stakeholder groups when devising comprehensive or targeted improvement plans for identified schools. The list of key partners grows longer for states that might wish to participate in the pilot program for developing innovative assessment systems, to include "stakeholders representing the interests of children with disabilities, English learners, and other vulnerable children; teachers, principals, and other school leaders; LEAs [local educational agencies]; parents; and civil rights organizations."[84]

State leaders in California, Georgia, Pennsylvania, Wisconsin, and elsewhere have held listening tours, created online portals for gathering public feedback, generated hashtags, convened advisory councils, and hired consultants to facilitate stakeholder engagement. Recognizing that coordinating such networks asks a great deal of state agencies, major associations have held webinars and published guides for states to support their efforts.[85]

This emphasis on inclusion builds on the legacies of the Obama administration's RTTT competition, which similarly opted to award points to states based in part on the extent to which they could demonstrate having open and participatory processes for crafting proposals, and strong support from diverse stakeholders. It reflects the deepening recognition among many public administrators and reformers that the success of their endeavors depends on the thoroughness with which they engage, learn from, and are supported by core constituencies.

Many groups are highlighted as important in ESSA's text and in support documents encouraging states to cultivate broad partnerships. Some stakeholder groups are in close, constant contact with schools; others are more indirectly connected to them. There are individuals and the organized groups who are actively engaged with schools: students, parents and guardians, and education professionals. There are those who maintain a consistent interest in schools and often a close relationship with them, but are not actively engaged with education on a daily basis: civil rights organizations and advocates, community-based organizations, and policy advocates. And there are those who may be concerned with schools but are also likely to have a large portfolio of policy activities: political parties, businesses, and philanthropic organizations. Of course, these categories are not always mutually exclusive. Policy advocates may also be organizations representing the interests of a particular student group. A philanthropic organization may also be a community-based group. These constituencies can and do organize and establish a presence at the local, state, and national levels.

An Opportunity and a Challenge

For these stakeholders and others, ESSA presents both an opportunity and a challenge. On the one hand, the new law has created an opening in which new student assessments, new indicators of school quality, and new systems for school accountability can be devised, and it has left a deliberate path for diverse state and local constituencies to participate in decision-making. On the other hand, the two years of planning for ESSA's implementation have proven fractious in many states, as long-simmering conflicts have been surfaced by the mandate to draft a document that lays out the future of the state's schools. As the locus of control over education shifts to state capitols, how ESSA unfolds over the long term will depend in part on whether or not activists and leaders can take advantage of the opportunities it creates, and work through the challenges it presents, to collectively support policies and programs that are tailored to the circumstances of their state. The following chapters describe state governance in greater detail, focusing on how differing state commitments to institutional fragmentation, political exceptionalism, and local control have mediated the impact of federal efforts and shaped state-level policy processes in the past.

4

School Districts, Fragmentation, and Inequality

One factor that has major implications for the way that ESSA will play out in different states is institutional *fragmentation*—the extent to which state school systems are broken up into larger or smaller numbers of districts. Despite the rise in federal and state authority and the massive consolidation efforts detailed in the preceding chapters, the district remains the foundational administrative unit of education governance. States rely on district governing bodies and superintendents to make important decisions about finance, academics, and personnel. States and the federal government allocate resources through local districts and task them with adapting and implementing state and federal policies and programs. Further, for more than 80 percent of public schoolchildren, district boundaries and residential attendance zones still determine which schools they will attend.[1] This chapter, the first of three exploring a specific dimension of education governance in the states, considers how institutional fragmentation shapes policy processes, how it structures inequalities, and finally why it has remained so stable in recent decades, despite the tumult occurring with respect to other aspects of educational policy and governance.

Fragmentation is a critical aspect of the institutional configuration of state school systems, because it shapes *how* policy is made and implemented. It also affects *who* is able and expected to participate in that process. In general, state systems that are more fragmented face more substantial hurdles to achieving good governance. Communication, coordination, and collaboration throughout the policy process are more difficult in fragmented states. Regional education service agencies (RESAs), stakeholder groups, advocacy organizations, and professional associations can help to bridge divides between state and local leaders, but since resources are often required to participate in and maintain these intermediaries, relying on them may contribute to inequalities in political engagement and influence. Regardless, those who hope to make change at the state level must recognize and account for these differences in process to avoid political backlash and decrease the likelihood of implementation failures.

Perhaps more importantly, fragmented systems establish institutional boundaries that perpetuate—and in many cases exacerbate—racial and socioeconomic segregation. This means that the institutional underpinnings of educational inequality, and consequently the stubbornness of achievement gaps linked to segregation, vary systematically. This variation in turn creates opportunities for mismatch, wherein the same policy implemented in more or less fragmented states is likely to yield different effects. And though fragmentation appears to contribute to higher levels of segregation overall, school district borders have proven to be remarkably durable over the last thirty years, due in part to Supreme Court decisions that required racial integration within school districts, but not between them.

HOW FRAGMENTATION SHAPES POLICY PROCESSES

During interviews with education leaders working in state education agencies (SEAs), legislatures, and gubernatorial offices of diverse states, I observed differences in the relationships between local and state authorities in more and less fragmented systems. The patterns I identify are largely consistent with previous studies. From the top down, large numbers of districts seemed to present a significant coordination challenge for the SEA in terms of providing consistent support to districts, monitoring the implementation of programs, and rallying local education agencies (LEAs) around new initiatives. From the bottom up, it appeared that large numbers of districts also created coordination challenges for local school boards or superintendents who want to advocate for their students or schools and influence a state's political process.

Communication and Cooperation Between State and Local Education Leaders

In less fragmented systems, leaders and bureaucrats in SEAs often felt that they were able to maintain close and frequent contact with district leaders, in many cases espousing a deliberate commitment to accessibility. One state chief proudly shared with me that every single district superintendent had their personal phone number and was encouraged to use it, meaning that local leaders had a direct line to one of the most important public school leaders in that state, someone with the authority to immediately modify programs and who could voice their concerns directly to the state legislature.[2] Such a leadership strategy would not be feasible in California or New York, where districts are so numerous, and it would probably not be advisable in states where there are several hundred districts. This chief also sought to foster a shared commitment to accessibility throughout the agency: "We have the culture of school districts depending on the department. Now, do they fuss at us? Oh, yes. Do they complain? Oh, yes. But, I said to staff, 'I want all district superintendents to believe that I value their opinion. I listen to them, and I'm in touch with them, and they can call me at any time.'"

These sentiments confirm what one might observe publicly in a state where the school system is more consolidated. For instance, Lillian Lowery, who served as the superintendent of schools for Maryland from 2012 through 2015, was widely known to meet monthly with the state's twenty-five local superintendents and its teacher union leaders.[3] Lowery also visited every county in the state twice during her first year as superintendent, working closely with schools and district leaders throughout the implementation of Common Core. These visits enabled her to quickly respond to challenges as they arose, which in one instance meant requesting the extension of federal deadlines for introducing a new system of teacher evaluation.[4] Lowery's successor, Karen Salmon, continued the practice of meeting monthly with local superintendents.[5]

New Jersey provides a contrast to Maryland. Though the two are similarly sized in terms of square miles, New Jersey's school system is extraordinarily fragmented, with more than six hundred school districts during the 2012–2013 school year. It is difficult to imagine how Chris Cerf, who served as the state's commissioner of education from 2011 until 2014, could have visited every district, nor is it clear that this would have been a wise use of his time. Instead, recognizing the importance of communication and cooperation between state and local leadership, Cerf fielded a survey of the state's LEA superintendents. Three-quarters of the respondents indicated that the state's education department did not play a major role in supporting districts to improve student achievement. As discouraging as these results were, the survey was the first of its kind in New Jersey, and established a mechanism for improving communications going into the future.[6]

Those working in SEAs that served less fragmented, more consolidated state systems believed that access was important, partly because it fostered trust between local and state leaders. Several interviewees emphasized that these trusting relationships helped to ensure that bureaucrats in the state agency were well informed about what was working or not in local systems. Discontent, frustration, or a mismatch with local needs could be addressed, and confusion about new programming could be cleared up quickly, improving—from the vantage point of state bureaucrats—the quality of program implementation. This closeness also enabled SEAs to identify opportunities for collaboration and innovation. One upper-level employee told me how knowing district leaders well made it possible to identify, recruit, and partner with districts in order to pilot new technology: "So, that one-to-one was all about figuring out how we would do a statewide rollout. What are the issues? Really, I like the approach, because I said, 'let's bite off a little chunk.' And I know that it's probably not going to be perfect, but we are going to learn a lot from it. We are going to learn about what the barriers are, and we are going to learn about what works well. We are going to learn about what we need to do, and what to make sure we do."

Fragmentation seems to shape connections between local leaders and state legislators somewhat differently. Even in fragmented states, state legislative boundaries are often small enough that they encompass a manageable number of districts. And though education is only one of the issues legislators must address, it is an important one. Schools are also common sites for reaching out to constituents. For local leaders, this avenue of bottom-up influence is available since it is often straightforward for constituents to obtain meetings with their legislators. Further, research on state-level policy-making suggests that simple phone calls from constituents can significantly influence a legislator's vote on an upcoming bill.[7] When local leaders and constituents reach out, they can also inspire legislators to craft new proposals. One legislator described their motivation for introducing a bill that proposed major changes to the state's testing and accountability system as "lots of conversations in the preceding year" in which "people—primarily parents and teachers—expressed frustrations with standardized testing." At the same time, legislators are typically removed from policy implementation and program support and generally less able to respond to immediate needs and requests, as compared with SEAs. This may explain why legislators reported hearing from constituents and organizations who identified as parents and teacher representatives and less often mentioned superintendents or local school board members.

RESAs, Organizations, and Associations

Those in more fragmented states, both in governor's offices and at SEAs, were less likely to describe having frequent and close contact with school district leaders. Instead, they were more likely to describe communicating with RESAs. Research on these agencies has been somewhat limited, but these comments were in keeping with past work suggesting that regional agencies can support public schools and governance in two directions, providing vital services to local districts as well as serving as a key source of information for SEAs. In all, estimates suggest there are at least five hundred RESAs located throughout the country, spread across at least thirty-three states.[8] While most states have established regional agencies, they operate in a variety of ways, sometimes focusing narrowly and sometimes providing more comprehensive supports.

Legislators who served on education committees, gubernatorial staff, and state chiefs also mentioned engaging in deliberate outreach to superintendent, school board, and educator associations both as a means of gathering information and providing access to key stakeholders. Several state chiefs (including some working within less fragmented systems) and legislators sitting on education committees described intentional efforts to attend the annual meetings of state associations as well as being contacted by the organizations. Associations, like RESAs, may play a particularly important aggregating role in fragmented states, bridging the gap between the many local actors and state leadership.

It is not clear how the elevated importance of associations and organizations is likely to shape policy processes in more fragmented systems of education governance. In part, this is because the nature of relationships between government and organized groups varies widely.[9] For instance, policy communities involving governmental institutions and nongovernmental actors can be characterized by cozy, closed relationships involving relatively few groups. Governance within such policy communities may verge on clientalistic, or corporatist, creating an exclusive policy-making process, largely captured by a narrow set of interests and shielded from broader political conflicts. Overreliance on a small set of organizations or groups to inform and direct policy processes might therefore solve a logistical challenge in fragmented states, but could simultaneously function to preserve a status quo, even a dysfunctional one.[10] Such insular arrangements were commonly observed in the United States through the 1970s, and within education governance especially.

However, policy communities can also be characterized by messier, more complex, open relationships that involve many groups and yield comparably volatile, more politicized processes. These competitive, pluralistic arrangements have become increasingly common in the United States and within education governance. At the national level, there were more than six hundred new lobbying organizations in 2006 compared with 1981; over three-quarters of these organizations existed in 1981 but lacked a formal political presence.[11] Accordingly, researchers have begun to investigate the increasing prominence of new and different interest groups in local and national educational politics, yet there is little recent attention paid to how the insularity or openness of policy communities differs from state to state.[12]

Regardless of the structure of policy communities, financial resources are necessary to establish and maintain organizations. Therefore, even when networks are more open, reliance on these nongovernmental organizations to facilitate policy processes carries the risk of privileging narrow interests and generating a political agenda that underrepresents the concerns and experiences of poorer constituencies.[13] This is not to say that organizations are not vital to advancing equity in policy. Quite the contrary: groups like the NAACP have been instrumental in building coalitions and applying political pressure on behalf of those who often go underrepresented. But systems that rely overmuch on nongovernmental actors to perform critical communication and coordination functions throughout the policy process may tend to accord undue influence to the groups that are best organized and funded.

Fragmentation and Race to the Top

Evidence beyond these conversations suggests that states with larger numbers of districts may be at a pronounced disadvantage when it comes to developing new policy proposals and gaining buy-in from local leaders, particularly at the speed that is often called for by federal initiatives. For example, during the Race to the Top (RTTT) grant competition, the US Department of Education (ED) scored state applications in part based on the percentage of school districts that agreed to endorse the proposed reform agenda and promised to participate in its implementation. From the standpoint of ED, as with any grant funder, this was just an important capacity check, intended to gauge whether or not state plans were feasible: Were local leaders willing to put the programs and projects in motion if the grant funding were to come through?

However, for states with large numbers of districts, this intuitive requirement—gaining signatures from thousands of school board members and superintendents—presented a significant logistical challenge. In an analysis of state scores on RTTT, those with larger numbers of operational districts scored worse on average, partly because they were less successful in obtaining a full set of signatures from LEA leadership.

The implications of fragmentation extended even beyond the application process during RTTT. States with larger numbers of districts struggled not only to create a coalition around reform efforts, but also to hold their coalitions together over the duration of the program. As implementation progressed from one school year to the next, states that were more fragmented saw districts opt out of reform efforts. During the first round of grant applications, there was a clear, negative correlation between the number of districts in a state and the percentage of LEAs that endorsed the state's reform plan. That relationship strengthened during the second round of applications; rather than enabling states to consolidate participation, the passage of time appeared to do the reverse. In the following years, as states implemented their plans, that correlation became even more pronounced as participation rates fell precipitously for more fragmented states. (See the appendix for more on this relationship.)

The application's scoring rubric did account for this in part by also including points for the percentage of a state's students, and specifically the percentage of a state's low-income students who resided in the participating districts. This ensured that states with low levels of LEA participation, but high levels of student inclusion, did not lose all possible points in that section of the grant. The challenges of compliance nonetheless remain for these more fragmented states, and will likely be an issue that shapes the development of state plans under ESSA. Indeed, early analysis suggests that states successful in winning RTTT funds have also been better prepared to plan for and implement ESSA.[14]

Large Versus Small School Districts

Regardless of whether or not a state was fragmented, state leaders consistently described being in closer contact with superintendents and representatives of larger school districts compared with smaller ones. In part, this is likely a result of resource differences between the central offices in large and small districts, though large urban districts are often subject to specific regulations, which may also increase their need to contact state policy makers.

One legislator in a fragmented state speculated that they heard more often from large districts because superintendents were more likely to have a budget that supported travel to the capital city. A gubernatorial staffer who worked on education in a fragmented state likewise described frequent encounters with lobbyists hired by city school districts. Indeed, according to data gathered by the Center for Responsive Politics, the Los Angeles Unified and Houston Independent school districts each spent $120,000 to hire lobbyists during 2016.[15] In Nebraska, Omaha Public Schools, the largest district in the state by population, spent more than $350,000 in the five-year period from 2012 through 2016. A report focused on Nebraska's school districts found that just 17 of 245 invested in lobbying and that those with lobbying budgets served the state's more urban areas.[16] There is little systematic research on school district lobbying efforts, but the practice has garnered attention in recent years from news agencies and conservative politicians and interest groups who describe the practice pejoratively as "taxpayer-funded lobbying."

Smaller and more rural districts were not as likely to directly communicate with state-level leadership. They may exert less influence over state politics than larger districts or may have to work through associations to ensure their voices are heard. Among state leaders, there was general recognition that smaller districts needed more support, either from RESAs or from the SEA itself. One state chief I interviewed explained that "small school systems do not have the people to review software, and to make decisions," but emphasized that a critical role of the state agency was to absorb some of those functions, providing support and technical assistance to LEAs with limited capacity.

HOW FRAGMENTATION SHAPES INEQUALITY

Fragmentation is significant not only because it shapes policy processes in the overt ways just described, but also because it can shape the very inequalities that policy makers purport to tackle, and which lay at the root of divisive political dynamics. State systems that are more fragmented at the local level magnify underlying economic and racial inequalities in several ways.

The larger the number of school districts in a given state, the smaller their size in terms of both square miles and population, and the easier it can be for families who possess the means to relocate, sorting themselves into enclaves where resources and opportunities can be hoarded. Far from interrupting this dynamic, the accountability systems that have been the focus of the last several decades seem to have provided parents with more and higher-quality information, which can be used to inform those choices. Because the historic legacies of racism and economic exclusion helped to establish school district boundaries, parents need not be acting from malice in order for their choices to perpetuate this dynamic but rather simply house- or apartment-hunting and factoring in online ratings for the local school system. Evidence also suggests that open enrollment and other choice policies that allow students to cross district boundaries have not typically ameliorated these dynamics; in a number of instances, they are linked instead to rising segregation.

Fragmented state systems do not simply facilitate segregation, they also establish administrative and legal constraints for addressing it. When segregation exists *within* a large and diverse district, the policy alternatives for achieving integrated schools are more diverse. When segregation exists *between* two or more districts, which today is more common throughout the United States, citizens and advocates confront a much more challenging policy environment for addressing it.

Federal policies also play out in this landscape and interact with these institutional configurations. For example, while large districts throughout the South were compelled by federal courts to integrate during the 1970s, 1980s, and 1990s, no such process took place in any consistent manner throughout the Midwest and Northeast. Districts in those regions are smaller and segregation between them typically more dramatic, so the signal provided by test-based accountability is therefore one that is even more easily acted upon. Throughout President Bush's and President Obama's time in office, economic and racial segregation in many American school systems has worsened. Since all measures of segregation are dependent in some way on the demographic diversity of a local population, some scholars have rightly pointed out that the increasing proportion of children who belong to racial and ethnic minority groups accounts for much of this increase. Yet the demographic transformation of the United States does not explain all of the shifts. By failing to consider how these structures of education governance vary from state to state and have created distinct geographic inequalities that turn up in schools, the federal government has promulgated policies that in fact impede the reduction of racial and economic achievement and opportunity gaps.

Island School Districts, Boundaries, and Segregation

A recent nationwide report illustrates how economic segregation is influenced by the drawing of district boundaries. In the summer of 2016, the nonprofit EdBuild published its second annual report on student poverty. Titled "Dividing Lines: Gated School Districts," the report was not a traditional think-tank publication.[17] Instead, it presented a dizzying map of the roughly 13,500 school district boundaries that crisscross the United States. Each local school district was highlighted in blue. The darkest shades indicated that more than 40 percent of the school-age children in that district during 2014 were living in poverty—a threshold used by social scientists to identify areas of concentrated poverty—while the lighter shades indicated that fewer than 10 percent of a district's children were living at or below the federal poverty line.[18] Districts reporting the lowest poverty rates often appeared adjacent to those reporting the highest.

A map of poverty in the school districts just across the bay from San Francisco, rendered in figure 4.1, reveals a particularly striking example of this phenomenon. Piedmont City Unified School District (PUSD) seems to be floating, like an island, in the middle of the much larger Oakland Unified School District (OUSD). PUSD is colored with the palest of hues, indicating a low poverty rate, while the entire area of OUSD surrounding it is a much darker shade. The sharpness of the contrast is striking.

When the city of Oakland first began to expand in the early 1900s, annexing other cities and towns as it grew, Piedmont City had already become an extraordinarily wealthy community. Nicknamed the "City of Millionaires" by the 1920s, it has fought hard to maintain both its independence and the exclusivity of its school system.[19] PUSD's boundaries proved extremely effective in locking out poor families. During 2015, only 1 percent of the roughly twenty-five hundred children in the district lived below the federal poverty line. In OUSD, an estimated 29 percent of the district's roughly fifty-seven thousand school-age children were living below the poverty line. Notably, the federal poverty line is set considerably lower than the bar for receiving free or reduced-price lunch, and because of this it classifies a smaller proportion of children as poor.

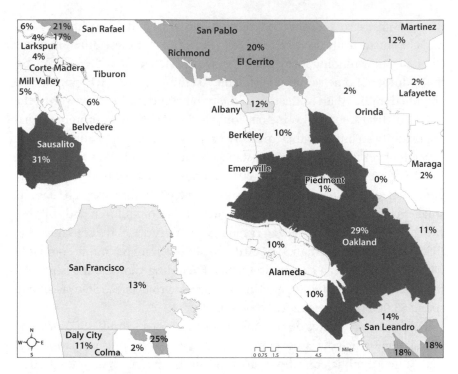

FIGURE 4.1   Poverty rates for families with children in Oakland area school districts

Source: United States Census, American Community Survey, 2011–2015.

A closer investigation of the two districts, using data from the US Census's American Communities Survey, makes clear that the PUSD boundaries have locked out not only the poor, but also all but a small number of black and Hispanic families. Therefore, the school district borders replicate multiple dimensions of inequality. Not only are PUSD households much less likely to be poor, they are much more likely to be white.

Other indicators suggest that there are concentrated advantages conferred upon children who grow up on the PUSD side of the boundary. It is not simply that poverty rates are higher in OUSD or that racial and ethnic minorities have been almost totally excluded from the community. Children who grow up in PUSD live in homes with incomes that are roughly four times those in OUSD. They are also much more likely to grow up in homes with adults who have finished college and who speak fluent English.

School districts draw their funding from the local, state, and federal governments, and while some states do a great deal to correct for the inequities that manifest across local school district borders, California's funding formula has historically done relatively little to adjust for these different needs (though a new funding formula may move the state in that direction).[20] So the additional home resources available to children in PUSD appear to be amplified, rather than mitigated, in the public schools. In other words, the school district boundaries in this context do not seem to promote equal opportunity so much as they magnify existing unequal opportunity.

Student-teacher ratios are substantially smaller in PUSD than OUSD, 16.72 versus 22.12 in the 2011–2012 school year, despite demonstrably greater need in OUSD. This alone is significant, given that research suggests smaller class sizes are particularly beneficial for poor children and children who belong to oft-marginalized racial minority groups.[21] In that same year, PUSD collected more than $18,000 dollars in revenues per pupil, compared with $12,000 for each student in OUSD. Excluding capital outlays, investments in district buildings, and infrastructure projects, PUSD was able to spend $3,000 more *per student* than OUSD.[22]

Further, these figures do not reflect contributions from PUSD's devoted foundation, which declares on its website (www.piedmontfoundation.org) that "a great public education isn't free," and explains that, among other benefits, the foundation's annual contributions have helped the district to maintain and expand programs, even at a time when state funding fluctuates year to year. These school- and district-focused foundations have become increasingly prominent in recent decades, enabling wealthy communities to deliver substantial resources directly to their schools, skirting state laws that might limit local property taxes.[23] According to the foundation's 2015 report, it granted more than $2.9 million to PUSD between April 2014 and March 2015—more than $1,000 per student—to support capital and safety improvements, extracurricular and enrichment activities, curricular innovation and design, professional development for teachers and staff, new technologies, and teacher and staff salaries.

Researchers have long shown that the cumulative effects of concentrated poverty on students' academic opportunities and outcomes are substantial. In other words, a child's opportunity to succeed academically is intimately connected not just to the child's own family background and resources, but also to the family backgrounds and resources of the other children with whom they attend school.[24] Economic segregation of the kind that exists between PUSD and OUSD has substantial and lasting effects on academic outcomes. In PUSD, the cohort graduation rate for the 2011–2012 school year was 99.5 percent, 40 percentage points higher than the one for OUSD.

These discrepancies are all too familiar to low-income families, professional educators, and students of educational policy. The EdBuild report highlighted a number of similarly large disparities between neighboring school districts, driving home just how frequently district boundaries segregate the wealthy from the poor. In New Jersey, the impoverished Freehold Borough School District is surrounded by the much more prosperous suburban school districts of Freehold Township. The two had separated in 1919 due to a dispute over how to distribute local tax income.[25] In the city of Columbus, Ohio, the well-off Bexley City School district is surrounded by the much larger district that serves Columbus. In each place, LEAs served students with vastly differing resources, right next door to one another.

The report referred to the completely surrounded districts as "island districts," a phrase that caught on rapidly with journalists and Twitter users, spawning local and national stories about the inequalities driven and preserved by nearby school district borders. Yet the report highlighted only a fraction of these districts. Across the contiguous forty-eight states, the map showed roughly 164 island districts, places where school district boundaries completely separated the wealthy from the poor.[26] Some of these islands were like PUSD, havens for the affluent, while others hemmed in the poor like Freehold Borough. The map and the data presented in the EdBuild report communicated just how starkly segregated the American school system is along economic lines.

Another similarly styled report published by EdBuild a few weeks later, "Fault Lines: America's Most Segregating School District Borders," reinforced the point, highlighting a different facet of school district boundaries. It listed the fifty most economically segregating school district borders in the United States, selecting them by the size of the difference in poverty rate on either side of the border. The average difference between two neighboring districts was seven percentage points. The most segregating border in the nation divided the Detroit City School District from the Gross Pointe Public School System. On the Detroit side of the border, the poverty rate for children under eighteen was 49 percent, compared with 7 percent on the Gross Pointe side of the border.[27] Nationally, about 20 percent of children are living in poverty at any given time, though that status is often in flux. Lower-income families may subsist just above the poverty line and then fall below briefly; estimates suggest that closer to 40 percent will spend at least one year of their childhood below the poverty line.[28]

Economic and Racial Segregation Between and Within School Districts

Taken together, the EdBuild reports illustrate well the fact that poor students often attend school districts populated by other poor students, and wealthy students often attend school districts populated by other wealthy students. The same is true with regards to white students and their black and Hispanic peers. Study after study has demonstrated that poor and minority students' academic achievement tends to be lower when students are attending highly segregated schools.[29] Decades of research have also demonstrated lifelong benefits for white children who attend integrated schools.[30] This persistent separation in schools is maintained in many ways, but made possible in part because the local school district remains a fundamental institution, the foundational unit of education governance throughout the United States.

As such, it has a significant effect on one of the key problems facing public schools today—not just in determining whether segregation levels are likely to be high or low, but also, and perhaps more importantly, in identifying the dimensions along which segregation is likely to occur. Segregation in school systems can occur through multiple sorting pathways. Wealthy and poor, black and white students may segregate between the public and private school sectors, between traditional public schools and schools of choice (magnets and charters), between traditional schools within a district, or between school districts.[31]

These variable pathways suggest differing degrees of entrenchment—and therefore of difficulty in disrupting the various drivers of segregation. For example, the segregation that arises between private schools and public schools is unlikely to be directly impacted by policy; however, the segregation that arises between traditional public schools and charter schools is something that a change in policy or practice may be able to shift. And many charters successfully and deliberately pursue diverse student bodies. Magnet schools also can have a substantial impact on integration, though this effect has been lessened in recent decades as requirements that they achieve racial balance have been relaxed.[32]

Where segregation of students occurs primarily within districts as a result of student assignment plans, open enrollment, or district-operated charter schools, motivated local school districts and citizens can effect some level of integration by demanding changes in school assignment, the redrawing of attendance zones, the introduction of magnet schools, or modifications to open enrollment policies. Battles to change school assignment plans within districts are likely to be contentious, district plans that explicitly seek racial balance must be carefully designed to comply with Supreme Court guidelines, and minority parents may well select a school for the availability of special programs or cultural awareness among educators. Yet these are matters over which most school districts have some exclusive authority and policy interventions for which there are positive models available.[33]

Where segregation of students occurs primarily between districts, states may advance integration only by involving multiple, autonomous institutions—redrawing school district boundaries, pursuing legislative acts, or suing for court intervention. Some advocates have suggested that between- or within-district open enrollment policies may facilitate integration. However, analysis of which students tend to use open-enrollment policies to switch away from their zoned school suggests that relatively privileged students take advantage of these choices more often than disadvantaged students, and that these switches tend to segregate districts further along racial and class lines.[34] Of all of these different pathways, school district borders account for the largest amount of segregation within public schools in the United States, and increasingly structure disparities in the distribution of students in public school systems.

Research by Ann Owens, Sean Reardon, and Christopher Jencks has found that on average around the country, income-based segregation for families with school-age children has increased by 15 percent between school districts from 1990 to 2010, reflecting a substantial increase in residential segregation by income and wealth over the same time period.[35] Similar patterns emerge for racial segregation. A study by Jeremy Fiel identified between-district segregation as the most significant contributor to race-based segregation in schools.[36] With regards to segregation between black and white students in particular, this dimension of racial segregation decreased *within* school districts in the aftermath of the 1954 Supreme Court decision in *Brown v. Board*, but increased *between* school districts. Despite decades of court cases and legislation aimed at equalizing funding and standardizing curricula across districts, a child's educational opportunity is still, unmistakably, determined to no small degree by where he or she is born and grows up.

Like other government institutions, school district boundaries, once established, have proven to be relatively stable entities. Also like other institutions, they shape individual-level choices, and from these aggregated actions emerge collective patterns. In the case of local school districts, wealthy parents increasingly factor in school quality when deciding where to live, choosing to buy homes based in significant part on these boundaries, driving the dramatic and disturbing inequalities just described.

While the deliberate study of political institutions fell out of favor among political scientists in the middle of the twentieth century, losing out to quantitative and survey-based research projects that focused on individual characteristics, identities, and rationality, the paramount import of institutional structures has never been far from the minds of education researchers. This is because districts have remained so critically important. Even as states and the federal government assumed a more assertive role in funding school systems, they have worked with and around the local school district.[37] And yet, in spite of the rise in segregation between districts, and the fact that the majority of segregation can be attributed to between-district divides, that is not the whole story. The extent to which segregation can be attributed primarily to sorting between-districts depends on the degree to which a state's school system is fragmented and how district boundaries are organized.

FRAGMENTATION AND SCHOOL DISTRICT ORGANIZATION

As chapter 2 made clear, school districts developed differently and thus vary in their character from place to place. Consequently, the island districts described by the EdBuild researchers are present in some states, but not at all in others. The particular way school district boundaries interact with and reinforce economic and racial inequality is not consistent from state to state. In some states, the way school district borders are drawn has facilitated segregation between districts. But in other cases, they have hindered it—or at least rendered it subject to policy change. And in some instances, borders have been deliberately maintained or drawn so as to preserve divides.

Local school districts therefore differ across states in their organizational structure—the logic that dictates how their borders are drawn, and also, critically, the number of districts in the state. For example, the 2015 school district maps for the states of Florida and Alabama, displayed in figure 4.2, show obvious variation both in the number of districts and the way boundaries appear.

Understanding these variations in the way that state governments organize local school districts is key to navigating education governance,

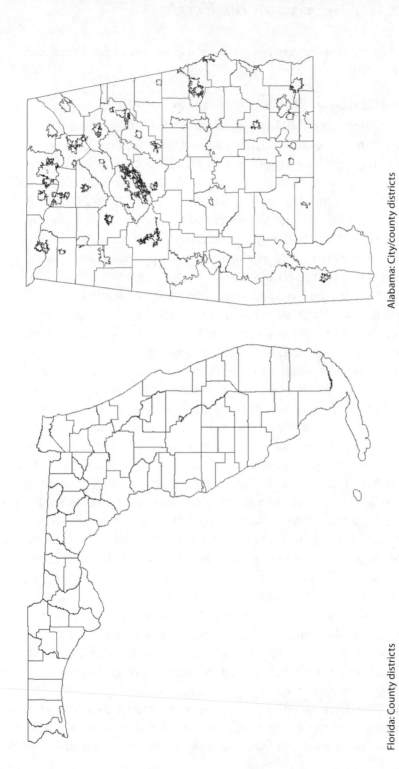

Florida: County districts

Alabama: City/county districts

FIGURE 4.2   Types of school district boundaries for Florida and Alabama, 2015

particularly for making sense of how racial and economic inequality in each state is structured.

County and City/County School District Systems

Though the EdBuild maps showed island school districts scattered around the country, there are no such districts present in nineteen states. In seventeen other states, there are only one or two such school districts. There are only fourteen states in which three or more island districts could be located. Not only are island districts concentrated in a minority of states, they are clustered in one region as well. Of the 164 island school districts that the EdBuild report identified in the contiguous forty-eight states, 137—or 83.5 percent of them—were located east of the Mississippi River, and most of those appeared in a swarm in the South.

Florida, Maryland, and West Virginia stand out as notable exceptions to this pattern. Not a single island district is visible in any of these states. Each of them, along with Nevada, organizes its school districts in a way that is coterminous, or congruent, with another government institution—the county. School district borders are drawn in these states along county lines. There are relatively few school districts in states that operate county-based systems, and the districts tend to be fairly large, both in terms of land area and enrollment. Florida and New York, for example, are the third and fourth largest states by population, but during 2012 the average county school district in Florida enrolled more than 40,000 students, compared with the 3,900 average enrollment in New York. The scale of county districts means that they often include urban, suburban, and rural communities, lessening the potential for dramatic differences in poverty and wealth between districts.[38]

The majority of the island school districts cited in EdBuild's analysis were located in just eight southern states, because these states have drawn school district boundaries to match those of counties and municipalities. Twenty-eight islands are located in Kentucky, nineteen in Alabama, eighteen in Tennessee, twelve in Virginia, eleven in Georgia, eleven in Mississippi, seven in North Carolina, and one in Louisiana. Another sixteen are located in Alaska. South Carolina also draws its school districts' borders along existing county and city lines, though none of its municipal districts are entirely surrounded by a single county.

In some of the states operating a city/county system, there are only a few city, or municipal, districts—Louisiana and North Carolina, for example. The overwhelming majority of districts in these states cover a geographically large area defined by county borders, making these states more similar to county systems than other city/county systems. Districts in these states therefore are also relatively few in number, fairly large, and geographically diverse. In Kentucky, Tennessee, and Alabama, city school districts are more common.

During 2012 there were 134 total school districts in Alabama, 67 organized along county lines and 67 organized along municipal lines. This mode of drawing school district boundaries has created districts that are large in terms of population or geography, but divided along racial and economic lines. Indeed, school district borders in Alabama appear to be more economically segregating than in any of the other contiguous forty-eight states. According to the EdBuild report, the average gap in child poverty across district borders in Alabama was 13.4 percentage points, while the average across school district boundaries in other states was 6.8 percentage points. Further, six of the fifty most economically segregating school district boundaries in the nation were borders shared by the Birmingham City Schools, where the poverty rate for children under eighteen was 49 percent, and its neighboring counties, where child poverty fell between 6 and 15 percent.[39]

School District Borders and Congruence in Noncounty Systems

Most of the remaining forty-eight states—all of those in the Northeast and Midwest of the country as well as quite a few in the South and West—operate school districts in a way that more closely aligns them with cities and towns. In some of these places, district boundaries follow, or closely follow, the borders. Using Google Earth to examine the congruence of school district and municipal boundaries in 2007, William Fischel found near-perfect overlap in Massachusetts, New Jersey, and Pennsylvania, and a generally high level of congruence between city and school district boundaries throughout the New England states where school districts have been organized around townships.[40]

Elsewhere, Fischel and others have observed that district boundaries may have overlapped substantially with cities or towns but also diverge from them, carving into other counties or cities, occasionally dividing up the area inside municipalities. Iowa is often cited as an archetype of this extraordinarily fragmented, incongruent system; more than three hundred school districts overlap all of its ninety-nine counties' borders. In two of the largest states, by both area and population—Texas and California—there appears to be little consistent overlap between cities and school districts.

This lack of congruence between school district and city or county boundaries is also very often found in midwestern states, including Illinois, Iowa, Michigan, and Ohio.[41]

This lack of congruence is also regularly apparent in many western states, though it differs somewhat in character. Rather than large numbers of districts that are incongruous because they cover small areas, districts in the western states are often incongruous with county and municipal boundaries because they include a large amount of territory. For example, in Utah a number of the larger districts in the state draw the majority of their enrollments from a single city, but the boundaries of the district are drawn expansively to include sparsely populated areas.

In ten states, including California, there is an additional layer of organization. Districts serve local communities but also are distinguished from one another by the education level of the students they serve. In these systems, some districts operate only elementary schools, some only high schools, and others—unified districts like PUSD and OUSD—serve the full range of students from preK through high school.

School District Numbers: Variable Fragmentation of State Systems

These various methods of organizing school systems across states are noted in table 4.1. Aside from the obvious connection with the city/county mode of school district organization, there is little that ties these other types of school districts to either the presence of island school districts or the presence of the most segregating school district borders.

Instead, the presence of islands and of highly segregating borders is clearly visible in the northeastern and midwestern states, near large cities—as in the South—and appears in states where there tend to be larger numbers of school districts that serve geographically smaller areas. Segregation between school districts today is connected not just to the different *ways* of drawing school district borders, but also to the sheer *number* and *size* of the school districts in a given state—though those aspects are certainly interconnected. As is evident in table 4.1, states that draw districts along county or city/county borders tend to operate school systems with relatively few school districts, while states that draw borders at the local level operate systems with far greater numbers.

Fragmented state systems, in which school districts are smaller and more numerous, as in the case of California and New Jersey, facilitate segregation

TABLE 4.1   Types of school district organization and number of districts (2012)

County systems[1]	City/county	Elementary/ high school/ unified	Other (26)
Florida (67)	Alabama (134)	Arizona (227)	Arkansas (238)
Maryland (24)	Alaska (54)[2]	California (939)	Colorado (178)
Nevada (17)	Georgia (180)	Idaho (116)	Connecticut (166)
West Virginia (55)	Kentucky (174)	Illinois (865)	Delaware (19)
	Louisiana (70)[2]	Montana (415)	Hawaii (1)[3]
	Mississippi (151)	New York (695)	Indiana (296)
	North Carolina (115)	Oklahoma (521)	Iowa (348)
	South Carolina (84)	Oregon (180)	Kansas (309)
	Tennessee (141)	Pennsylvania (500)	Maine (239)
	Virginia (132)	Wyoming (48)	Massachusetts (329)
			Michigan (550)
			Minnesota (336)
			Missouri (521)
			Nebraska (249)
			New Hampshire (179)
			New Jersey (616)
			New Mexico (89)
			North Dakota (178)
			Ohio (611)
			Rhode Island (36)
			South Dakota (151)
			Texas (1,029)
			Utah (41)
			Vermont (294)
			Washington (295)
			Wisconsin (423)
Average (40.75)	**(123.50)**	**(450.60)**	**(308.76)**

[1] If there is only a single city district, the state is placed here. This is the case of Maryland with Baltimore and Nevada with Carson City.

[2] County equivalents in Alaska are dubbed *boroughs*; in Louisiana, they are referred to as *parishes*.

[3] Hawaii is not included in the average listed here.

between school districts rather than within them in much the same way as does drawing school district borders around cities.[42] Families with children and resources will be able to relocate into a wealthier or whiter school district without needing to travel far, paying a substantial cost, or losing access to the benefits that come with being near a large city. Fragmented governance subsidizes residential and educational segregation. Kendra Bischoff suggests that smaller school districts "activate or enable racial differences in preferences or resources to dictate residential location."[43] In Jefferson County, Alabama, as new districts were created within the county lines, families sorted and school districts became increasingly racially homogeneous.[44]

The variation between states along this simple dimension is vast. While Hawaii operates a single-district school system, California operates a system of more than one thousand school districts, and between those two extremes are states placed somewhat evenly along the distribution of possible values (illustrated in figure 4.3). The most fragmented states by raw number of districts are Texas, California, Illinois, New York, and New Jersey, with Ohio and Michigan following closely behind. These are states where high levels of segregation have been observed.[45] The least fragmented states by raw number of districts are Hawaii, Nevada, Delaware, Maryland, and Rhode Island.

Notably, many of the more fragmented states are also the largest states in the nation, and a number of the least fragmented states by number of school districts also happen to be some of the smallest states in the country, whether by population or area. To some extent, fragmentation may be expected in states with larger geographic territories and larger populations. However, states differ considerably from one another even when the number of school districts in the state is adjusted based on its population and area. Figure 4.4 illustrates this. Given its population and area, Florida, with sixty-seven regular school districts, appears to be the least fragmented state school system in the country as of 2012. Illinois emerges as the most fragmented state in the nation for its population size and area.

Segregation is not just structured differently (between versus within districts), but all else equal, it is actually higher today in states with more fragmented systems. After adjustments for region and demographics of the state's student population, multiple measures of segregation are likely to be higher in state school systems with larger numbers of LEAs. For example, a higher proportion of black students attend schools where 90–100 percent of the student body also belongs to other underrepresented minority groups. After demographics are controlled for, measures of black and white *isolation*, which estimates what percentage of a student's schoolmates share his or her racial or ethnic identity, are also higher in more fragmented states. For each additional school district, there is a small but consistently higher proportion of black students attending segregated schools.[46]

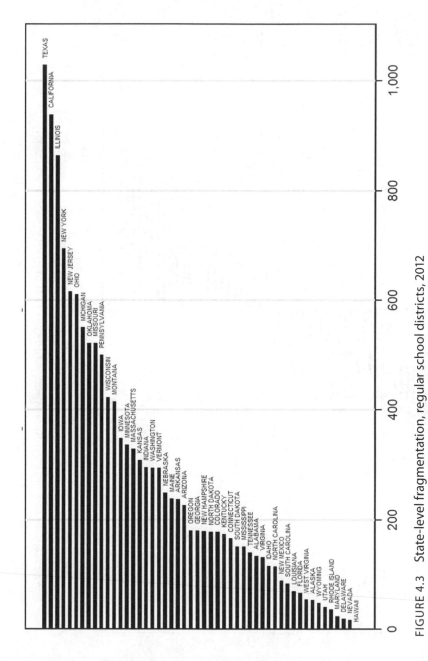

FIGURE 4.3   State-level fragmentation, regular school districts, 2012

Source: "Local Education Agency (School District) Universe Survey Data," 2012–2013, National Center for Education Statistics, https://nces.ed.gov/ccd/pubagency.asp.

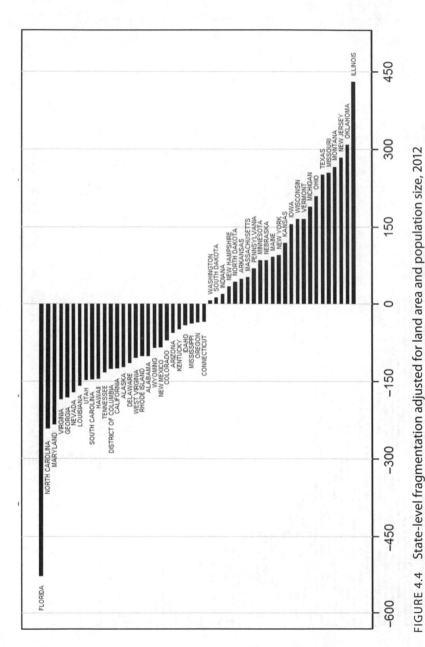

FIGURE 4.4 State-level fragmentation adjusted for land area and population size, 2012

Source: Author calculations using data from "Local Education Agency (School District) Universe Survey Data," 2012–2013, National Center for Education Statistics, https://nces.ed.gov/ccd/pubagency.asp, and the 2010 US Census.

PERSISTENT DISPARITIES IN FRAGMENTED SYSTEMS

The persistence of disparities in fragmented systems can be traced in part to the series of Supreme Court cases that followed *Brown v. Board of Education*. This sequence of decisions simultaneously interrupted the process of school district consolidation and created legal barriers to pursuing integration across school district borders.

From *Brown* to *Milliken*

In *Brown*, the court upended *Plessy v. Ferguson* (1896), judging the racially based segregation of public schools illegal, and required that school districts take deliberate actions to achieve racial balance. School district consolidation at the time was still very much under way—there remained roughly sixty thousand school districts still spread out across the country.

There is good reason to think that the decision in *Brown* may have immediately slowed consolidation efforts. While practical and ideological imperatives of efficiency and modernization had driven consolidation advocates and state leaders to attempt these transformations of state systems, school district consolidation efforts have implications that go beyond those considerations. They bring two or more different communities together. Consolidation has frequently met with fierce resistance, and there can be little question that much of this conflict has revolved around race, ethnicity, and class. Consolidation efforts have been consistently opposed whenever merging school districts meant that diverse communities might be forced to come together.[47]

Initially, though *Brown* met with considerable resistance nationwide, most of the federal efforts to enforce it were concentrated on the more violent resisters in the South. Consolidation of school districts, especially but not exclusively in the midwestern states where they were most abundant, proceeded, as did litigation over how to implement integration efforts. Two cases proved rather important.

The first case emerged out of North Carolina: *Swann v. Charlotte-Mecklenburg Board of Education* (1971). Notably, the city and county school systems had consolidated only in 1960—after a multiyear process of negotiation and planning that took place throughout the late 1950s. Several years later, in 1964, Vera Swann and her husband, Reverend Dr. Darius Swann, had attempted to enroll their son, James, in an integrated elementary school near their home in Charlotte. James was denied entry and directed to enroll in an all-black school in another neighborhood. The NAACP supported the family in bringing a suit, the case moved to the federal courts, and in 1969 Judge James McMillan ruled in favor of the Swanns, directing the Charlotte school district to implement a large-scale busing program. The case was challenged, and when the Supreme Court issued its decision in 1971, it upheld McMillan's ruling. The Charlotte-Mecklenburg schools became the flagship school district for racial integration.[48]

The ruling in *Swann* established clearly that school districts would have to invest significant time and resources in order to achieve integration within their boundaries by busing students out of their home neighborhoods. White parents who viewed this as burdensome—and those who plainly sought to avoid sending their children to integrated schools—began searching for ways to circumvent the ruling and eventually began moving out of urban areas and into more homogeneous school districts.[49]

Three years after *Swann* the Supreme Court issued another landmark decision, in *Milliken v. Bradley* (1974), this time regarding interdistrict integration in Michigan. In 1970, the NAACP and a group of parents in Detroit brought suit against Michigan state leaders, including Governor William Milliken. They alleged that the city of Detroit and the surrounding counties had fostered policies—specifically, redlining and exclusionary zoning—that had created residential racial segregation and therefore segregation within the school system. The lower courts found in favor of the plaintiffs, the state officials appealed, and eventually the federal appeals court ruled that the state was responsible for ensuring integration across district borders. The Supreme Court reversed the finding in 1974, emphasizing that there was no evidence that the fifty-three districts outside of Detroit had perpetrated any illegal action or intentionally sought to foster segregation. Therefore, they and the state leadership were not obligated to participate in an interdistrict integration effort, even though the court acknowledged that the rights of the black students in Detroit had been violated. This ruling tied the hands of state officials, who could no longer pursue interdistrict busing remedies without clear determinations of wrongdoing or voluntary agreements to participate.[50]

Short of consolidating with school districts or investing in voluntary magnet programs, urban school districts had little mechanism for combating white flight. For families seeking to avoid integration, crossing and preserving school district boundaries took on a new flavor, and this appears to be the moment at which district consolidation slowed.

Reasons for the Slowdown of Consolidation: Avoiding Integration, or Achieving Optimal Scale?

There is, of course, another possible explanation for why the pace of district mergers slowed. School districts were consolidating in pursuit of greater efficiencies of scale; perhaps it was simply coincidence that district consolidation slowed after *Milliken*. Perhaps states and districts had managed to create public school systems that were optimally scaled, and so they ceased their efforts. Policy scholars have used innovative econometric strategies to study school district consolidation from an evaluator's perspective, attempting to identify the efficiencies obtained in terms of students' academic and life outcomes, as well as those having to do with the daily operations of a school system.[51] One evaluation identified modest increases in wages for white men who had attended school in consolidated districts. Another estimated that Arkansas's consolidation efforts, which targeted districts enrolling fewer than 350 students, yielded small but statistically detectable improvements in student achievement.[52] One review of this work estimates that significant, substantial cost savings can be achieved from consolidating small districts (three hundred to fifteen hundred students), but notes that these benefits are likely to diminish once districts grow larger than a few thousand students.[53]

Given these findings, it is possible that in the early 1970s, average school district size in many states approached these optimal enrollment levels, and the potential benefits of further consolidation were minimal. Indeed, by 1971, all but sixteen states had achieved an average district enrollment of at least two thousand students. The states that did not meet this threshold could be found mostly in less populated states: Nebraska, Montana, North Dakota, Vermont, and South Dakota reported the smallest average enrollment numbers. By 2012, twelve states reported average enrollments of less than two thousand. There may also be costs that arise when districts grow too large. In 2012 average district enrollment in Florida, Louisiana, Maryland, Nevada, North Carolina, and Utah exceeded fifteen thousand students. Higher transportation costs, larger schools, and diminished access to teachers and principals are often cited as challenges for larger districts.

To evaluate whether district consolidation slowed due to resistance to integration or because districts had reached optimal enrollments, I gathered data on the number of school districts in each state, spanning from 1931 to 2010, and matched these data to a series of other indicators likely to affect whether a state was adding school districts or consolidating them. These data enabled me to estimate a statistical model, described more fully in the appendix, which tested the influence of each of these factors on the number of districts in the state. The results of this effort offered some support for both hypotheses: that concerns about efficiency and scale, in combination with the *Milliken* decision, contributed to the slowing—and in some cases the reversal—of district consolidation efforts. In both instances, however, the interpretation of these outcomes requires some care.

With regards to efficiency and scale, average enrollments did not appear to impact consolidation. Instead, as population density increased, so did the expected number of school districts within a state, suggesting that population growth may be a more important factor in slowing down consolidation—and spurring fragmentation—than explicit concerns about efficiency. Consolidation was also more likely to proceed during national recessions, when resources were limited and concern about efficiency was elevated.

With regards to *Milliken*, on average the estimated number of school districts in a state increased in the aftermath of the decision, or rather the rate of decline slowed markedly. Racial diversity was also a predictor of fragmentation. The higher the percentage of a population that was identified as white during this time period, the more school districts a state was expected to have. It does appear that this latter result is driven largely by the states in the Midwest, which are not becoming as rapidly diverse as the states in the South, West, and throughout much of the Northeast and which have maintained larger numbers of districts.

The core finding, however, that the rate of district consolidation slowed significantly and perhaps even reversed in some states, holds across all sensitivity analyses. In other words, that finding appears quite robust. To describe in more qualitative terms how *Milliken* might have affected school district consolidation, and in the process institutionalized racial segregation between school districts, I turn now to Shelby County and the city of Memphis in Tennessee.

Memphis After *Milliken*: Splitting and Merging the Memphis City and Shelby County School Systems

In 1954, there were four separate school systems included in the boundaries of Shelby County: a black and a white school system operated by the county, and a black and a white school system operated by the city of Memphis. Part and parcel of Jim Crow, anyone attempting to operate an interracial school at the time would have been subject to a fine and a stint in prison under Tennessee laws of the era. So, though the state's supreme court invalidated these statutes in 1957, both the city and the county were steadfast in their efforts to avoid integrating, or unifying, the two systems within each of their boundaries. As a result, the black citizens of those districts partnered with the NAACP and brought cases against the districts in federal court. Both districts dragged their feet in response to court orders, implementing only the most limited transfers throughout the 1960s, during which time the population of Memphis became majority black, and the population in outlying Shelby County majority white.[54]

By 1971, little progress had been made on integration in either district, and when the *Swann* decision was handed down, negotiations began over how to structure a busing program in Memphis, to begin in the 1973 school year. By the time the busing order took effect, thousands of white families had pulled their children out of the Memphis City Schools (MCS) district, and in an effort to avoid the integration mandates, they moved into Shelby County or enrolled their children in private schools.[55]

The *Milliken* decision came shortly thereafter, reassuring those families that crossing district borders was an effective way to avoid the cross-city busing in Memphis. Like MCS, Shelby County Schools remained under court supervision, but in contrast maintained a more white, economically affluent majority. Meanwhile, throughout the state, district mergers seemed to stop rather abruptly. In fact, several communities established new, special districts (the slight uptick visible in figure 4.5) that could then operate separately and independently from merged county and municipal systems.[56]

In response, in 1982 a Democrat-controlled legislature passed a law prohibiting the establishment of new special districts and encouraging existing special districts to consolidate or merge with one another. Another Democrat-controlled legislature enacted another law in 1998, also blocking the establishment of new municipal school districts. Gradually, district consolidation resumed, and no new school districts were formed during this time period.[57]

Meanwhile, the demographic and wealth disparities between Shelby County and MCS grew, becoming progressively more acute. By 2010, nearly 86 percent of the students in Memphis identified as black, and 87 percent of them were from low-income families. In Shelby County, 37 percent of students were black, and 37 percent were from low-income families. While Shelby County was not a wildly affluent district, it was very much

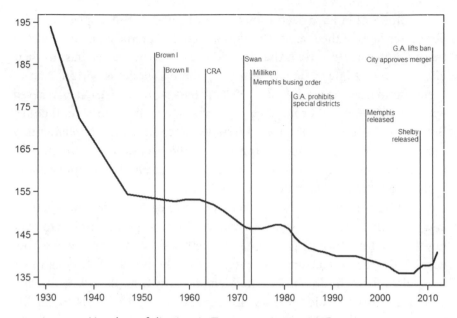

FIGURE 4.5 Number of districts in Tennessee, 1931–2012

so compared to Memphis, with median family incomes of $92,000 and $32,000, respectively.[58]

Shelby County and Memphis property taxes were pooled at the county level and divided among the districts. MCS, as the larger district, collected a larger portion of those revenues, but it had struggled nonetheless to meet its students' needs and to maintain schools during the fiscal crisis in 2008. In the aftermath of the November 2010 elections, which granted Republicans large majorities in the statehouse, Shelby County Schools began to discuss pursuing status as a special school district with the state legislature, a step that might legally allow it to secede from the county, preserve its borders, gain taxing authority, and potentially cease sharing property tax revenues with MCS.[59]

In November 2010, an MCS alumnus and a prominent member of its school board proposed relinquishing the MCS charter, a move that would make the school system part of Shelby County Schools.[60] The state constitution would obligate the Shelby County system to absorb MCS, a special school district and a far larger system. MCS board members hoped the laws prohibiting the creation of new districts would prevent Shelby County Schools from seceding and itself becoming a special district. In

March 2011, an overwhelming majority of Memphis residents voted to support the proposal, but the state legislature had already acted. In February 2011 the General Assembly repealed the statutes that prohibited the creation of new districts, stipulating in the bill that the repeal applied only to communities in Shelby County.[61] Worried suburban residents acted quickly, and by late 2011, six municipalities in Shelby County had begun the process of creating special districts, just as a twenty-three-member board was planning how to resolve the many differences between the Memphis and Shelby County school systems—ranging from textbooks to teacher evaluations to school bus operations.[62]

Though a federal judge briefly put a stop to the small district secessions, in April 2013 the state legislature acted again, this time freeing municipalities to establish special districts statewide. That July, the merger between Shelby County and Memphis became official, and by August 2014, the six municipalities had seceded and were preparing to open the doors to brand new school systems.[63]

An in-depth study of the district by the Center on Reinventing Public Education suggested that the new Shelby County/Memphis City Schools district had many resources, including a 2009 grant of $90 million from the Bill & Melinda Gates Foundation, but simultaneously a lot of hurdles to overcome.[64] Since the merging of the two districts and the exit of the suburban communities, the new district has confronted consecutive budget shortfalls and been forced to close schools and lay off teachers.[65] Though data are somewhat limited on these recently split districts, initial reports suggest that the secessions have effectively exacerbated racial and economic segregation in the Memphis metro area. The more than one hundred thousand students of the new district, which now includes Memphis and only some of the old Shelby County system, confront considerably more obstacles than their peers in most of the other districts: 73 percent are identified as being from low-income families, compared with 24 percent in the seceding districts; 6 percent are English language learners, compared with 2 percent in the seceding districts; and 8 percent are white, compared with 67 percent in the seceding districts.[66]

CONSEQUENCES OF FRAGMENTED SCHOOL SYSTEMS

The recent efforts to merge the Memphis and Shelby County school systems illustrate the contemporary challenges associated with consolidation efforts as well as the importance of examining the specific history of consolidation or fragmentation in the state.

School district boundaries were in flux throughout much of the twentieth century; this was true of Tennessee and most other states in the country. In Tennessee, that pace of change slowed after the 1973 busing order, the 1974 decision in *Milliken*, and the 1982 legislature's attempt to keep new districts from forming. Boundaries also hardened because the state and its school districts were under the supervision of federal courts. As a result, jurisdictional lines became more fixed and harder to shift. In many places where this occurred, districts were large and under court order, and the firming up of these boundaries had the potential to support sustained integration efforts. This was true in some parts of Tennessee. When districts were smaller and close to one another, the hardening of boundaries created a straightforward exit for wealthy and predominantly white families who were uninterested in working through the difficulties of integration. Similarly, when the legislature chose to lift the ban on the creation of new districts, better-off and white communities sought to place boundaries between themselves and their neighbors.

In recent years, consolidation has reemerged as a salient policy issue. Significant legislative measures have been adopted or introduced to mandate or encourage district consolidations in Arizona, Arkansas, Indiana, Illinois, Iowa, Kansas, Maine, Nebraska, Pennsylvania, New York, New Jersey, and Vermont.[67] This renewed attention is likely due, at least in part, to the recent economic recession, which left many states and school districts searching for ways to stretch every dollar just a little further.

At the same time, a wave of rising fragmentation, or rather a secession of communities from existing districts, has occurred in Alabama, Maine, Tennessee, Utah, and Wisconsin. In Alabama, these efforts have been particularly consistent and threaten to exacerbate already-high levels of racial and economic segregation within the school systems. Between 2000 and 2015, ten new districts were formed, a process made fairly easy by the state's permissive statutes.[68]

In northeastern states and midwestern states like Wisconsin, where school districts have typically been greater in number and smaller in average enrollments, achievement gaps between black and white students have grown or remained stagnant. This finding is particularly stunning when compared to the narrowed gaps between black and white children in the South, where school districts have been larger—and until recently—prevented from fragmenting as a result of federal supervision. This relationship, and the persistence of income and racial segregation, means that the stakes of school district consolidation and fragmentation efforts are incredibly high. More than ever, state policy makers and advocates considering consolidation or fragmentation should be mindful of the impact school district boundaries may have on increasing or decreasing racial and economic stratification—though, again, the nature of these considerations should differ from state to state.

At the same time, it is equally important to acknowledge that these boundaries organize educational opportunities throughout the country. Policies that fail to account for that fact will leave more or less unchecked a critical underpinning of educational inequality. ESSA, for example, requires that district report cards show—to parents and the public—the disparities present within their districts across schools. In places where districts are smaller and the majority of segregation exists between districts, this offers very little in the way of actionable information to parents. Only in places where districts are larger might this reporting requirement yield actionable local intelligence. Oddly enough, once more, federal pressure might help to provoke greater equity in the South and parts of the West—but not so in the North.

Both policy makers and advocates must recognize and respond to the way that fragmented state systems reinforce racial and economic segregation in the public school system, concentrating students who are wealthier, more educated, and white in one district and cutting them off from their poorer, black and brown neighbors. Large numbers of small districts make it easier for families to self-segregate, and school district boundaries formalize these divisions, raising institutional barriers for states and localities to pursue policies that might encourage integration or redistribution.

5

Exceptionalism, Partisanship, and Democracy

This chapter continues exploring the shifting foundation of state school systems, turning from the subject of fragmentation to focus on the institutional structures that drive or prohibit *exceptionalism*—that is, the extent to which education governance is conducted separately from (versus integrated with) general governance—and how those structures in turn shape democratic accountability in education politics and stability in policy.[1]

Whether governance is exceptional or integrated is a function of how leaders are chosen, the authority they possess, and the divisions or linkages created by these two factors. Each approach comes with pitfalls as well as possible advantages, and affects states' capacities to devise, implement, and support education reforms for their specific context. Moreover, this aspect of education governance is more and more influenced by a rising partisan polarization that has grown beyond Congress to permeate state governments, producing state policy regimes that are increasingly distinct from one another and sharpening divisions within states between members of the two major parties.

As described in chapter 3, exceptionalism took root with Progressive Era reformers, who believed that the people and agencies making key decisions about schools should be, and could be, insulated from the unpleasantness of politics. However, the Progressive institutions that were created to serve as bulwarks against partisan conflict have increasingly been challenged. Asserting variously that institutional barriers protect an unacceptable status quo, privilege only organized interest groups, and create inefficiencies, partisan actors including legislators, governors, and mayors have attempted to legally and formally dismantle the structures that have kept education and politics separate for the better part of a century. Less formally, elected leaders from both major parties have worked to transcend barriers by becoming more active and vocal on education issues than was common in decades past.

Reform-minded groups, particularly those affiliated with mega-philanthropists, business leaders, and the Republican Party, have also endeavored in recent years to draw education debates into larger public forums, where teacher unions—consistent Democratic Party allies—and other professional educator and administrator associations exert less influence and face more competition from other pressure groups. Whether motivated by a desire to weaken political opponents, improve schools, or some combination of the two, these efforts are changing the politics of education governance—broadening the scope of conflict, even as the school district borders that were the subject of the previous chapter remain remarkably fixed.

FRAMING POLITICS AS A PROBLEM FOR GOOD, RATIONAL GOVERNANCE

Every year, in most states across the country, legislatures hold joint sessions in order to hear governors report on the "State of the State," an analogue of the president's annual State of the Union address. Governors reflect on policy achievements and failures of the past year, and put forward platforms and budget proposals for upcoming legislative sessions. State of the State addresses also offer governors a perennial venue in which they can disavow the supposedly dirty and childish business of politics and partisanship, particularly when it comes to education policy.

Excerpts from the gubernatorial addresses of 2016 offer up archetypal examples of such public repudiations, voiced by governors across the spectrum of political ideology and party. Arizona's governor, Republican Doug Ducey, called upon the members of the legislature to "put politics and partisanship aside, and put our kids and teachers first."[2] The following month, Maryland's governor, Republican Larry Hogan, asked legislators to "set aside political gamesmanship and work together for the sake of our children."[3] West Virginia's governor, Democrat Earl Tomblin, went a step further, chastising members of both parties for using public education as a "political football," calling the legislature's actions "disappointing" and "unacceptable," and emphasizing that "we cannot allow politics or red tape to get in the way of providing our kids with a thorough and efficient education."[4] And in Minnesota, Democratic governor Mark Dayton, speaking about early childhood education, characterized political disputes as petty, telling law-makers that "sixty thousand Minnesota four-year-olds" needed the state's "grown-ups to go beyond their big self-interests and place those little interests first."[5] Similar comments can be found in other years and other states.

This rhetoric is often present at the local as well as the state level, though it tends to be employed more defensively, in an effort to stop or reverse a new initiative rather than to advance one. In the spring of 2017, in Onslow County, North Carolina, five members of the school board penned a letter to the local paper in which they responded to a proposed bill that would convert local school board elections from nonpartisan to partisan contests. They declared: "There is nothing political about providing resources for students to maximize their academic potential. There is nothing political about educating children in safe and appropriate classroom settings. There is nothing political about recruiting, hiring and retaining highly qualified teachers, who are the most important element in fostering student success. *Politics and education just don't mix!*" [Emphasis added.][6]

In the fall of 2017, in Syracuse, New York, Republican mayoral candidate Laura Lavine announced that as mayor she would seek authority over the city's struggling school district. Retired superintendent Robert DiFlorio fired back quickly, calling her proposal "nothing more than a political gimmick" and asserting that "the district has incredible teachers and administrators" whose efforts to improve student outcomes "should not under any circumstances be curtailed by the nuances of a mayor."[7]

In part, these comments may be evidence of wishful thinking on the part of frustrated, ambitious public officials who seek policy process with less conflict. More often, they are strategic efforts to characterize opposition as illegitimate, or to defend against a proposal that threatens the status quo of governance, by labeling some group or action as political and thus suspect or unreasonable. However, such comments are also powerful, because they speak to a long-standing tendency to eschew politics where schools are concerned.[8] In 1964, Nicholas Masters, Robert Salisbury, and Thomas Eliot wrote that "in the eyes of the public, schools and their operations are removed, or should be removed, from the arenas where other governmental decisions are made."[9] For them, the notion that politics and education ought not to mix presented a problem, first because it was untrue, and second because it functioned to keep important debates out of the public eye.

The Ubiquity of Politics

Certainly, it is true that partisan polarization, gridlock, and personalized conflicts on local and state boards and in state legislatures can hinder policy debates and may introduce greater conflict and volatility into the policy processes that shape schools.[10] At the same time, serious disagreements cannot be settled by exhortations to "put our kids first." Characterizing political disagreements as inherently petty, unnecessary, and avoidable obscures the reality that they are often significant, consequential, and indicative of fundamentally divergent visions for how public education should be organized and conducted. Democrats and Republicans regularly disagree on basic issues concerning school finance, choice, teacher hiring and firing practices, discipline, LGBTQ student rights, and curricula.[11] So, while some employ "politics" as a synonym for partisanship, politics is ubiquitous even when it does not revolve around the two major parties. In addition, partisanship and ideology often creep into nonpartisan contests whether or not liberals and conservatives, Democrats and Republicans, are named explicitly.[12] Whether those who condemn politics realize it or not, they are ultimately engaging in a legitimate, though often misrepresented, debate over what form politics should assume in the realm of education.

Nonetheless, the idea of exceptionalism in education governance is compelling. More than in other policy arenas, Americans have long imagined that education can be apolitical, and that good governance of schools is achieved through rational, professionally determined policy. In other words, many leaders and citizens believe that there are clear, best choices to be made about how schools should be funded and operated, and that the *correct* decisions about education can be made consistently when policy-making processes are designed to circumvent the partisan fray. Though this idea can be traced back to eighteenth- and nineteenth-century policies in New York and Massachusetts, exceptionalism is most clearly a mark made upon the landscape of school governance by the Progressives at the start of the twentieth century. It was a core ambition of their movement to ensure that local governments would be able to offer basic public services to communities, especially public schools, without the corrupting and dividing influence of partisanship.[13] Education governance today is still shaped by this ideal of separate, single-issue governance; by the institutional mechanisms that Progressives established at both the local and state levels to promote it;

and by the teacher unions and associations that were empowered by those mechanisms.[14]

One such mechanism focused on electoral politics. For instance, rather than local school board elections being scheduled in November to coincide with congressional and presidential contests, they were often held in odd years and during other seasons. This prevented them from being overshadowed by state and national contests in which partisan cues were likely to be especially salient. Further, school board seats were declared nonpartisan, weakening even more decisively the grip of parties on education governance. A parallel process happened in some states with state-level educational leadership, though it was not as common.[15]

A second mechanism focused on authority, setting school boards and educational leaders apart, outside of the hierarchy of general government. Hence, mayors or other agents of general government—for example, county boards—might have had no formal authority over a school system serving the same community, or governors might have had no authority to appoint or dismiss members of a state board. Local school boards in these cases were empowered to independently make decisions about crucial issues, including school finance, rather than having to seek approval from city councils or county boards.

The Return of Partisan Politics to Education Governance

Though they were never adopted equally around the country, institutional markers of exceptionalism, by and large, continue to characterize most systems at the local level and many at the state level. Nonpartisan, off-cycle local school board elections are the norm. State chiefs and boards often possess considerable independence, operating outside public spotlights, empowered to make important decisions such as adopting new content standards. Yet this aspect of education governance is in flux. Reformers today assert that the persistently low voter turnout in local school board elections, reliably sparse attendance at hours-long school board meetings, and generally slow pace of policy change in education are the problematic legacies of the Progressive Era. They believe that lack of engagement is engendered by these exceptional mechanisms and contributes to preservation of the status quo.[16]

Legislatures all over the country have enacted or considered laws that would either convert local and state school board elections from nonpartisan to partisan, or alter their schedules so that the contests are held on even-year Tuesdays in November, along with other major state and national partisan elections. In theory, these changes would ally school board members with like-minded public leaders to facilitate coordination among them, and to help the public more easily draw conclusions about the priorities of candidates and sitting members. In many instances, then, efforts to shift the timing of school board elections or explicitly insert partisanship into local contests wrest debates over educational funding and policy out of arenas dominated by organized interests—where only the most attentive stakeholders, often teacher unions and associations, participate—and into more public arenas where the scope of conflict is broader. These changes theoretically will increase engagement and pressure for reform.[17]

In a number of cases, rather than focus on indirectly aligning educational politics with general politics through elections, legislators have placed school systems directly under the authority of executives or other agencies of municipal, county, or state government. Mayors, assisted by legislatures, have assumed control over major urban school systems from California to New York.[18] Governors have also sought to consolidate authority over chief state school officers and state school boards, in addition to asserting more informal influence through increased advocacy as "education governors," particularly in the South.[19]

Across the board, these efforts seem to be part of a cyclical process that is driven by, and serves to reinforce, the rising prominence of education on public agendas and in public budgets. This process is fueled partly by the nationalization of politics, efforts to curtail labor union influence, and bitter partisan polarization that have increasingly infused American life in recent decades. Though efforts to reform local elections are most often supported and proposed by Republican legislators, political leaders from both major parties have sought to expand their authority over schools.[20]

EXCEPTIONAL AND INTEGRATED SCHOOL GOVERNANCE AT THE LOCAL LEVEL

This section takes a closer look at the ways in which the exceptionalism or integration of school governance plays out at the local level, and how those differences impact each state's capacity to initiate or implement education reforms equitably and effectively.

Elected Versus Appointed School Boards

Exceptional, single-issue education governance can be said to predominate at the local level in the United States. Of the more than thirteen thousand regular public school districts in the country, nearly all are governed by local school boards (alternately dubbed *committees, boards of directors,* or *school trustees*). Of the school boards in the United States, more than 90 percent include only elected membership, and these local elections are most often conducted in a way that dampens the effects of partisan politics. School boards also typically possess the authority to operate somewhat independently from other local, general-purpose governments. Because elected school board leaders are accountable most directly to voters, rather than to governors and legislatures, county executives and boards, or mayors and city councils, they are able to act more with more autonomy than appointed leaders. In other words, elections attenuate the leverage that a state agency might prefer to have over a local agency, or that a county agency might prefer to have over a local district.

But there are, and have long been, exceptions to the rule of elected school boards in a number of states. These boards are composed either entirely of appointed members or of some mix of appointed and elected representatives. Appointment typically coincides with other dependencies that ensure these school districts are supervised by—and beholden to—municipal, county, or state governments.

Appointment of local boards signals that there is limited authority and scope held by the appointed body. Local board leaders, when they are appointed, tend to be selected by a supervising local government with corresponding geographical boundaries, a county or city board, or a mayor (though in the case of extreme underperformance in a large district, governors may also play a role in appointing local board members). Appointment indicates that districts are not autonomous governments but rather dependent on and accountable to the locality.

In 1972, thirty-three states provided exclusively for the election of local school boards, and as of 2016, that number remained unchanged. Among the twenty-seven states that allow for appointed boards today, there are typically just a few across the entire state. In California, for example, only the Los Angeles County School Board is appointed, and in New York, only the school boards for New York City and Yonkers are appointed. Throughout the South, appointment was persistently challenged throughout the 1970s, 1980s, and 1990s and became increasingly rare. Teacher unions and civil rights groups were often particularly instrumental in fighting to convert appointed boards to elected ones, describing appointment as a relic of the Jim Crow era.[21] This shift from appointment to election runs somewhat counter to the conventional wisdom that education governance is becoming more integrated and less exceptional.

However, the shift precedes more recent changes. In addition to their efforts to convert local school board elections into partisan, on-cycle affairs, some state legislatures have been returning to appointment as a useful tool for establishing mayoral or state control over school districts. Since most of these are large, urban districts, many children are educated in systems that feature an appointed board. The demographic composition of large, urban districts means also that children who belong to racial and ethnic minority groups are disproportionately likely to be educated in systems governed in part by appointed boards. As community activists have pointed out, this means that parents who belong to racial and ethnic minority groups are more likely than white parents to be unable to vote for local school board members, a fact that has major implications for the equitable implementation of education policy.[22]

Election Timing and Partisanship

Historically, election processes for school board members have been separate from other political contests throughout much of the country. However, as noted earlier, the timing and partisanship of local school board races appear to be two aspects of state education governance most obviously in flux. Efforts to alter timing have succeeded more often than efforts to introduce partisanship.

In more than twenty states, school board election dates still vary from district to district. Partly due to the higher cost of holding elections off-cycle, and partly to encourage increased turnout, in many of these states a growing percentage of local board elections are held on-cycle. In Minnesota, where timing has varied, the number of districts holding odd-year elections has been steadily declining. In 2003, 46 percent of the state's school districts held odd-year elections, and by 2015 that number had fallen to 13 percent.[23] California, where timing has also varied, passed a law in 2015 stipulating that if the voter turnout in local elections is consistently lower than average turnout in the statewide general election, they must align their timing with statewide general elections. The law, which takes effect in 2018, prompted the cancellation of most school board elections that were originally scheduled for November 2017.[24]

Bills to change election timing have been introduced in at least thirty-five states. Most often, these initiatives have been sponsored by Republican legislators and staunchly opposed by school board and educator associations, who fear the intrusion of partisanship and seek to preserve their sway in school board elections. Democratic legislators have usually voted against these bills.[25] Presently, just twelve states administer local school board elections on-cycle, in November of even-numbered years. Two of these states, Indiana and Michigan, only recently embraced this schedule. Both initiatives were spearheaded by Republican leaders and followed by the passage of right-to-work laws in 2012.

Partisanship is even less common than on-cycle timing for local board elections. In only five states—Connecticut, Pennsylvania, Alabama, Louisiana, and Utah—are these contests partisan. Recently, the nonprofit organizations VoteSmart and Ballotpedia have devoted resources to tracking school board elections, making it possible to more closely monitor patterns in the aggregate. According to their tallies, in 2016, just 8 percent of the races in the one thousand largest school districts by enrollment were classified as partisan contests.[26]

In six states—New York, Rhode Island, Georgia, North Carolina, South Carolina, and Texas—at least some school board elections are administered as partisan contests. A relatively high percentage of counties in North Carolina and Georgia administer partisan local school board elections, a number that has risen dramatically in North Carolina since a Republican-controlled legislature began to consider changes in the status of districts. Since 2013, school board contests in twenty districts have been declared partisan, sometimes at the behest of the districts' local legislative representative but more often against the protests of the existing local school board, as in the aforementioned case of Onslow County.[27]

In only two states, Pennsylvania and Utah, are local school board elections both partisan and on-cycle. Pennsylvania's law, however, allows candidates to run in the primaries for both parties, so there is some question as to the real salience of partisanship in most races. Utah's law was passed in 2016, following several years of heated debate over how to select state board members. Not scheduled to take effect until 2018, the law was recently ruled in violation of the state constitution and thus may never be implemented.[28]

Low Voter Turnout and Low Turnover

Though there has often been little state or federal monitoring of candidacies or turnout in local school board elections, the available evidence suggests that the theoretical benefits of single-issue governance (e.g., increased civic engagement, and more accountability from elected representatives) are not borne out. In 1974, a comprehensive survey of local governance found that turnout rates among voters were low and that school board members often ran unopposed. In 43 percent of districts surveyed, no incumbent had been voted out of office in respondents' recent memory. The authors concluded that Progressive reformers had been too successful, unintentionally protecting the board members from the voting public as well as from partisan interference.[29]

In 2002 and 2010, surveys sponsored by the National School Boards Association (NSBA) reported a near-identical set of findings. In 2002, turnout rates of 20 percent or less were common.[30] State school board associations also regularly reported low turnout; in 2006, the New York State School Board Association reported a 14.2 percent turnout rate statewide.[31]

When turnout rates are low, small coalitions of parents, businesses, civic leaders, or teacher unions can often mobilize just a few hundred voters and determine the outcome of school board elections. However, these local governing coalitions appear to be quite stable; turnover on school boards is low. The NSBA surveys indicated that incumbent school board members were rarely challenged and rarely voted out when they did face an opponent. In 46.8 percent of districts, no incumbent had been voted out of office in the previous five years.[32] In the largest one thousand US school districts by enrollment, spanning thirty-eight states, 82 percent of incumbent school board candidates who chose to run won reelection in 2016, slightly lower than the 83 percent of incumbents who won reelection during 2015, and slightly higher than 81 percent in 2014.[33] These numbers suggest a consistent degree of safety for school board candidates even in the largest districts, a striking fact given that many of these boards oversee schools where racial and socioeconomic achievement gaps are pronounced, at a time when education and educational inequality are higher on public agendas than in past decades.

Turnout in school board elections is reliably higher when elections take place on-cycle. Though many express concern that larger state and federal issues will drown out local voices, turnover among school board leadership increases in response to local conditions. Julia Payson found that California voters were more likely to oust an incumbent school board member over poor academic performance when elections coincided with presidential election years.[34] Similarly, the passage of bills to change school board election timing has been linked to an increased likelihood that voters will oust an incumbent.[35]

Transitioning local school board elections from off- to on-cycle may also have unanticipated consequences that do not always increase accountability. In New Jersey, Republican Governor Chris Christie signed a law encouraging local school districts to hold elections in November rather than in April. Following the law's enactment in 2012, more than half of the state's school districts decided to move their elections. In the years since, there has been a demonstrable drop in the number of candidates for school board; 130 of 805 seats during 2015 had no candidate on the ballot.[36] This may be a temporary effect resulting from confusion about new calendars, or potential candidates may be uneasy about the higher profile of November contests. New Jersey's small districts and the lack of compensation for school board members also contribute to the difficulty attracting candidates. Data from the largest school districts in the country suggest that competition for school board seats elsewhere is actually growing, as elections are increasingly on-cycle and a rising number of districts hold partisan contests. In 2014, only 66 percent of races included at least two candidates for each seat. That proportion increased to 72 percent in 2015, 74 percent in 2016, and 86 percent in 2017.[37]

While these trends toward increasingly integrated electoral politics for education—more on-cycle and partisan elections, higher turnout, and competitive races—are quite clear in the aggregate, variation between and within states persists. In 1998, voters in Florida chose to adopt a constitutional amendment mandating that all county school board elections be conducted in a nonpartisan fashion after the year 2000. Moreover, large, urban districts within states where education governance is otherwise exceptional are often politicized informally. Campaign expenditures and lobbying efforts in recent contests in Los Angeles, Denver, Wake County (North Carolina), and Fairfax (Virginia), for instance, have attracted major endorsements and outside spending in recent years.[38]

School District In/Dependence

Just as important as how local school board members are selected is whether or not boards are authorized to make important policy decisions. In particular, if local school leaders are to be influential, and if electoral accountability for them is to be meaningful, local education agencies must be independently able to determine their own budget, levy taxes, and carry a debt burden.[39] Withholding this kind of fiscal authority is one mechanism by which connections are established or preserved between education and general governance, but also a way in which electoral accountability for school boards can become muddled.

As with election of school board members, exceptionalism—in this instance, independence—remains the norm. Thirty-one states operate school systems in which 100 percent of school districts can be classified as independent. An additional ten states operate school systems in which more than 90 percent of local districts are independent. Only five states—Maryland, North Carolina, Virginia, Alaska, and Hawaii—operate systems in which school districts are considered to be entirely dependent on local or state governments. An additional four states—Connecticut, Maine, Massachusetts, and Rhode Island—operate systems where between 50 and 90 percent of local districts in 2012 were considered fiscally dependent.

Dependent school districts are therefore primarily located in New England and the Mid-Atlantic states. For the most part, the dependent school systems in these states rely on township or municipal governments for revenues and budgetary approvals. School districts in Maryland, North Carolina, Tennessee, and Virginia are classified as dependent, primarily on county governments. Notably, no states in the Midwest operate public school systems in which there are a majority of dependent districts. Likewise, there are no dependent systems in the contiguous Western states.

Altogether, as of 2012, more than 90 percent of local school districts around the country had the autonomous power to levy taxes and determine their own budgets, while just 9.1 percent were classified as dependent. This number represents a gradual increase over sixty years in the proportion of districts that are classified as dependent; however, this increase is largely an artifact of where most consolidation occurred. Northeastern and midwestern states with large numbers of small districts also tended to be states where independence was the norm, so the proportion of independent districts across the country increased. There is a great deal of constancy within states with regards to this aspect of governance, with the important exception of fiscal dependency among large, urban districts.

Dependence can be a complicating aspect in education governance, or one that creates opportunities for coherent reform. When local school boards sit at the head of a dependent school district and are charged with responsibilities similar to those of a more independent board, they must go through another local agency or the state itself to obtain permission to raise or spend funds. For superintendents, school boards, and the voting public, this can extend and complicate the process of drafting and approving budgets by introducing more actors and more veto points. In cases where a board is elected but lacks independent authority, voters may have more difficulty sorting out which public leaders are responsible for finding and allocating resources to schools.[40] On the other hand, when local school boards in a dependent school district are charged with a clearly defined set of responsibilities—for instance, under a carefully designed version of mayoral control—they may be able to achieve both coherence and transparency.[41]

Diverse Local Systems Among the States

Mechanisms for selecting school board members and fiscal dependence interact to shape local policy processes for school districts, especially the manner and extent of their connection to general governance. Taken all together, there are diverse configurations among the states with regards to the degree of integration or exceptionalism in local education governance. Some patterns emerge within regions, however.

Throughout the midwestern states, most school districts remain politically separate and fiscally independent. Local district elections continue to be nonpartisan, and with the exception of Michigan and Indiana, they occur out of sync with major, partisan national contests. It does seem likely that school board elections in both Indiana and Michigan will assume a more partisan flavor in the coming years, and momentum in this region is building toward aligning general elections and school board elections, yet local education governance in these states appears relatively exceptional.

In the northeastern states, it is more common for school districts to be fiscally dependent on townships or other supervisory unions and therefore for budgeting processes to include local municipal leaders. However, partisanship is still a very uncommon feature of local school board elections, turnout is often low, and seats regularly go uncontested. The dates of school board elections are also highly variable within states. Only Pennsylvania and Rhode Island, where local board elections are on-cycle, administer school board elections on a consistent schedule.

In the southern states, most school board elections are off-cycle and nonpartisan and most states maintain independent systems. In the several states where school districts are dependent, education governance is aligned with general governance through county-district or municipal-district fiscal oversight. North Carolina stands out as the state where education governance at the local level is most closely and consistently in sync with general governance and partisan electoral contests. Its districts are dependent, all school board elections take place on-cycle, and a growing number of its local school board elections are designated as partisan races.

Among the western states, with the exception of Alaska and Hawaii, local education governance is independent from other local agencies. Nearly every school board is elected, and with the exception of the contested law in Utah, elections are nonpartisan. There is also great variability in timing, though several are in sync in spite of being nonpartisan.

EXCEPTIONAL AND INTEGRATED SCHOOL GOVERNANCE AT THE STATE LEVEL

At the state level, there are similar dynamics at play as at the local level. State boards of education (SBEs) and chief state school officers (CSSOs) are the designated leaders of state school systems. All but a very few states have constitutional or statutory provisions for these two offices, with the expressed intent that they direct school policy and oversee the school system in the state. What varies most notably across the states are the mechanisms by which these potentially influential leaders are chosen. The means of selection in turn affect their autonomy, relationships with the governor and legislature (who control the purse strings), and how accountable they are to the public—in short, whether state-level governance tilts toward exceptionalism or integration.

SBEs are present in forty-seven states (the exemptions being New Mexico, Minnesota, and Wisconsin), though they are sometimes known as commissions, boards, or councils. SBE members can be elected in partisan or nonpartisan statewide elections, appointed by the governor or the legislature (or a joint effort between the two), or granted a position on the board through their election to another state office. State constitutions may, for example, designate governors and lieutenant governors as members or even chairs of the SBE.

CSSOs are present in all fifty states, and this title also differs throughout the country: some CSSOs are superintendents of public instruction, others are commissioners of education, and still others are secretaries of education, the latter usually designating a CSSO who serves at the pleasure of the governor. CSSOs can be elected in partisan or nonpartisan elections or appointed by the SBE, the governor, or the state legislature. Partisanship is, however, far more common in these state-level contests.[42]

Common Models for Selecting State Boards of Education and Chief State School Officers

At the state level there are four common configurations for selecting the CSSO and the SBE, which account for thirty-nine of the fifty states (see figure 5.1). In the first model, the governor asserts clear and direct authority over a state's school system, while the voters' influence over this level of education governance is less direct. Governors directly appoint both the CSSO and the SBE in eleven states.

The second model is the most common throughout the country. In twelve states, the governor appoints the SBE, and its members in turn appoint the CSSO. The governor maintains a strong influence over the school system, but gubernatorial authority is indirect and therefore slightly weakened by the intervening position of the SBE. The voters have only indirect influence, exercised via their ability to elect the governor, whom they must presumably hold accountable for many policy outcomes. This model is similarly employed by at least one state in each of the four major Census regions.

In the third model, the governor appoints the SBE, but the CSSO is elected by the voters. Voters therefore have direct influence over education governance in the state. The governor and the members of the SBE must negotiate with the elected CSSO in a manner akin to the way that a county board might negotiate with elected school board leaders in a fiscally dependent district. In eight of the ten states characterized by this model (marked in bold and underlined in figure 5.1), the elections for the CSSO are partisan; the only two states where this is not the case are California and North Dakota. Though partisanship may not centralize policy-making in the same way that gubernatorial authority seems to do, it may centralize the political process and raise the public profile of educational issues. Turnout among the voting-age population for CSSO elections is approximately 40 percent on average, but ranges from 15 to 62 percent. The turnout rate is roughly five percentage points higher for partisan contests, and sixteen percentage points higher when they take place during a presidential election year.[43]

In the fourth model, currently operating in six states, governors have no direct authority over the public school system. Instead, the voters elect an SBE, which in turn appoints a CSSO, mirroring the model at the local level wherein an elected school board appoints a local superintendent. SBE elections in these states are partisan, with the sole exception of Nebraska. Alternative models offer slight variations on these common approaches and similarly shape gubernatorial and voter influence over the educational

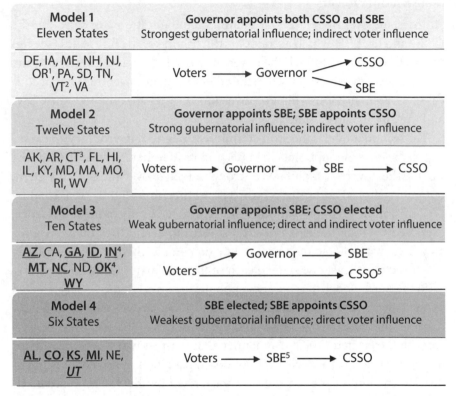

FIGURE 5.1   Common state models for choosing educational leaders (thirty-nine states)

[1] Oregon: A chief is appointed by Oregon Education Investment Board, an entity that oversees education, preK–20. The governor of Oregon appoints a deputy superintendent to lead the state's K–12 system.

[2] Vermont: Governor appoints the CSSO from among three candidates who are chosen by the SBE.

[3] Connecticut: SBE makes a recommendation to the governor about the CSSO. Governor makes final appointment.

[4] Indiana and Oklahoma: CSSO also serves as the chair of the SBE.

[5] For states marked in bold and underlined, elections are partisan. CSSO is chosen in a partisan ballot in Arizona, Georgia, Idaho, Indiana, Montana, North Carolina, Oklahoma, and Wyoming. SBE is chosen in a partisan ballot in Alabama, Colorado, Kansas, and Michigan. The status of the SBE elections in Utah remains uncertain.

system. In New York and South Carolina, for instance, the state legislature appoints members to the SBE.

Growing Gubernatorial Influence

Gubernatorial influence in the selection of the SBE and CSSO is growing. Governors have been widely recognized as newly prominent policy leaders in education. Many researchers have written about governors' extraordinary struggles to exert informal influence on education and to obtain formal authority over state school systems, steps that may be motivated by increasing public expectations that governors demonstrate leadership in this arena.[44]

For SBE members, gubernatorial appointment is by far the most common mode of selection; thirty-two state boards were chosen in this fashion in 1972, and thirty-three as of 2016. The governor shares the selection of the SBE in another four states. Of the thirteen elected SBEs in 1972, seven were partisan contests, while six were chosen via nonpartisan ballot. Of the ten elected SBEs in 2016, eight were chosen in partisan contests. The SBE was eliminated in Minnesota during 1999 in favor of increased gubernatorial control, and the SBE in New Mexico was stripped of all but its advisory capacity in 2003. Otherwise, there have been few major alterations to selection of SBEs.

For CSSOs, the story is rather different. There is substantially less continuity between 1972 and the present. The number of CSSOs elected between 1972 and 2016 declined from nineteen to fourteen, while the number of CSSOs appointed by a governor increased from six to thirteen. This of course represents only successful attempts by governors to change formal lines of authority. Failed efforts are plenty. In 2009, the Democratic governor of North Carolina, Beverly Perdue, appointed her own chief to helm the state system, but was thwarted when the recently elected superintendent, June Atkinson, sued and won in state court.

The active reform of the last several decades is frequently attributed to the increased attention governors have paid to education policy since the early 1990s and to their greater collective advocacy, often through groups like the National Governors Association. Governors were major leaders in the standards-based reform movement and the adoption of accountability systems.[45] To the degree that governors have more control over school governance in a state, school governance will be more integrated with other state institutions, and adoption of innovative—or disruptive—policies may be more likely.

LINKING THE POLITICS OF STATE AND LOCAL EDUCATION GOVERNANCE

Exceptionalism and integration with general governance at both the state and the local levels combine to shape the political dynamics of education within a state. Partisan elections and on-cycle election timing can broaden participation and expand the scope of conflict in education elections, but elected education leaders and leaders in general politics will have to negotiate with one another later in the policy process. Strong gubernatorial influence over the CSSO and/or the SBE, and the dependence of school districts on other agencies, may lead to the inclusion of educational issues in partisan general elections or ensure that they are subsumed beneath other issues. Post-election, however, the hierarchical relationship engendered by these arrangements will shape policy processes and ensure that the connection between education and general policy continues.

Table 5.1 illustrates the prevalence of partisanship in education elections at both the local and state levels. In the upper-left cell of the table are the states where both local and state board elections are designated as partisan. This turns out to be quite rare. Only Alabama and Utah hold elections for local and state boards of education and treat them as partisan contests; and, as noted earlier, the legal status of Utah's electoral structure is uncertain. In 2017, in both states the Republican Party controlled both houses of the state legislature in addition to holding the governorship. In Utah, this control has been long-lasting. In Alabama, Republican consolidation of power is more recent, dating to just 2011.[46]

Among states that hold elections for education positions at the local and state level, it is most common to hold nonpartisan local elections and partisan state-level elections. For nine states, this is the case. There are only six states, shown in the middle-right cell of table 5.1, where nonpartisanship characterizes local board and state level education elections. Nebraska voters choose SBE members through nonpartisan contests, and Ohio and Nevada voters choose some members of the SBE through nonpartisan elections. In California, North Dakota, and Wisconsin, the CSSO is chosen through a nonpartisan contest. For twenty-three states, shown in the bottom-right

TABLE 5.1   Partisanship in education elections at the local and state levels

State elections for SBE or CSSO	Local school board elections				State totals
	Partisan	**Some partisan**	**Nonpartisan**		
Partisan	Alabama Utah[1]	Georgia North Carolina South Carolina Rhode Island Texas	Arizona Colorado Idaho Indiana Kansas	Michigan Montana Oklahoma Wyoming	16
Nonpartisan	Louisiana		California Nebraska Nevada[2]	North Dakota Ohio[2] Wisconsin	7
No election	Connecticut Pennsylvania	New York	Alaska Arkansas Delaware Florida Hawaii[3] Idaho Illinois Kentucky Maine Massachusetts Maryland Minnesota	Mississippi Missouri New Hampshire New Jersey New Mexico Oregon Pennsylvania South Dakota Tennessee Virginia Washington West Virginia	27
Local totals	5	6	39		50

[1] The partisan status of state and local board elections is pending in Utah as of this writing due to court challenge.

[2] In Ohio, voters choose a majority of SBE members through nonpartisan elections. In Nevada, voters choose a minority of the SBE members through nonpartisan elections. The remainder are appointed by various leaders and organizations.

[3] Hawaii does not hold local school board elections.

cell of the table, there are no state-level education elections and local elections are nonpartisan.

Table 5.2 illustrates dependence or independence of education leaders at both levels. In the lower-left cell are the nine states where gubernatorial influence is weakest, and local school districts are also fiscally independent. These are states in which education leaders are elected at both levels, local districts are not subordinate to other local agencies, and the governor's direct control over the school system is limited. In short, these are states where exceptionalism predominates, though it may be moderated by partisanship.

Alabama and Utah, with their partisan elections, are included among these states, as are Colorado, Kansas, Michigan, and South Carolina, where state-level elections are partisan.

In the upper-right cell of the table are the four states where gubernatorial influence is strongest and where the majority of school districts are fiscally dependent on town or county governments, systems characterized by integrated governance. In these states—Maine, New Hampshire, Tennessee, and Virginia—governors are stronger, districts are dependent, and clearer lines of hierarchical authority may speed the adoption of new programs and policies. Such processes may also ease the implementation of new programs, provided the broader partisan environment is not mired in gridlock.

TABLE 5.2   Hierarchical integration between educational and general governance at the local and state levels

State-level gubernatorial influence	Local school district fiscal status			State totals
	Independent		Dependent	
Strongest	Delaware Iowa Minnesota New Jersey New Mexico	Oregon Pennsylvania South Dakota Vermont	Maine New Hampshire Tennessee Virginia	13
Stronger	Arkansas Florida Illinois Kentucky	Missouri Nevada West Virginia	Alaska Connecticut Hawaii[1] Maryland Massachusetts Rhode Island	13
Moderate	Louisiana Mississippi	Ohio Texas		4
Weak	Arizona California Georgia Idaho Indiana	Montana North Dakota Oklahoma Wyoming Washington	North Carolina	11
Weakest	Alabama Colorado Kansas Michigan Nebraska	New York South Carolina Utah Wisconsin		9
Local totals	39		11	50

[1] Hawaii's system is a single district entirely dependent on the state.

Nonpartisan local school board elections, also a feature of governance in each of these states, may also complicate municipal and county control.

Altogether, these features of state and local governance are not determinate. Instead, they shape the likelihood that certain actors and organizations will be able to win advantage or choose to participate in the policy process, and they structure the types of conflicts that are likely to arise throughout the process. Brief case studies of educational politics in two states, one exceptional and one integrated, offer some insight into how these institutions shape process.

Wisconsin: Nonpartisan Electoral Politics and Independent Education Leadership

Education governance in Wisconsin is firmly separated from general governance at both the state and local levels with regards to authority and electoral politics. At the state level, the Wisconsin Constitution empowers the superintendent of public instruction to make major decisions without having to consult a legislative body. Neither is there a state board with whom the CSSO must cooperate.

The superintendent is also buffered from traditional partisan electoral politics in a number of ways. Candidates for the position compete in nonpartisan elections held during the spring of odd-numbered years, when neither gubernatorial nor presidential elections are likely to draw extreme partisans or ideologue voters to the polls—or even a great deal of media attention to the campaign. Instead, the statewide election syncs up with the schedule for local school boards. These local school board elections are also nonpartisan affairs, likely to draw only the most motivated to the polls and to be heavily influenced by the preferences of the state's teacher unions.

In 2001, the superintendent's election drew just under 14 percent of voters to the polls, and in 2013, despite increased attention to the race, just 20 percent of the voting-age population came out.[47] Since 1902, when the election for superintendent became nonpartisan, there have only been ten superintendents, meaning the average tenure in office is more than ten years. Leadership of the Department of Public Instruction (DPI) has been characterized by a great deal of stability. Superintendent Tony Evers won election to his third four-year term in 2017.

The Wisconsin superintendent must collaborate with the legislature, particularly during the budgeting process, but as an elected official is directly accountable to voters. This has enabled superintendents in the state to act independently, and to push back against gubernatorial and legislative efforts to play a larger role in determining important school policies. Dividing power in this manner has further ensured that education policy at the state level is often considered on its own terms, rather than constantly weighed against other priorities. This also slows the pace of change and contributes to stalemate when the superintendent and other state leaders are at odds with one another.

In 2011, the Republican state legislature, working alongside Governor Scott Walker, enacted a law requiring that state agencies, including the DPI, seek the governor's approval before issuing any new regulation. Superintendent Evers challenged the law in court as a constitutionally empowered state official, and in May 2016, the Wisconsin Supreme Court upheld his challenge, affirming his ability to issue regulations without gubernatorial oversight. In 1996, the Wisconsin Supreme Court similarly blocked Governor Tommy Thompson's efforts to establish a new state secretary of education.[48]

Exceptionalism extends down to the local level in Wisconsin as well. School board members are chosen through nonpartisan, off-cycle elections in more than four hundred school districts throughout the state. Turnout in these contests tends to be low, averaging just 14 percent across the state in 2010. It is lower, on average, in districts where teachers constitute a larger share of voters. Though multiple mechanisms might account for this pattern, it is possible that other voters are less likely to view their participation as worthwhile when the educators constitute a larger voting bloc. Candidates in Wisconsin's local board elections often run unopposed: 53 percent of seats were uncontested in 2012.[49] Local agencies have little in the way of legally established relationships with other entities of local government. Partnerships, coordination, and negotiations must be established and negotiated between school leadership and other agencies.

Overall, these factors have combined to cultivate an education politics in the state characterized by relatively uncompetitive elections, stability in local and state leadership, and insular policy processes, all of which have led to incrementalism in reform. There are benefits and drawbacks to such a system. Innovative proposals have been negotiated and adopted in the state, and allowed time to take root, grow, and evolve. Yet the state also boasts some of the largest racial gaps in academic outcomes in the country, and the urgent, coordinated action they warrant remains to be seen.

Virginia: Appointed State Education Leaders and Dependent Local School Systems

Unlike Wisconsin, in Virginia education governance is more firmly integrated with general governance at both the state and local levels. The state board of education and the superintendent of public instruction may be officers enshrined in the state constitution, but they are accountable directly to the governor rather than to voters. The governor appoints both the members of the SBE and the superintendent of public instruction, after which the state legislature votes on whether or not to confirm the governor's selections. Virginia is a closely divided state in which governors are term-limited, partisan control of the governor's office has changed hands between the two major parties on multiple occasions, and the SBE and superintendent typically change when the governor does. Since 1870, there have been twenty-four different superintendents, an average tenure of roughly six years, suggesting greater turnover among leadership relative to Wisconsin.

Since the state's educational leaders report to the governor, he or she has the authority to effect a significant transformation over the school system. This authority, combined with the governor's singular visibility as a public leader, means that constituents will expect action in the realm of education. Drivers of educational politics and policy in Virginia are therefore more likely to be connected to, and weighed more explicitly against, other major issues in the state, tying educational policy more closely to partisan politics and even national conflicts.

During the fall of 2017, education featured prominently in Virginia's gubernatorial contest. In one poll, leading up to the race, roughly a third of voters cited improving K–12 education as their top concern.[50] As one of the first major elections after President Donald Trump's surprise victory, the stakes of Virginia's gubernatorial race were unusually elevated, but the race is illustrative nonetheless.

Both major candidates, Republican Ed Gillespie and Democrat Ralph Northam, devoted considerable attention to public schools. Gillespie promised to work toward expanded school choice, including more charter schools, a virtual school, and tax credits to support private school attendance. Though he promised to raise teacher pay, his agenda closely matched that of controversial Secretary of Education Betsy DeVos; indeed, members of the DeVos family contributed more than $100,000 to his campaign. Gillespie avoided campaigning with President Donald Trump and sought to carefully limit his connections to the president, but teacher unions spent more than $450,000 effectively making the case in campaign materials that Gillespie's and Trump's agendas for education were one and the same. Thousands of teacher union members knocked on doors in support of Northam, who eventually beat Gillespie by nearly nine percentage points. Northam opposed the expansion of charter schools, called for an increase in teacher pay, endorsed investments in early childhood education, and promised to reduce the state's emphasis on standardized testing.[51]

Despite the significant attention paid to education throughout the hard-fought and closely watched campaign, neither candidate devoted a great deal of attention to the more idiosyncratic and challenging issues confronting the state's school system, mostly leaving aside difficult questions regarding segregation and racial tension, and failing to flesh out details of their core proposals. Gillespie, for instance, promised vaguely to work with legislators to develop his plans for tax credits, and Northam's plan for a less test-reliant accountability system was similarly unclear. Education was therefore high on the public agenda for both leaders, but the conversation was very much driven by and in response to national debates, clarifying who each leader stood with and what he stood against more clearly than what he stood for.

At the local level, Virginia's school system is one of the few where school districts are dependent on the coterminous city or county government. The state was also the slowest to transition away from appointing school board leaders, and the last in the nation to legalize elected school boards.[52] In 1987 the American Civil Liberties Union led a lawsuit, alleging, in part, that the prohibition on elected school boards was a Jim Crow–era policy designed to preserve white control over local institutions and disenfranchise black communities. Starting in 1992, state law was modified—not to require that school boards be elected, but to allow localities to hold referenda on adopting an elected school board. The new law did not, however, expand school boards' legal authority. Voters in most school districts rapidly ratified referenda to install an elected board rather than one appointed by the supervising county or municipality. By 2009, there were 108 elected boards, with 26 remaining that were appointed; as of fall 2016, the Virginia School Board Association reported that there remained only 20 appointed boards. Most school boards are now elected in nonpartisan contests, held in May or November, but none are fiscally independent. This means that elected school board members can fulfill their campaign promises only with the approval and support of county boards of supervisors.[53] And so at this level too, educational and general politics often comingle, though turnout in local school board elections is often lackluster.

In several of the remaining districts where appointment continued as the mode of selection, switching to an elected board has been on the local ballot several times. Typically these initiatives are supported financially and rhetorically by educators' associations, and opposed by the county leaders who appoint the board.[54] Superintendents who experienced the transition from appointed to elected boards perceived an increase in conflict during budgeting processes as the elected school and county board members competed for influence.[55] In essence, Virginia's system shifted from one where education and general governance were fully integrated to one where lines of authority at the local level were somewhat fractured by process.

Overall, these factors have combined in Virginia to ensure that education politics in the state is closely connected to general politics, a fact that creates opportunities for conflict but also ensures that schools remain high on public agendas. At the state level, divided party control of the legislature and the governor's office has meant that, in spite of power changing hands at the highest levels, major swings in policy have often been blocked. For instance, Virginia was one of a few states that resisted adopting the Common Core State Standards, and during his tenure in office, Democratic governor Terry McAuliffe vetoed multiple bills related to school choice.[56]

EDUCATION GOVERNANCE IN AN ERA OF GROWING PARTISAN POLARIZATION

Changing governance in recent decades means that education, schools, and teachers are increasingly at the center of extraordinarily partisan fights in many states. In June 2016, Pew reported record animosity between people who identified as Democrats and those who identified as Republicans. Compounding this animosity, party identification aligns ever more closely with racial identity, ideology, attitudes toward labor unions, rural/urban residence, and religious beliefs, threatening to further strengthen those divides.[57] This rising polarization has had a dramatic effect on state governments. In 2013, for about half of states, there was greater ideological distance between Democratic and Republican members than could be found in Congress. Those gaps have been growing. In most chambers, it is Republicans growing more conservative and driving polarization, though in a smaller but significant number of states, it is Democrats who are becoming more liberal.[58] Political scientists worry about polarization because, as Nolan McCarty explains, it gets in the way of "negotiation, compromise, and good governance."[59]

In education, violating norms of nonpartisanship has often provoked a backlash, particularly in states where exceptionalism is most firmly established. However, the form of polarization that has gripped American politics is characterized less by a strongly shared sense of purpose among copartisans than by an intense animosity toward those on the other side.[60] This means that political leaders are able to win votes by scoring points against opponents, a tactic that weakens constituents' ability to hold leaders accountable for advancing a positive agenda.[61]

As polarization has increased, so too has the incidence of unified government, wherein a single party controls both houses of the legislature in addition to the governor's mansion. In 2014, thirty-six state governments were operating under unified party control. Prior to 2005, that number regularly hovered around twenty. Unified control creates opportunities for parties to enact more extreme policies, including ones that dramatically depart from the status quo.[62] To the extent that a single party maintains control over a long period of time, policy regimes in red and blue states are likely to grow more and more distinct from one another, particularly in light of the expanded autonomy granted to states under ESSA. Conflicts between conservative districts and liberal state governments, or more often the inverse, are also likely to increase. To the extent that unified party control is short-lived, ushered in by "wave" elections, reform efforts from extreme partisans may be especially subject to political and legal challenges, provoke electoral backlash, or be quickly reversed. These possibilities increase uncertainty for teachers, parents, and students and incentivize states to delay implementing a program that many expect or hope will be repealed.

Scarce state resources, common in the aftermath of the Great Recession, have combined with polarization to increase the likelihood of conflict between parties with different spending priorities for education and different electoral constituencies.[63] In states where control of state government is both divided and polarized, budget delays are also increasingly likely, which presents a significant challenge for local school systems dependent on state aid.[64] Virginia's legislators only narrowly avoided a state government shutdown in 2014.[65]

Polarization seems to have affected education politics most dramatically in "purple" states like Colorado, Wisconsin, and North Carolina, where parties are far apart ideologically but have roughly similar levels of support from voters and have recently found themselves in close, fierce contests for control of state government. Party leaders locked into such battles identify electoral advantages of reforming (or preserving) exceptional institutions in education governance. Realigning elections, emphasizing partisan issues, and drawing new lines of authority offer a particular advantage to Republicans, while Democrats reap indirect advantages of protecting exceptional institutions. Party-line votes to alter or defend these long-standing institutional arrangements are likely to deepen antipathy and distrust among political opponents and threaten future opportunities for cooperation.

For a century, Progressive mechanisms have made voting in school board elections more difficult, kept turnout low in state and local education elections, and produced advantages for the most organized and interested groups, which has often meant teacher unions and associations. Generally, this has isolated education from broader partisan debates, creating policy change that is slow, incremental, and negotiated. By and large, these institutions remain, dampening voter engagement and preserving the influence of educators even in the most integrated of states. However, as these institutions are challenged, educational politics is becoming more closely tied to national politics and connected to partisan debates. On the one hand, this means that education is higher on public agendas. On the other hand, the growing rancor of partisan politics is increasingly likely to introduce gridlock and volatility into school governance, and abstract ideological differences or tangentially related issues threaten to subsume concrete debates in states and districts. Among more integrated states and large, urban districts, the entry points for partisan politics are clear, but even in more exceptional states conflicts between general government and education leaders are also likely to be sharpened. Ultimately, while politics may be ubiquitous and unavoidable, the politics of a polarized society pose serious challenges for public schools.

6

The Rhetoric and Reality of Local Control

This chapter turns to the third and final key factor shaping the role of the states in education governance: local control. The fragmentation of a state's school system and/or the degree of exceptionalism—the aspects of state education governance discussed in chapters 4 and 5, respectively—are often assumed to indicate levels of local control, yet the term encompasses something more: local autonomy over budgets, curricula, and personnel decisions.

Historians and education scholars have regularly described the desire for local self-determination as one of the most important and enduring features of public school systems in the US. Professor Michael Feuer writes, "if there is a civil religion that binds us, then its sacred texts include stern commandments on the dispersion of power. We have distributed accountability not because it was forced upon us, but because we designed it that way—and fought for it."[1] Throughout their history Americans have often viewed local authorities as most legitimate; defended local control of schools as a right; and struggled to ensure that decisions about schools' curricula, leadership, staffing, and budgets remained with the citizens of the towns and communities they serve. Yet local autonomy is largely contingent on states' willingness to support it, as the following case study from New Jersey illustrates.

LOCAL CONTROL RETURNS TO NEWARK

In September 2017, the New Jersey State Board of Education voted unanimously to end the state's twenty-two-year takeover of the Newark Public Schools (NPS). It was a dramatic moment, welcomed by a gathering of local activists and community leaders who embraced and cheered outside of City Hall. Standing with the crowd was Mayor Ras Baraka, who had campaigned fiercely as a candidate in 2014 to "take Newark back." Earlier in his career Baraka had worked as a teacher and principal in NPS, so for him the vote was a personal victory as much as a political one. He declared: "We now have control over our own children's lives. . . . It doesn't mean that we don't make mistakes. . . . What it does mean is that we have the *right* to make mistakes; we have the *right* to correct them ourselves. We think that we know what's best for the kids in our city."[2]

The return of power from the state to the school board marked the end of a long and difficult chapter in Newark history. In 1995, citing corruption, fiscal mismanagement, neglected school buildings, and poor academic performance, the state launched an emergency takeover of NPS. The largest school system in New Jersey, NPS served a city that was majority-minority and among the most impoverished in the country, a place traumatized by the twin plagues of deindustrialization and white flight. Though it was widely acknowledged that the district central office and its schools were in dire straits, the takeover was resisted and resented from the start. There was no clear objective, elected local school board leaders were unceremoniously stripped of their power, and voters felt disenfranchised. The takeover seemed like merely one more in a long history of injustices heaped upon the city by outsiders.[3] Some viewed it as a sort of annexation, executed in response to—or retaliation for—a 1994 New Jersey Supreme Court ruling that required the state to dramatically increase funding to public schools in impoverished urban districts.[4] In the first decade of state control, test scores and graduation rates remained dismal; questions about financial mismanagement persisted; and state-appointed superintendents clashed repeatedly with parents, teachers, and community organizations.

Fifteen years into the takeover, in the fall of 2010, Governor Chris Christie and Mayor Cory Booker announced a renewed push to improve Newark's schools, granting Facebook founder and billionaire Mark Zuckerberg a seat at the table in return for his pledge to contribute $100 million. The reform agenda was determined with little input from community members or leaders. It included an array of within-school initiatives, such as new principals and curricula, but also structural changes that promised to upend Newark residents' experience of K–12 education. These latter measures included the closure of low achieving schools, the rapid expansion of nondistrict charters in their place, and the establishment of a citywide enrollment system. The whirlwind of change was disruptive; it ignored fundamental needs (e.g., transportation), exacerbated distrust between state and local leaders, and accelerated a financial crisis within the district-run schools, which in turn contributed to a shortage of support staff for the highest-poverty classrooms. Altogether, these rapid changes triggered a measurable decline in student achievement.[5] In a 2014 *New York Times* op-ed, Mayor Baraka decried state leaders for failing to prioritize real investments in local capacity and instead treating Newark as "a laboratory for experiments in top-down reforms." He went on to argue that "successive state-mandated initiatives came and went," a cyclical process that "hurt teachers' morale and bred cynicism among parents."[6]

In the aftermath of this effort, graduation rates eventually rose, test scores in English language arts began to improve, the financial condition of NPS stabilized, and the state-appointed superintendent, Chris Cerf, sought to mend fences with community members and leaders.[7] Nonetheless, Newark residents, including Mayor Baraka, were committed to winning local autonomy and celebrated the decision to end state control. They looked back on the takeover as a painful period in which the city's mostly black and Hispanic citizens, and their elected representatives, were excluded from major decisions about the direction of the public school system. "We never had an opportunity to say what we wanted. . . . We have been a shadow in our own community," Baraka lamented.[8]

STATE AUTHORITY AND LOCAL CONTROL OF PUBLIC SCHOOLS

A takeover like the one executed by the state of New Jersey represents one of the most extreme—and targeted—ways in which states can deny local control, but commitments to and conceptions of local control vary in subtler ways between states, over time, and within states. To investigate these variations, I examine a subset of state policies related to spending, teacher certification, curricula, standards and accountability, and state takeover.

Common to most demands for local control is a plea for autonomy at the local level. Of course, the impact of local autonomy on educational outcomes and opportunities depends on the nature of that autonomy, on the capacity of local districts, and on the inequalities that surface between them. Therefore, the policies I focus on here are ones that arguably contribute to the density of the states' policy environment, limiting local schools' and districts' ability to independently determine whom they will hire as well as what and how students will learn.[9] Rather than capacity-building endeavors to empower localities, these policies come across as efforts to control local priorities and actions and establish coherence across local jurisdictions.

Considering this set of policies as a whole allows for approximating, tracing, and comparing relative levels of local and state control across states over time. Such an analysis is useful for several reasons. First, though it is clear that commitments to local control vary in strength and influence between states, there is no consistent metric for distinguishing "local control states" from those where state control is the norm. Second, rhetorical commitments to localism are prolific but increasingly unreliable as an indicator that local autonomy is respected in state policies and practices. In fact, as a norm, it is often violated, even in ostensibly local control states. Over the last forty years, states have increasingly asserted their authority, often in service of complying with federal policies or in pursuit of federal funds. This means that many states now find themselves in a position where today's policies and practices seem to be in conflict with dominant narratives about the states' political culture and traditional commitments to localism.

New Jersey serves as a critical example of these increasingly common incongruities. Like many other states, it has been described as a bastion of localism, a state comprising hundreds of "political fiefdoms," where local control is more religious precept than political concept.[10] The state's more than five hundred school districts and the sustained two-decade fight in Newark suggest that local autonomy is a deeply entrenched part of the state's political culture and that claims rooted in localism carry weight (eventually) in state politics. State policy, however, tells a different story. In 1983, New Jersey was among the earliest to adopt a high-stakes high school exit exam, and in 1989 it was the first state to take over a local district, Jersey City, because its students were struggling academically.[11] It has since used that authority to take over the Newark, Patterson, and Camden districts. The reality of governance, shaped by policy, contradicts the rhetoric of political leaders and activists who lift up the state's tradition of local control.[12]

Incongruities between rhetoric and policy, long-frustrated appeals for self-determination, and messy implementation of top-down reforms have spurred a resurgence of localism around the US. State leaders have acquiesced to community demands and taken steps to end state control in cities including Newark, Philadelphia, Detroit, and New Orleans. This revival of localism engendered by these contradictions is also evident beyond just urban districts. For instance, the Ohio Department of Education (ODE) explicitly advises parents that the agency's authority is limited because "Ohio is a local control state."[13] The state nevertheless embraced the Common Core State Standards (CCSS) in 2010. Parent activists mobilized in opposition, forming Ohioans for Local Control, and in 2015, forty-one Ohio school districts organized the Ohio Public School Advocacy Network (OPSAN) to call for reduced testing and greater local autonomy. The results of a survey commissioned by OPSAN indicated that 81 percent of Ohioans believed the state should reduce mandates and return greater authority to local school boards.[14] Responding to these pressures, in 2017, twenty-eight of the ninety-nine members of the Ohio House of Representatives cosponsored a bill to broadly eliminate state authority on several issues.[15] By 2018 the OPSAN had grown to include more than 130 member districts, representing roughly a fifth of the more than six hundred districts in the state, and a bill to deregulate school districts and restore local control had earned strong support in the legislature.

Local frustrations with No Child Left Behind (NCLB), Race to the Top (RTTT), and CCSS in part drove state efforts to ensure that provisions for flexibility and limitations on federal power would be written into the Every Student Succeeds Act (ESSA). This moment—in which states have been granted greater autonomy by the federal government under ESSA, and in which local districts are often demanding greater autonomy from states— requires more than an examination of how local control varies in degree across states and over time. It also requires that we consider what communities and political actors mean when they praise or condemn local control, and what happens when it is granted or refused.

Exploring these nuances is critical, because demands for local autonomy arrive at different times from different communities in pursuit of different policy goals. Without question there is an obvious and earnest longing to be civically empowered. This is a potent, affirmative sentiment that can ensure local schools are well supported by an engaged citizenry. At the same time, the desire for local autonomy is also deeply rooted in collective place-based identities. While this, too, can serve to sustain community involvement with schools, the many dimensions of segregation that characterize American housing patterns mean that place-based identities are inextricably bound to race and ethnicity, socioeconomic status, and even political ideology— in other words, power, wealth, opportunity, and influence. Granting local control or refusing it can therefore reinforce or challenge historically produced inequalities. In Connecticut, for instance, local control is sometimes described as the "third rail" of education politics—a roadblock that has made it difficult for policy makers to confront segregation and unequal funding.[16]

HOW STATE POLICIES DETERMINE LOCAL AUTHORITY

Despite the frequency with which local control is referenced in public debates about education governance, there has been no consistent metric for determining which states' systems are in fact characterized by high levels of local autonomy. Often, the extent to which a state's school system is fragmented has been used as a proxy for local control, and yet as a quick examination of New Jersey and other highly fragmented states reveals, the two are not synonymous. Fragmentation does ensure that local school districts serve geographically small areas, and in doing so, it fosters racial, economic, cultural, and political homogeneity within them, simultaneously reinforcing the differences between them. Therefore, fragmentation is an institutional structure that should affect local control only *indirectly*, by reinforcing place-based identities and fortifying desires for local autonomy. Exceptionalism, too, may sustain local control indirectly, by decreasing the likelihood that local concerns will become intermingled with broader national debates. Yet neither fragmentation nor exceptionalism should be assumed to coincide with local autonomy. To evaluate the real balance of power between local and state governments, we must look beyond those aspects of education governance.

Several attempts to formally classify the states with respect to local and state authority stand out in the education governance literature. Two are found in the 1970s scholarship of Tyll van Geel and Frederick Wirt, both of whom explicitly classified state school systems as characterized by a greater or lesser degree of local or state control.[17] In a third, more recent effort, researchers at the Thomas B. Fordham Institute attempted in 2015 to evaluate whether policy authority was concentrated at the local or state levels.[18] Taken together, these three works (the results of which are summarized in table 6.1) suggest that there is some consensus regarding how to evaluate local and state control—a focus on *enacted policies* and *authority* rather than the institutional structure of fragmentation or the exceptional or integrated political processes by which leaders are chosen and held accountable.

van Geel's typology, the roughest classification of the three, effectively distilled the conventional wisdom of the era regarding the status of local control in each state. Avoiding a false precision, he categorized states into three groups. *Decentralized* states were characterized by weak state authority over curriculum; *moderately decentralized* states by slightly more robust state-level power to review and approve curricula and establish graduation requirements; and *centralized states* by stronger state control over curricula, particularly the ability to select and prescribe textbooks. van Geel focused on statutory authority and the specificity of state academic requirements and regulations, though he observed that most decentralized states were also ones with a greater number of school districts and elected state chiefs or boards.[19]

Frederick Wirt's assessment was a far more systematic and comprehensive evaluation of local and state control. His work was possible due to the efforts of the Lawyers' Committee for Civil Rights Under Law (LCCRUL), which had catalogued state school policies across thirty-six areas in 1972.[20] Relying on these in-depth descriptions, Wirt scored state and local authority in each area independently, on a scale from 0, indicating the complete "absence of state authority," to 6, indicating "total state assumption" of responsibility.[21] He then averaged state scores across all of these policy areas to create an index, and ranked states in order to distinguish those with high or moderate state control over education governance from those with high or moderate levels of local control.

In 2015 researchers at the Fordham Institute examined a set of policies relating to states' handling of school district takeovers and charter school authorization, teacher evaluation and collective bargaining, textbook selection, taxes, and the adjustment of district boundaries. States that preserved local district control over these functions were awarded higher scores than those where authority was assumed by state-level agencies. The scores for each policy were then added together to create a summative index ranging from 0 (stronger state) to 30 (stronger local), with scores of 15 or higher characterized by the authors as states where local control over education policy-making predominates.[22]

While there are some conflicting assessments of the relative strength of local and state authority among these three classification schemes, there is a striking degree of agreement in spite of their different methodologies and timespans. The position of the states relative to one another seems somewhat stable. For instance, the Wirt and Fordham indices both rank local control strongest in Wyoming and state control strongest in Hawaii. Yet none of these three rankings depicts change over time—neither the absolute increase in state power nor the shifts in the states' relative position. Since the time of van Geel and Wirt's touchstone efforts, the overall balance of power between states and localities has shifted dramatically even if there may be a great deal of relative stability.[23] To capture these changes requires examining and tracking policy proliferation across states and over time.

STATE POLICY PROLIFERATION

In the 1970s and 1980s, the failure of local control to live up to democratic ideals in terms of participation, the slow pace of progress in the context of the Cold War, and the persistence of racial and economic disparities in academic opportunity combined to weaken political and cultural commitments to local district autonomy, most decisively among federal and state policy elites, including many in business communities. While the federal government enforced desegregation, increased its financial stake, supported the development of state capacity, and provided major boosts to the standards and accountability movement, it is arguably state governments that took the most consistently active role in regulating classrooms and schools in the ensuing decades.

As they assumed responsibility for larger proportions of school funding during the 1970s and 1980s, states began to regulate schools and classrooms more thoroughly and more deliberately: what is learned, who is teaching, how they teach, how schools and teachers will be evaluated, and the conditions under which credentials can be awarded.[24] As the previous chapters have established, states have mostly respected the institutional and political underpinnings of local control while narrowing local authority in myriad ways. Fragmentation, elected school boards, and nominally independent districts remain largely intact, though few can entirely escape the increasing politicization of education. In contrast, every state has adopted more detailed standards, introduced assessments, and established more stringent criteria for teacher qualifications.

These policy changes shed light on the reality of local control across the fifty state school systems through several waves of reform. The balance of power between states and local districts is shaped by the sum total of statutes and regulations. In particular, as state policies proliferate, they gradually create a denser space within which local schools and boards maneuver. The following discussion details several policies that have been cited as evidence of state authority: state textbook adoption, testing requirements for teacher certification, testing and credit requirements for high school graduation, standards and accountability systems, and legislation that facilitates state takeover of local districts. These form the basis of a *policy density index* spanning forty years (1974–2013), the results of which are presented alongside the aforementioned assessments in table 6.1.

State Textbook Adoption

State-level textbook adoption is one of the oldest ways in which states have worked to influence the content and quality of what is taught and learned in schools. By 1897, eighteen states engaged in the practice, and by 1927 that number had grown to twenty-five.[25] Textbook adoption laws were aimed at achieving coherence across state curriculum, guaranteeing a baseline of quality, controlling the cost of materials, centralizing the process of public engagement, and allowing states to review and control controversial content.[26] In fact, the proliferation of state-level textbook adoption laws was driven in part by post–Civil War efforts among white, southern leaders to guarantee that history textbooks included positive depictions of the Confederacy.[27]

State-level adoption places clear limitations on local decision-making. Though only nineteen states held this authority as of 2017 (see figure 6.1), this number included three of the largest states by population—California, Florida, and Texas. Each selects textbooks and provides lists to local districts from which they may choose. Typically, the state education agency (SEA), a specially designated textbook commission, or a subcommittee of the state board of education (SBE) will examine textbooks, invite public and expert comments, and publish a list of approved books. Often this happens on a regular cycle, specified in statute or regulations. A number of textbook-adopting states even provide approved textbooks to local districts at no cost. As with every state policy, the specifics of the program design vary, granting differing degrees of flexibility to local districts. For instance, in California, the state constitution provides for the review only of K–8 materials, while in Texas materials are reviewed K–12.

Though state-level textbook selection narrows the range of texts from which local schools and districts can choose, it offers potential benefits that may provide disproportionate relief to poorer districts. State-level adoption creates larger economies of scale through bulk purchasing, and states may have more resources to devote to evaluating textbooks. It may also increase coherence and alignment to standards across schools and districts. A study conducted by the RAND Corporation found that in Louisiana, where textbooks are selected at the state level, teachers had a stronger understanding of the CCSS than teachers in non-textbook-adopting states.[28]

TABLE 6.1   Comparing measures of state and local control

Region	State	Van Geel, 1976 Classification	Wirt index, 1972 Score	Wirt index, 1972 Classification	Fordham index, 2015 Score	Fordham index, 2015 Classification	Policy density index, 2013 1980	1990	2000	2013	Classification*
NORTHEAST	CT	Decentralized	2.68	High Local	11	State-centric	0	3	5	5	Moderate
	MA	Decentralized	2.73	High Local	14	State-centric	0	1	3	4	Moderate
	ME	Moderate	3.09	High Local	19	Local-centric	1	2	2	4	Moderate
	NH	Decentralized	3.13	High Local	22	Local-centric	1	2	2	4	Moderate
	NJ	Moderate	3.87	High State	12	State-centric	0	5	5	6	Dense
	NY	Moderate	3.63	Moderate State	16	Local-centric	2	4	6	6	Dense
	PA	Decentralized	3.75	High State	13	State-centric	1	3	4	5	Moderate
	RI	Decentralized	3.21	High Local	11	State-centric	1	2	4	5	Moderate
	VT	Decentralized	3.17	High Local	16	Local-centric	0	1	2	4	Moderate
MIDWEST	IA	Decentralized	3.80	High State	17	Local-centric	0	2	1	3	Open
	IL	Decentralized	3.32	Moderate Local	19	Local-centric	1	2	3	4	Moderate
	IN	Centralized	3.90	High State	14	State-centric	2	3	4	5	Moderate
	KS	Decentralized	3.38	Moderate Local	17	Local-centric	1	3	3	4	Moderate
	MI	Decentralized	3.85	High State	14	State-centric	0	0	3	4	Moderate
	MN	Decentralized	4.10	High State	23	Local-centric	1	3	4	4	Moderate
	MO	Decentralized	2.84	High Local	21	Local-centric	2	3	4	5	Moderate
	ND	Moderate	2.89	High Local	25	Local-centric	1	1	2	4	Moderate
	NE	Decentralized	3.81	High State	24	Local-centric	0	3	3	4	Moderate

Region	State											
MIDWEST	OH	Decentralized	3.65	Moderate State	18	Local-centric	1	2	4	6		Dense
	SD	Moderate	3.08	High Local	21	Local-centric	1	2	3	5		Moderate
	WI	Decentralized	3.62	Moderate State	13	State-centric	0	2	3	3		Open
SOUTH	AL	Centralized	4.67	High State	12	State-centric	3	4	7	7		Dense
	AR	Centralized	3.57	Moderate State	16	Local-centric	2	5	6	7		Dense
	DE	Decentralized	3.15	High Local	14	State-centric	1	2	4	5		Moderate
	FL	Centralized	4.19	High State	16	Local-centric	3	5	6	6		Dense
	GA	Centralized	3.24	High Local	8	State-centric	4	5	6	6		Dense
	KY	Centralized	3.90	High State	14	State-centric	2	5	6	6		Dense
	LA	Centralized	3.19	High Local	15	Local-centric	4	4	6	6		Dense
	MD	Decentralized	3.56	Moderate State	11	State-centric	2	4	6	6		Dense
	MS	Centralized	3.93	High State	13	State-centric	3	4	5	7		Dense
	NC	Centralized	3.80	High State	2	State-centric	3	5	7	6		Dense
	OK	Centralized	4.91	High State	12	State-centric	2	4	6	7		Dense
	SC	Centralized	4.61	High State	9	State-centric	2	6	7	7		Dense
	TN	Centralized	3.48	Moderate Local	10	State-centric	2	4	7	6		Dense
	TX	Centralized	2.88	High Local	17	Local-centric	2	6	7	7		Dense
	VA	Centralized	3.88	High State	7	State-centric	3	5	6	6		Dense
	WV	Centralized	3.94	High State	9	State-centric	2	5	6	6		Dense

(Continues)

TABLE 6.1   Comparing measures of state and local control (*Cont.*)

Region	State	Van Geel, 1976	Wirt index, 1972		Fordham index, 2015		Policy density index, 2013				
		Classification	Score	Classification	Score	Classification	1980	1990	2000	2013	Classification*
WEST	AK	Decentralized	3.38	Moderate Local	16	Local-centric	1	2	3	6	Dense
	AZ	Centralized	2.91	High Local	20	Local-centric	2	3	3	5	Moderate
	CA	Centralized	3.65	Moderate State	15	Local-centric	1	3	5	6	Dense
	CO	Decentralized	3.79	High State	20	Local-centric	0	1	1	3	Open
	HI	Centralized	6.00	High State	2	State-centric	2	5	4	6	Dense
	ID	Decentralized	3.26	Moderate Local	15	Local-centric	2	4	3	7	Dense
	MT	Decentralized	3.47	Moderate Local	23	Local-centric	1	3	3	3	Open
	NM	Centralized	3.79	High State	9	State-centric	3	6	7	7	Dense
	NV	Centralized	2.84	High Local	13	State-centric	2	5	6	6	Dense
	OR	Moderate	4.30	High State	19	Local-centric	3	4	5	6	Dense
	UT	Centralized	3.42	Moderate Local	18	Local-centric	2	4	3	5	Moderate
	WA	Decentralized	4.37	High State	11	State-centric	1	1	2	6	Dense
	WY	Decentralized	1.86	High Local	26	Local-centric	1	1	1	2	Open

Sources: Tyll van Geel, *Authority to Control the School Program* (Lexington, MA: Lexington Books, 1976); Frederick M. Wirt, "What State Laws Say About Local Control," *Phi Delta Kappan* 59, no. 8 (1978): 517–20; Frederick M. Wirt, "School Policy Culture and State Decentralization," in *The Politics of Education: The Seventy-Sixth Yearbook of the National Society for the Study of Education, Part II*, ed. Jay D. Scribner (Chicago: University of Chicago Press, 1977); Dara Zeehandelaar and David Griffith, *Schools of Thought: A Taxonomy of American Education Governance* (Washington, DC: Thomas B. Fordham Institute, 2015), https://bit.ly/2NMh3DJ.

* This is a relative classification of state systems as dense, moderately dense, or open, useful for comparisons among the states in 2013. It should not be thought of as an absolute classification, where a score from 0 to 3 would always merit an assessment of open. Consider that, in 1980, a 3 would signal a relatively dense policy environment, whereas in 2018 it would signal a relatively open policy environment.

Some states that do not select textbooks do provide local districts and schools with instruments and standards intended to support local selection processes and to increase transparency for local citizens. Ohio has long regulated textbook publishers rather than the textbooks directly. The Ohio Department of Education allows only publishers that have agreed to sell their textbooks to districts at the lowest wholesale price available to any school district in any other state. In this way, districts in Ohio have control over content, but are relieved of the burden of negotiating for prices. Ohio's SEA otherwise avoids endorsing textbooks or publishers. The department functions as a regulator, not a decision maker. Rhode Island similarly tracks this process and makes available lists of other districts' choices and purchases, also functioning as a regulator in a market where districts may lack the capacity to vet and negotiate with textbook vendors.

Teacher Licensure and Exams

As with state-level textbook selection, state control of teacher licensure is both a signal of state authority and a policy with a long, specific history. This history is characterized by a greater degree of back and forth between state and local governments, compared to the relative stability of state (or local) control over textbook selection. Though state requirements for teacher

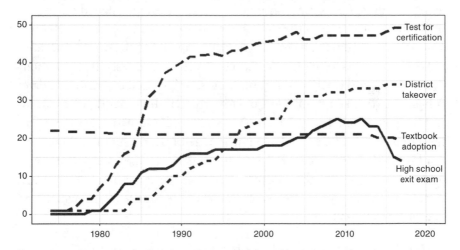

FIGURE 6.1   Number of states with policy in place, 1974–2017

Note: Author calculations based on reports from the Education Commission of the States, the National Council of State Legislatures, the National Center for Education Statistics, news, and data collected in Eric Grodsky, John Robert Warren, and Demetra Kalogrides, "State High School Exit Examinations and NAEP Long-Term Trends in Reading and Mathematics, 1971–2004," *Educational Policy* 23, 4 (2009), https://doi.org/10.1177/0895904808320678.

credentialing are numerous, often complex, and notoriously difficult to compare from state to state, certification exams stand out as a clear indicator that is traceable over time, and their use or lack thereof has largely corresponded to fluctuating state regulation of teacher licensure.

During the nineteenth and early twentieth centuries, states assumed progressively more control over teacher certification. Initially, states used exams as the primary mechanism for evaluating teacher candidates, but shortly thereafter turned away from exams and toward mandated and lengthy formal training, effectively devolving authority over teacher certification to normal schools and universities.[29] By 1937, forty-four states were exercising primary control over certification, and twenty-eight states had eliminated the use of examinations.[30] These policies, along with the introduction of salary schedules based on seniority, were supported by teacher unions and the NAACP as ways of addressing inequalities between black and white school systems.[31] They were also attractive to southern state lawmakers who hoped to forestall integration and saw these efforts as a way to demonstrate that racially divided school systems were in fact equal.[32]

The onset of World War II interrupted state proliferation of requirements for teacher certification. Teacher shortages swept the country, and state-level testing requirements virtually disappeared. The relatively lax regulatory environment in most states continued until the shortages abated during the 1970s and 1980s, around the time the *A Nation at Risk* report also elevated concerns about educational quality.[33] One response to the report's findings in many states was to reintroduce teacher certification tests. In 1974, many local districts and teacher education programs required teacher candidates to pass standardized exams, but only North Carolina mandated them for initial certification. By 2017, forty-nine states had adopted at least one testing requirement. Exams evaluate knowledge of pedagogy or specific content knowledge in the teachers' area of expertise, or they are performance assessments in which teachers' practice is observed and evaluated.[34] Though some states require only one exam, others require more for licensure, and thresholds for passing vary.

High School Exit Exams and Graduation Requirements

As noted in chapter 3, state-mandated high school exit exams are a more recent policy innovation than state-level textbook selection and regulation of teacher licensure. During the late 1970s, state policy makers began to advocate for establishing and testing minimum competencies—the most basic skills a student might need in order to be a contributing member of society—across all of a state's schools. This burgeoning movement, concerned initially with equality and eventually with quality, spurred numerous states to establish minimum competency exams for high school students. States with exit exams withheld diplomas or offered lesser diplomas to student who could not pass them.[35]

In the 1974–75 school year, New York was the only state to administer some form of high school exit exam. As of the 2017 school year, exams were in place in fourteen states, down from twenty-five in 2009 (see figure 6.1). As with textbook adoption and teacher certification, states in the South and the West were early adopters of exit exam policies.

State efforts to increase the rigor of student learning did not end with exams. Over time, states have adopted and raised credit requirements for graduation from high school. State policies have typically included both a minimum number of total credits required to graduate from high school and specific credit requirements in key subjects including math, science, social studies, and civics. These requirements, which have been regularly cited as evidence of increased state authority, were intended to shape district requirements for high school graduation, school course offerings, and students' courses of study. Again, the overall number of credits required to graduate has been consistently higher in the South and the West than the number required in the other two regions of the country. There is also greater volatility in the Northeast and the Midwest, as requirements there have been more subject to repeal once they have been adopted.

As with textbook adoption and licensure exams, coursework requirements have a long history. Even in 1932, thirty-four states had enacted some coursework requirements for high school graduation.[36] By 1974, forty states had enacted minimum total credit requirements for high school graduation.[37] In the 1980s, responding to *A Nation at Risk* and the growing moral panic about low-quality schools, states began to increase graduation credit requirements. Raising graduation requirements seemed a low-cost, commonsense means of improving students' academic outcomes.[38] As of 2013, forty-eight states had established total credit requirements for graduation.

In Colorado and Massachusetts, high school graduation requirements are set at the local level, and local boards have tended to establish relatively high standards. Among states with total credit requirements, the total varies widely, just thirteen in Wisconsin and Wyoming, compared with twenty-four in a number of states, though the average number of credits required has risen steadily over time (see figure 6.2). In states with few mandated requirements, statutes often encourage localities to require more of their high school students, but laws clearly stipulate flexibility for local boards. For example, Wisconsin state statutes encourage boards to adopt additional requirements. In North Dakota and Nebraska, until recently, a certain number of credits were required to earn a high school diploma, but the state allowed localities to determine the composition of those credits. Some state requirements are relatively new. Both Michigan and Iowa enacted minimum credit requirements that took effect in 2011.

Standards, Accountability, and Takeover

Finally, evidence of the increased power of states, relative to local districts, can be found in the standards and accountability policies that proliferated during the 1990s. Following the 1989 governors' education summit held by George H. W. Bush, professional organizations and states began to develop content standards.[39] Specifying what students should know and be able to accomplish for a given subject at a given grade level, these standards offered potential for states to influence the day-to-day teaching and learning taking place in classrooms and schools, particularly when complemented by performance standards and aligned assessments. State adoption of content standards was accelerated when Congress passed the Goals 2000 act in 1994.

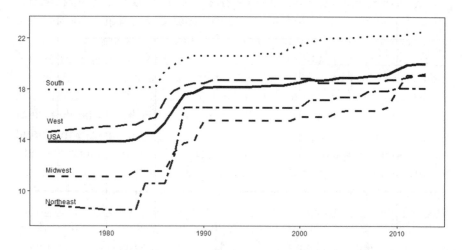

FIGURE 6.2   Average credits required for high school graduation, 1974–2013

Note: Author calculations based on reports from the Education Commission of the States, the National Council of State Legislatures, the National Center for Education Statistics, news, and other historical records.

In 1994, there were just four states with any type of high-stakes account-ability systems in place; by 2000, thirty had written standards, begun administering tests, and adopted some form of NCLB-like consequential accountability system.[40] When NCLB was enacted in 2002, the remaining states were compelled to follow suit. Although many of these states worked hard to protect local autonomy by manipulating the design and implemen-tation of their exams and performance standards, even the most reticent states assumed greater authority over and responsibility for their public school systems.

Boosted by the standards and accountability movement, and by NCLB in particular, a slow wave of laws has also been enacted allowing for state take-over of academically distressed districts (the ability to take over financially mismanaged districts often goes back further in time). Though the federal government had taken over school districts in the 1960s in order to enforce desegregation, the passage of statutes empowering state education agencies, state boards of education, chief state school officers, or some other delegate of the state to take control of a district has been a more recent trend. In 1987, just six states possessed the authority to enact an academically motivated district takeover. Of these, and as noted earlier, New Jersey was the first to actually take over a district.[41] Several states in the South—Texas, South Carolina, and Kentucky—were among the first to enact legislation facilitat-ing a district takeover. However, the pattern of regional adoption is much less clear for this policy than others: New Mexico, Iowa, Massachusetts, and New Jersey were also among the early adopters.[42]

By 2002, when NCLB was signed, twenty-four states—excluding Hawaii, which technically needs no such statute—had created a process for the take-over of a district in the event of chronic academic failure. By 2008, nine-teen states had utilized that authority to take over at least one district. As of 2017, thirty-three states and Hawaii held takeover authority. In that same year, scholar Kenneth Wong reported that there were approximately sixty school districts around the country operating under the supervision of a state agency.[43]

HOW POLICY DENSITY VARIES OVER TIME AND ACROSS THE STATES

In combination, state textbook adoption, teacher licensure examinations, high school graduation requirements, content standards, assessments, accountability systems, and the expansion of state takeover authority have altered the functional—and often the legal—nature of the relationship between states and local school districts. As more of these policies are adopted, education policy environments have become increasingly cluttered and dense, the state's role has strengthened, and the scope within which local schools and districts are able to maneuver has narrowed, increasingly determined by state-level leaders. However, not all states have embraced this scheme with equal fervor, and so the sum of those choices can be used to infer the relative strength of state and local authority.

To create an index that measures the density of the state policies that control the academic aspects of school and district operations, I reduced the aforementioned policies to a series of simple indicators: (1) whether or not states engage in textbook selection; (2) whether or not states require testing for initial teacher certification; (3) whether or not states require an exit exam of high school students; (4) whether or not states set credit requirements for high school graduation; (5) whether or not states set these credit requirements at twenty or higher; (6) whether or not states have adopted a high-stakes program of standards and accountability; and (7) whether or not states have the legal authority to take over school districts that are struggling. For each state, I assigned each indicator a value of 0 if the policy was not in place, and a value of 1 if it was in place. I gathered data on every one of these policies between 1974 and 2013 for all fifty states. The minimum possible score is therefore 0, while the maximum possible score is 7.[44]

Rising State Control

As shown in figure 6.3, policy density has increased in every state, across every region, over time. At the beginning of the time period in question, the average score across all fifty states hovered around 1.34. That across-state average rose steeply during the 1980s, somewhat more gradually during the 1990s, and instantaneously after NCLB. In 2013, the last year of these data, the average was 5.26. This result supports other scholarly assessments, which emphasize that states are increasingly powerful and active in education governance.[45]

Beyond the rising average policy density, the range of possible scores has shifted considerably. The most open state policy environments today—where local control appears most intact—are nevertheless denser than they were in the past. Similarly, the densest state policy environments today—where state control appears strongest—are even denser than they were in the past.

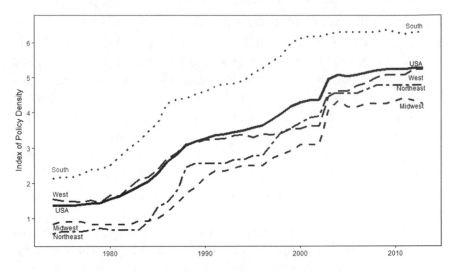

FIGURE 6.3   Average state control by region, 1974–2013

Note: Author calculations based on reports from the Education Commission of the States, the National Council of State Legislatures, the National Center for Education Statistics, news, and other historical records.

In 1974, the minimum observed score was 0, indicating an absence of state control over the policy set studied here; ten states fell into that category. That same year, the maximum observed score was 3, indicating a stronger level of state control for the time, though less state control relative to the present day; only four states fell into that category. By 1991, the minimum observed score had risen to 1, meaning that every state had at least one of these policies in place; the maximum observed score had climbed to 6.

After 2002, when NCLB was enacted, the minimum observed score climbed to 2 when every state was compelled to adopt accountability measures (the maximum had already reached 7 in 1994, when Texas implemented its high-stakes accountability system). By 2013, the minimum observed score was still 2, but only Wyoming fell into this category. In that year, four states' observed score was 3—Colorado, Iowa, Montana, and Wisconsin—suggesting a high level of local control and an open policy environment relative to other states. At the other end of the scale, in the top two categories, with scores of 6 and 7, there were eighteen and eight states, respectively; denser policy environments and stronger state control therefore appeared more common than local control. States' scores on this metric, as well as scores from selected earlier points in time, are presented in table 6.1.

Regional Differences and Relative Stability

Between 1974 and 2013, regional differences among the states were substantial and persistent. The across-state average for policy density was highest for states in the South during 1974. It remained highest among these states in 2013, by a substantial margin. State policy environments in the Northeast appear to have been most open at the beginning of this series but consolidated state authority more so than states in the Midwest, which was the most open region on average in 2013 (see figure 6.3); these differences persisted even when textbook selection was excluded from the analysis. It is also rather striking in this analysis that the relative position of the regions remains roughly the same over time.

Similarly, the states where local control seemed strongest in the early years of the series appeared more likely to maintain open environments over time, and vice versa. For instance, Wyoming scored a 2, the lowest observed value on the index of policy density in 2013, and could also be found at or near the bottom in earlier years. On the opposite end of the spectrum, states including Alabama and Florida scored relatively highly on the index in the early years and continued to do so over time. State scores on the index for 1980 were strongly correlated with state scores for 2013 (.66), suggesting a high degree of reliability over time (between 2000 and 2013, the correlation was .80).

State Characteristics Associated with Higher Levels of Policy Density

States with higher and lower levels of policy density have also tended to share other characteristics beyond geographic proximity. For instance, larger populations are associated with denser policy environments; the most populous states in the country—California, Florida, New York, and Texas—all had comparably dense policy environments in 2013. Though it is rather difficult to tease out independent effects of various state characteristics on policy density, given that geography, population size, poverty rates, racial composition, political culture, and academic outcomes are closely interwoven, it is possible to describe associations that suggest why state control is stronger in some states compared to others. (See the table of pairwise correlations in the appendix.)

One of the strongest and most consistent associations with policy density is educational attainment. In states where the proportion of young people (ages eighteen to twenty-five) who hold a high school diploma or its equivalent is lower, policy density has been higher on average. The correlation has grown stronger over time, suggesting a closer relationship between educational attainment and state policy choices. The states that have been more apt to assert their authority are those where students and schools have struggled most; those that have been less inclined to intervene are those where local districts have been successful in fostering high levels of academic attainment.

Academic outcomes are strongly related to rates of poverty and per-capita income, both of which are also strongly and consistently associated with levels of policy density. Where a higher proportion of the population falls at or below the poverty line, state policy environments tend to be denser, signaling greater state control over the state's public school system. Conversely, where per-capita incomes are higher, policy density tends to be lower. Local districts are more likely to lack capacity when poverty is higher and incomes are lower, which may motivate state policy makers. At the same time, poorer communities are less likely to hold political power and so the potential political toll of asserting state authority may be weaker. State leaders may also be more apt to view poor communities as less capable of self-governance.[46]

The racial composition of a state's population is also strongly and consistently associated with policy density. In states where a higher proportion of the population identifies as black, policy density is higher on average. Conversely, where a higher proportion of the population is white, policy density is lower on average. Without question, this relationship is partly a function of the tendency toward stronger state control in the South, an overlap between higher rates of poverty and a more diverse population. Yet it is also likely that the relationship is driven in part by the racial paternalism that has been linked to state policy-making in recent decades across a range of issues.[47] As with those in poverty, salient stereotypes mean that lawmakers are less likely to view nonwhite communities as capable of self-governance. Many have argued this paternalism is on display in the instances where states have taken over majority-minority school districts, including Newark. Further, the history of specific state policies, including high school exit exams and textbook adoption, would similarly indicate that the association between a state's racial composition and policy density is not purely a mathematical artifact of the overlap between racial composition and other state-level characteristics.

Finally, some aspects of states' political institutions and culture also appear linked to policy density, though less strongly and consistently than the academic, economic, and demographic factors just highlighted. More fragmented states were less likely to proliferate policy in the early years of the series, but this relationship appears diminished in the present day. More Democratic states have historically reported higher levels of policy density, though this association is likewise weaker in recent decades, as many Republican states have also enacted standards and accountability policies, granted themselves the authority to take over struggling school districts, and decided to require testing of teachers for certification. Conversely, states in which unions are stronger have tended to maintain more open policy environments. Though the association between union membership and policy density has also weakened in recent years, it is consistently stronger than the relationship between policy density and state partisan and ideological leanings.[48] In states where public sector unions became weaker, policy density rose more dramatically.

Limitations, Tradeoffs, and Categorical Funds

Measuring state policy density in this manner does mean that nuanced information regarding policy design and policy implementation is lost. For instance, Ohio's regulation of the textbook industry disappears from this analysis. Since the state does not adopt textbooks for districts, that indicator is assigned a simple value of 0. Similar subtleties vanish with respect to teacher examinations and state accountability laws. Activists and policy makers must concern themselves with these details, but here the simplification proves an acceptable tradeoff in order to cover the forty years included in this analysis. It was not feasible in this study to evaluate the relative strength of each policy with precision over such a long duration.

In addition, several of the measure's components were either very uncommon at the beginning of the time period studied (e.g., high school exit exams), or they achieved near-universal, or universal, adoption by its end (e.g., teacher examination requirements and accountability systems). The index is based on a sample of major policies for which basic data was available over a long period of time, rather than replicating the type of comprehensive survey of all areas of state education policy undertaken by Frederick Wirt. Thus, the measure is not as sensitive as it could be to differences between the states at the very beginning of the time period, when few states had these policies in place, and toward the end when most did. (See the discussion of this variation in the appendix.)

The index of policy density is also not as fine-grained as the ones produced by Wirt in 1978 and the Fordham researchers in 2015, though it is more specific than the classification scheme created by van Geel in 1976. Even so, the four measures do largely corroborate one another (see table 6.1). Their assessments of state and local authority overlap fairly closely, despite different methodologies and time periods, which provides further evidence of stability among the states regarding the relative, if not absolute, extent of local or state control. (See the discussion of these correlations in the appendix.)

Where the measures do diverge from one another, a closer examination of governance in those states offers up information about different mechanisms by which they exercise authority over schools and districts. For instance, in 1978, Wirt characterized education governance in several midwestern states, including Iowa, Michigan, Minnesota, and Wisconsin, as marked by a moderate or high level of state control, breaking from stereotypical expectations about governance in that region and conflicting with van Geel's assessment of governance in these states as decentralized. Iowa and Wisconsin are classified as relatively open in terms of policy density in 2013, while Minnesota and Michigan are classified as moderately dense. While time explains these differences in part, the measures also differ in what they capture. Policy density focuses on the more academic aspects of school and district operations, and van Geel's assessment appears to have been similarly based on laws pertaining to academic operations and content.

Wirt's evaluation considers finance, as states can exert control over school and district operations by regulating the way that funds are spent. Recent studies have demonstrated that midwestern states, including those just listed, have been more likely than states in other regions to regulate schools and districts through categorical funding programs, even as they tended to be more reticent to adopt other policies.[49] Categorical state funds provide aid to school districts, but funds are differentiated based on priorities established by the state, and thus their use is narrowly restricted. Bilingual education, special education, and transportation are commonly funded via categorical programs across the states. Ideally, this ensures that critical services are funded adequately and not sacrificed when times are lean. However, the more categorical funding programs a state operates, and the larger the proportion of state funds provided to districts in that form, the less flexibility districts have to make determinations about how to allocate their budgets.

Data on categorical funds are not available across the states during the entire time period in question, but two surveys conducted in 2008 and 2013 offer insight. The average number of categorical programs across midwestern states during 2008 was thirty-one, higher even than the average for southern states (twenty-seven), and far larger than the average for states in the Northeast (nineteen), and in the West (twenty-two). These regional averages and distributions are displayed in figure 6.4. In 2008, Iowa reported having thirty-seven categorical programs, Michigan reported fifty, Minnesota reported fifty-eight, and Wisconsin reported thirty-six.[50]

Further, in spite of a nationwide effort to reduce the number of categorical programs, and the repeal of many between the 2008 and 2013 surveys, the highest average number continued to be found among the states in the Midwest. Iowa was one of very few states that added programs, raising the total number to sixty-four, Michigan's remained steady at fifty, Minnesota's declined but remained far above the national and regional averages at thirty, and Wisconsin reduced its number but likewise remained well above average with twenty-nine.[51] These numbers indicate that, despite the fact that those states have refrained from directly making policy about how schools and districts operate academically, they nonetheless exert considerable control via the way they structure state aid.

In spite of these limitations, the measure of policy density captures real growth in state power over time, and the widespread adoption of state-level policies that seek to shape the work of teaching and the operation of schools. Moreover, it describes real differences between the states. The few states that have most staunchly maintained open environments stand out all the more clearly as a result. Further, while the measure captures the change in state authority both before and after NCLB, the years just prior to NCLB may particularly evince states' underlying preference for local or state control given that adoption of accountability was more voluntary then.

MAKING SENSE OF THE RHETORIC OF LOCAL CONTROL

Though the balance of power has shifted away from localities and toward the states over the last several decades, local control boasts an impressive staying power in public discourse. In 1980, when asked whether the federal, state, or local government "should have the greatest influence in deciding what is taught in the public schools," 68 percent of Americans named

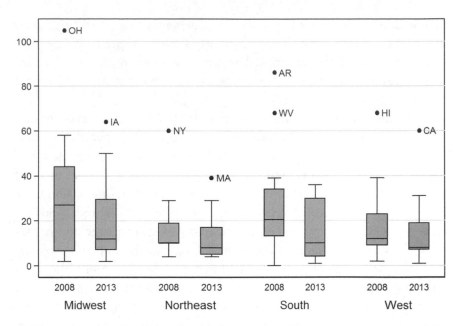

FIGURE 6.4   Categorical programs by region, 2008 and 2013

Sources: Amy M. Hightower, Hajime Mitani, and Christopher B. Swanson, *State Policies That Count: A Survey of School Finance Policies and Outcomes* (Bethesda, MD: Editorial Project in Education, 2010); Joanna Smith et al., *Categorical Funds: The Intersection of School Finance and Governance* (Washington, DC: Center for American Progress, 2013), https://ampr.gs/2NMi2nl.

their local school boards as the most appropriate authority to make those critical decisions.[52] In 2014, when asked this same question, 56 percent of those surveyed similarly named local school boards over federal or state governments, including majorities of Republicans and Independents and a plurality of Democrats.[53] Support for local district control of schools was diminished from thirty-four years prior, but the decline was not so dramatic as one might have expected given the record of active federal and state pol-icy-making during the intervening decades.

These statistics capture an important truth about informal norms of local control in education governance: it is not as dominant an idea as it once was, but it remains a persistently and broadly held value, and it continues to be deployed to mobilize political support for, or more often against, new policies and programs. Local control persists in part because it is venerated as a quintessentially American tradition of participatory democracy and in part because it is so versatile. Local control demands that power be granted to a local community; it does not inherently align with specific policy goals and has therefore been conscripted by groups with vastly different agendas and interests. Understanding these nuances is important, as calls for local control seem to be on the rise.

One education policy advisor I interviewed in 2014, when asked how he defined local control, who he heard it from, and how it impacted his work, replied, "local control is every day." He had plenty to share on the topic, though he admitted to being tired of it. Working in the governor's office of a state where the policy environment was dense, but the traditional fondness for local control remained strong, he heard the term daily from a diverse array of people including concerned citizens, professional associations, parent groups, and legislators. Most of these constituents wanted to be reassured that new state policies would not infringe on local control. Others had made the trip to the state capitol to demand that some older program be amended or repealed in order to restore local control. When they endorsed local control, this advisor generally understood them to mean that "local school boards are best situated to make decisions for their districts, and should be free from constraint to do so, as much as possible." This captures the term's most common usage at present and in recent history—a system in which mostly autonomous, elected school boards govern public school districts without interference from state or local officials. However, he had a different, personal perspective on the concept.

How Local Is Local?

To the reform-minded policy advisor I spoke with, local school boards were too far removed from the teachers and school leaders best situated to make use of broader autonomy. He explained that while many people assume that school board members possess special expertise in education, most do not. Referencing his mother's experience as a lifelong educator, he declared that "most members of local school boards aren't teachers, and they do not always know what they're doing." For him, local control, as an ideal, should be less about locally elected school boards and school districts, with their attendant central offices, and more about directly supporting and empowering teachers and principals—and by extension, parents who might be more likely to engage with decision-making at their children's schools. If the state could do a better job of getting money and resources directly to educators and school leaders, helping them to build capacity at the school level instead of at the district level, then, he thought, local control was worth fighting for.

This interpretation of local control has gained momentum in recent years, earning the endorsement of Secretary of Education Betsy DeVos.[54] It is a definition that favors school-level governance, school choice, and proposals to eviscerate central district offices and to extend charter-like freedom to traditional public schools. Collective bargaining agreements, even negotiated at the district level, are viewed as an impediment to schools' flexibility and autonomy. Such a reimagining of local control is especially popular with ambitious reformers who view school boards as incompetent, incremental, and irrevocably captured by teacher unions. For these individuals, school-level governance is a critical component of a choice-based system, because it allows schools to become differentiated from one another over time, which in turn renders parental choice more meaningful.[55]

However, choice advocates often fail to consider the way in which this vision may be at odds with many of the values that have lent local control its lasting appeal. The local district system is predicated on a vision of schools at the center of communities, accessible to parents, and strengthening bonds between neighbors. That vision continues to attract support from many. When asked which they wanted more, 71 percent of parents chose a "good quality neighborhood school" over "more choice."[56] Geography is central to that ideal, and choice threatens to disrupt those connections.[57]

School level governance is not, however, an idea that has always been linked with school choice, nor is it exclusively the province of twenty-first-century reformers. While the most common usage of local control references local district autonomy, many share this school-level vision of local control in education governance. In fact, several states and large cities have operated school-based governance projects for decades, establishing local school councils that enable parent representatives, teachers, and school leaders to make decisions about schools collaboratively. In general, such efforts have shown promise, but also struggled to maintain enthusiasm and engagement over the long term.[58]

Mythologizing Local Control

The idea of local control has staying power in political discourse in part because it is mythologized. Not only does it call to mind a nostalgic vision of neighborhood schools, but it is also viewed as a bedrock of pluralist

American democracy wherein regular citizens engage deeply and grapple sincerely with the difficult public processes of decision-making, and through those deliberations build civic capacity and community.[59] Faith in local control as profoundly democratic perseveres, in spite of the fact that it has often fallen short, especially with regards to producing any semblance of equitable opportunities.[60]

Local control of schools is also framed, wrongly, as a legal right. It is true that the federal government abjured control over schools in the Constitution and that many of the nation's school systems can trace their origins back to community initiatives in which local groups cooperated to fund and build one-room schoolhouses for the children of their town or village. However, it was quite rare for local control to be explicitly protected by states until the early twentieth century, and even then these protections tended to be quite limited. As Campbell Scribner explains, "For most of U.S. history, a community's right to control its own affairs was mythical because it was legally baseless. State constitutions assigned localities few responsibilities and construed those narrowly, with legislatures retaining the right to reorganize or dissolve local agencies at will."[61]

Writing in 1967, Laurence Iannaccone went further, arguing that wrongly understanding local control as a legal right—and imagining local communities as the primary architects of public education—constituted a misreading of the history of public education. He believed that the emphasis on localism functioned to obscure the reality that states had long been active participants in the construction and the expansion of state school systems, often spurring local school boards to form, mandating longer school years, adding hours to the school day, expanding the required age range for compulsory attendance, establishing colleges to train teachers, and providing critical financial supports along the way. He described local control as a "hazy folklore" that "customarily underestimates the role played by [state] legislation in directly limiting and shaping educational activities" in early US history. For Iannaccone, the rhetoric around local control confused "what is valued, as *reality*," when in fact "the deep-seated value placed on localism in American life is not easily reconciled with the fact of state mandates in educational matters."[62]

From a legal standpoint, state constitutions placed the obligation of providing public education on the state governments, and surprisingly few included clauses that safeguarded the autonomy of localities within those systems.[63] In most states, local school districts derive what powers they do possess from the state, are formally subordinate to state governments, and can accurately be described as arms or agencies of the state with powers that can be expanded or rescinded at will. Indeed, most states possess the constitutional authority to dissolve and consolidate local districts or even to authorize institutions other than local districts to operate schools—for instance, the Achievement School District in Tennessee and the Recovery School District in Louisiana, both of which the state created to take over and reform academically struggling schools.[64]

Local Control as a Floating Signifier

Nonetheless, the "hazy folklore" surrounding local control renders it a powerful term, one that evokes core American ideals of liberty, antipathy to centralized government, egalitarianism, and civic engagement. At the same time it is nonspecific enough to be conscripted by vastly different political coalitions—left and right, strong and weak, majority and minority—in support of proposals that are in opposition to one another. It is a versatile slogan.

Throughout the early twentieth century, white, middle- and upper-class citizens have often invoked local control to protect privilege and power. During the 1950s, when suburban communities sought to resist integration orders, local control, like state's rights, served as a facially race-neutral justification for opposing federal and state policies—and a value that fed opposition to school district consolidation.[65] More recently, strengthening local control has been cited as the reason for carving new school districts from existing ones in Alabama, Massachusetts, Idaho, and California, among other states. The communities seeking to secede are typically whiter and wealthier than the neighbors they hope to leave behind.[66]

During the 1960s, young leaders of the Black Power movement called for black and minority communities to seek control of schools. At a 1968 rally in Oakland, California, Stokely Carmichael condemned white-led public school systems and their failure to support black youth, suggesting that new leadership and greater autonomy were key parts of redressing inequality and overcoming marginalization: "When our youth—who are more intelligent than all those honkies on those [school] boards—drop out of that school 'cause they recognize it's not going to help them, then we turn around and yell at them, dividing our community again. . . . We have to understand that unless *we* control the education system, where it begins to teach us how to change our community, where we live like human beings, no need to send anybody to school."[67]

Across the country, inspired and frustrated by the state of educational opportunities in their schools, minority parents in the Ocean Hill-Brownsville neighborhood sought, and won, control over their schools, launching a rare and short-lived experiment with autonomy inside the massive New York City school system.[68] Ultimately, a union strike in response to a mass dismissal of teachers contributed to the undoing of community control there.

In the twenty-first century, teacher unions have often stood alongside poor and minority parents and community leaders as vocal proponents of local control in major cities. In Philadelphia, the city's Federation of Teachers has been a key part of a coalition seeking an end to the state takeover of the school district.[69] And yet, throughout the Midwest, teacher unions have been struggling to fight off the attempts of state legislatures to curtail collective bargaining rights, also in the name of local control. In 2017, Republican legislators in Iowa cited local control as justification for stripping public sector unions of collective bargaining rights, asserting that doing so expanded the scope of authority for local school boards.[70]

Local control has been called upon to buttress claims brought by reformers advocating the expansion of school choice; states defending inequitable and inadequate systems of finance in court; districts opposing parental empowerment laws; parents seeking to curtail standardized testing; and Black Lives Matter activists searching for alternatives to school closures, accountability, and choice. Local control is more than a buzzword for educators, school leaders, policy makers, and reformers, but the term has become a floating, or shifting, signifier.[71] It is at once vague enough that it can be employed by vastly different groups and yet specific enough that it is effectively able to mobilize supporters. To understand what local control means in public discourse, one must consider the specific political context and conflicts in which the demand for local autonomy is being advanced.

Localism's appeal in the US is strongest among those who feel they can press their advantage better within a smaller jurisdiction than a larger one, or avoid an intergroup conflict altogether. Often in US history, this has meant that the most vehement advocates for local control were local elites demanding autonomy, at least partly to preserve their status and safeguard local resources. Yet local control cannot be easily written off as something that functions only to buttress the power and privilege of local elites and majority groups. Minority communities that have been historically disenfranchised have also demanded local control as a way to secure influence and exercise power over the public schools their children attend. The ideal of local control may be inflated, but the persistence of calls for it and the diverse quarters from which they come suggest that communities have a sincere desire for empowerment with respect to the governance of local schools—a desire that policy makers and reformers must take seriously.

Conclusion

Toward More Sustainable, Equitable Education Reform

IN TEXAS, SCHOOLS TRUMP FOOTBALL

In late August 2012, Governor Rick Perry called up Michael Williams to ask if he might assume leadership of the Texas Education Agency (TEA) and serve as the state's commissioner of education. At the time, Williams had just ended a primary bid for the Republican nomination in Texas's Twenty-Fifth Congressional District, but prior to that failed campaign he had won several statewide elections to serve consecutive terms on the Railroad Commission of Texas (RRC).[1] The RRC is a powerfully influential body that today has little to do with railroads; instead, it is responsible for regulating the state's massive oil and gas industry. The agency employs over seven hundred people to do this work and draws an annual operating budget in excess of $70 million. Williams was widely regarded as an experienced and adept politician, a strong partisan ally to Governor Perry, and an affable leader—known for his ever-present bowties, big smile, cowboy boots, and strong support for school vouchers.

Though many Democrats and educational advocates panned Williams's limited involvement with education policy, others believed that the administrative skills he had cultivated steering the RRC would serve as ample preparation for managing TEA's eight hundred staffers, overseeing the state's annual educational budget of around $20 billion (most of which is transferred to local and regional education agencies), and managing its special programs. Williams's supporters likewise believed that the political acumen he had developed over multiple campaigns would prepare him to negotiate the preferences and demands of the state legislature, the state board of education, and the governor's office, since he was accountable in some fashion to all of them.

Indeed, Williams was asked to helm the state's school system at an extraordinarily difficult time, and it was apparent that anyone leading the state of Texas's schools would need some degree of personal and political agility to navigate an especially challenging economic and partisan climate. The years of 2011 and 2012 were difficult for public schools in Texas and beyond. States around the country, still reeling from the economic downturn, confronted budget shortfalls brought on by diminished revenues and the looming end of federal stimulus aid. With limited ability or political will to raise revenues, most state legislatures were forced to adopt budgets that enacted massive cuts to education spending.[2]

Texas was no exception. In 2011, the Texas legislature voted to allow a cut of more than $4 billion to the state's public schools budget. By December 2011, more than twelve thousand teachers and support staff had been laid off, and more than three hundred school districts were suing the state, a number that ballooned to six hundred by October 2012.[3] Amidst these cutbacks, TEA lost 36 percent of its operating budget, and just a month before Governor Perry called Williams, the agency announced its second round of layoffs for the year, bringing the total number of positions lost to more than three hundred.[4] Commissioner Robert Scott, who preceded Williams as the head of TEA and presided over the bulk of these layoffs, had been torn between coaxing school leaders throughout the state—as well as his direct subordinates—to make do with less, and petitioning legislators to restore badly needed funds. Frustrated by both the increasing weight of high-stakes tests and the lack of forthcoming funding for the schools and the agency he led, Scott had stepped down from his leadership role in July, the month before Governor Perry called Williams.[5]

When I sat down with Commissioner Williams during the summer of 2014, he was approaching his two-year anniversary as the state's education chief and had weathered criticism and earned praise from many quarters for his handling of these seemingly incessant calamities and controversies. I asked him about his experience in education, his priorities for the agency, how heading up the state's education system was different from leading the state's most important energy agency, and whether he had observed anything particularly unique about educational politics.

He smiled and leaned back, chuckling wryly, and said, "Let me tell you a story." The first Sunday after Governor Perry announced that Williams would be TEA's leader, the new commissioner sat at home, preparing to watch preseason football, but found himself unable to enjoy the game because his phone kept ringing. Each time he hung up with one person, another called. He explained, "In all of my years on the Railroad Commission, I never once received a phone call about work during Sunday football—in Texas. I learned quickly that schools are different. Everybody has children. Everybody has a school. Everybody cares."[6] Sunday football may be close to sacred in the state of Texas, but in Texas state politics, schools trump even football.

EVERYBODY CARES

In telling his story, Commissioner Williams articulated a fundamental truth of American education governance: everybody cares, in some way or another, about public schools. This may not look the same from state to state, but it is ubiquitously true. And, in contrast with political arenas like defense or energy, nearly everyone knows something about education as a direct result of their own experience.

A mother votes to support the expansion of voucher programs, which allow children to attend private schools using public funds, citing her own rewarding experiences in private school as her motivation. A young man is passionate about the racial integration of public high schools because of the lifelong friendships he formed in a diverse classroom—connections he might never have made otherwise, living in a segregated city. After witnessing friends and family who are devoted public school teachers struggle to send their children to college on salaries that have been frozen for seven years, a local activist attends a school board meeting to demand a pay raise for the district's teachers.

The fact that these personal experiences occur early and often throughout individuals' lives—when they are children, and later as they become parents—means that everyone has an informed, detailed, and dearly held idea about education: what its core purposes are, what priorities should drive reforms, and who should be empowered to make decisions. Thus, public schools occupy an extraordinary niche in American political and social life.[7] They educate fifty million children in a given year and employ roughly eight million faculty and staff. K–12 schooling is second only to Medicaid in most states' annual budgets. School board members are the most common elected leaders in the country. Teacher unions are the largest organized interest group in the country and an undeniable force to be reckoned with come election season.

In the midst of a historically profound recession, President Obama suggested that maintaining and improving public education was a key component of a lasting economic recovery, and in the wake of budget shortfalls, the federal government provided an unprecedented $100 billion to ensure that state education spending remained equivalent to 2006 levels.[8] Schools are intrinsically important to parents and communities, but they also are public institutions with political significance beyond their immediate effects on children's academic and personal well-being.[9]

Schools' centrality to our communities and to our polity is not, and likely will never be, matched by satisfaction with their performance, however. In the twenty-first century, the next educational scandal or fiasco never seems far away. A solid 61 percent of Americans surveyed by Gallup in January 2016 reported that they were somewhat or very dissatisfied with the quality of public education in the United States.[10] And, although Americans are generally far more satisfied with their local schools than with the nation's as a whole, in 2015 just 51 percent of Americans surveyed would assign A or B grades to their local schools, a percentage that is remarkably constant going back to 1985, while 14 percent would assign them a D or F grade.[11] Harnessing Americans' energy and engagement to promote more sustainable and equitable approaches to education reform, then, requires grappling with the reasons for their widespread dissatisfaction with schools.

The Catch-22 of Great Expectations

Americans around the country not only care about education, they also have incredibly high expectations for what schools will be able to accomplish. They invest in schools emotionally and financially as doors to opportunity, in the same way that other developed nations have invested in welfare-state programs that instead establish floors (i.e., minimum levels of well-being).[12] This great commitment to and knowledge of public schools predisposes US citizens to be especially critical of them, and to some degree, the dissatisfaction many Americans feel is a function of this inescapable tension between sky-high hopes and a reality that will never quite live up.

Americans believe fervently, passionately, that public schools can assimilate immigrants, create equal opportunity for people from all ethnoracial and economic backgrounds, cultivate shared civic values in young people, ensure the health and well-being of children, and, in doing all of this, sow the seeds of a strong economy and a vital democracy. Every reader of this book could add many more items to this list. In short, schools throughout the United States are expected to be more than simply academic institutions, and they are judged on an endless number of criteria.

Citizens also define educational success in varying ways, placing different weight on these many ends. So expectations are not just high, they are also frequently in conflict with one another. Schools are tasked not only with creating better human beings and a better society, but also with resolving our collective differences about how to define "better." Educational historian Jack Schneider argues that the scale and complexity of the tasks set before public education represent "perhaps the nation's most ambitious collective project; as such it advances slowly."[13] The slow pace of this collective progress is unlikely to ever match up with public ambitions.

High hopes for public schools are a long-standing feature of American culture. Leaders all the way back to John Adams and Thomas Jefferson have seized on the idea that schools could fundamentally alter individuals and society for the better.[14] Public schools today provide and distribute social services and function as anchors for the many aspirations, ideals, and competing values enshrined in the American dream.[15]

It almost goes without saying that schools around the country do not universally, and cannot consistently, achieve all of these lofty aims. Set against infinite, herculean expectations—expectations that frequently pit individual and communal goals against each other and which often reflect vastly different aspirations for society—it is all but certain that schools will fall short in some fashion and that political conflicts will emerge around the kinds of outcomes and values that should guide important policy decisions.[16] And so educators, policy makers, and citizens find themselves coping with the inevitable contradictions that emerge from great expectations and an always-imperfect reality.

Describing these contradictions, David Tyack and Larry Cuban have argued that education reform has happened in cycles, driven alternately by crises, utopian ideals, and disillusionment.[17] As several chapters of this book have demonstrated, it has also bounced back and forth between centralizing and decentralizing. However, public accountability reporting, changes in media coverage of educational issues, and the rise of a dedicated and public relations–savvy group of education reformers (many of whom live by the Teach for America credo of "relentless pursuit") mean that schools' failure to measure up against these many yardsticks is perpetually on display.

In the most prominent periodical devoted to education, *Education Week*, the number of articles and blogs referencing some crisis has marched steadily upward since 1980. Between 2000 and 2015, there were only four years in which fewer than 150 pieces included such a reference.[18] Though journalist staffing has declined around the country, education reporting appears to have escaped the worst of these cuts.[19] The most well-known reformers similarly insist that schools in America are in crisis, citing dropout rates and test scores that, when deconstructed, actually show gradual progress over the last forty years. The sense of crisis today therefore seems more constant than cyclical; it has even come to colonize a great deal of education research as scholars consciously or unconsciously take in this narrative.[20]

Perpetual Crisis as Justification for Ill-Conceived Reform

This explanation for the failure of American schools is important. On the one hand, it cautions against a particular kind of hyperbolic rhetoric that can leave even highly qualified, well-paid, hard-working teachers feeling unfairly maligned, an alienating experience that makes more difficult the task of building coalitions and forging partnerships to improve educational opportunities. This is important since engaging teachers is a crucial step for effecting real change in classrooms and schools and better serving an ever-changing group of students in a rapidly evolving society.[21]

This explanation is also important to bear in mind since crisis rhetoric—rhetoric that fails to recognize either the enormity of the task at hand or the progress that has been made—invites opportunists to co-opt reform efforts and can justify the hasty deployment of half-baked innovations, the sort driven by a sense that "things are so bad, something must be done" but which may have little positive impact. Pausing to consider and acknowledge the scale and complexity of what we demand of schools, the consequences this has on public perception and discourse, and the real accomplishments of US schools over the last several decades should not be regarded as a weak stance. Likewise, it is critical to account for state and local contexts. This type of analysis is a vital bulwark against unnecessarily divisive rhetoric and poorly conceived proposals, and for those reasons can only help to focus policy makers and advocates on more strategically sound approaches to school reform. That said, recommending that leaders and activists pause to evaluate and contextualize ongoing inequalities and struggles within schools is not to imply that they should approach education reform with anything other than a profound sense of urgency, or that reforms cannot help American systems of education become something greater than what they currently are, or even that change must be incremental.

On the contrary, there are decades of evidence that legitimize American optimism about the potential power of schools. With the right resources, support, and pedagogy, teachers can help students from disadvantaged, low-income families achieve academic success. Educational achievements have been linked to improved wages and reduced race-based wage disparities in adulthood. The greatest schools not only create spaces for individual children to grow into self-determined adults, but also have spillover effects into other arenas of communal life. Social scientists have shown that high-quality schools and programs can drive up property values and rents, lower the need for welfare assistance, reduce rates of crime, increase civic knowledge, boost political engagement, and strengthen commitments to democratic and communal values, including a willingness to engage with ideas and values that differ from one's own.[22]

TAKING STOCK OF STATE DIFFERENCES

Setting aside the rhetoric of crisis, and accepting that no single reform effort will function as a magic bullet to improve academic outcomes, ameliorate civic malaise, or reduce inequality, provides breathing room to examine the differing challenges facing state and local systems as well as the underlying dimensions of governance that will make or break reform efforts. While there are many factors that determine the quality and character of a child's education, the state in which they reside is of tremendous significance.

Differences in both opportunities and outcomes are visible from prekindergarten through high school completion, and they are nontrivial. In 2013, for example, just 29.5 percent of three- and four-year-old Idaho children were enrolled in early-childhood education, compared with 62 percent in Connecticut. Racial gaps in access to early-childhood learning are also evident, and the states differ greatly in the extent of their opportunity gaps. In Arizona, Nevada, and North Carolina, white three- and four-year-old children are substantially more likely to enroll in school than are black children, while the inverse is true in Mississippi and Oklahoma.[23]

By fourth grade, when students across the country first sit for the National Assessment of Educational Progress (NAEP, colloquially known as the

"Nation's Report Card"), large differences in overall achievement on both math and reading achievement become apparent.[24] On the 2015 assessment, more than 50 percent of students in Massachusetts, Minnesota, and New Hampshire met the rigorous benchmark for proficiency in mathematics, compared with fewer than 30 percent of students in Mississippi, California, New Mexico, and Alabama. Similarly large differences between states are present in fourth-grade reading and in later NAEP assessments, administered to eighth-grade students. And the extent to which there are differences between white and black, white and Hispanic, and poor and nonpoor students also varies by state.[25] By high school, the accumulated differences in opportunity and achievement between the students yield stunning variance across the states in terms of attainment and high school graduation.[26]

These differences are not simply a product of the fact that states serve different populations of students, some who have greater need and fewer resources. Demographic factors do explain some of the differences across the states; however, even when those differences are accounted for statistically, some states clearly outperform or underperform others. For teachers, states shape the conditions under which they labor, from the time they begin their training until they retire. For parents, states shape the kinds of choices they can make about their children's schooling. States make their mark on schools in an infinite number of ways.

If educational opportunities in the United States are envisioned as emerging from a series of nested structural inequalities, states are the highest level structuring those inequalities: classes within schools; schools within districts; districts within states; and finally, states within the country.[27] Most parents, teachers, and students can explain how classes in a school vary from one another. From an early age, children know which class is full of high achievers and which is full of students who need to catch up, which teachers are the stars and which are just okay. Similarly, though their evaluations may not be based on perfect information, parents and teachers can identify differences between schools and school districts. The total impact of state governance, policy, culture, and finance on school operations, educational outcomes, and inequality is less obvious, but estimates suggest that about one-third of the variation in student achievement can be attributed to the state in which a child attends school.[28]

Evaluating state governance has traditionally presented scholars and analysts with a challenge of scope and scale, given that there are fifty different state systems of public education, each with its own idiosyncratic history, institutional structure, policy regime, challenges, and resources. Often, scholars writing about state-level education governance and policy have been forced to choose between conducting an in-depth, holistic study of a small number of states and producing broad surveys of all the states that focus narrowly on a specific policy.[29] Yet governance is more than the simple sum of its parts. This book has attempted to navigate those challenges and to offer a way to begin making sense of complex but important state systems, examining how school governance at the state level varies with respect to three foundational dimensions: the extent of institutional fragmentation, the degree of integration with more general local and state politics, and the balance of local and state control. These can serve as starting points for mapping and navigating the terrain of a state's system of education governance.

Fragmentation

The US system of education governance is often described as fragmented, layered, and complex. In the aggregate, this is true. Yet state systems vary substantially in the extent to which their systems of public education are organized into smaller or larger numbers of school districts. In Hawaii there is a single statewide district; in Delaware there are 19, in Nebraska there are 227, and in California there are more than 900. Governing education in Delaware is a different task than governing education in Nebraska. In general, the smaller the number of school districts, the more likely a state will be able to operate schools as part of a single, coherent system. The greater the number of school systems, the more likely a state will struggle with communication, coordination, and collaboration between the state and local leadership, vital at any stage of the policy process. Local actors, other than those who hail from larger and well-resourced districts, may have difficulty communicating their needs and priorities to state leaders when they are but one small voice in a large chorus. Rural district leaders and leaders of small districts may be especially limited in this regard, given the higher likelihood that they will be professionally isolated and too occupied with operational tasks to set aside time to lobby state officials.

For their part, state leaders in highly fragmented states may struggle to transmit their priorities, ensure faithful implementation of policies, or accurately evaluate public programs. These bottom-up and top-down challenges with communication and monitoring combine to threaten legitimacy, the collective sense that all stakeholders have a fair voice in the process. At the same time, many state leaders in fragmented systems are aware of these hurdles and have leveraged both formal and informal mechanisms to address them. Leaders gather and share information through regional education service agencies (RESAs) and county governments; they invite direct comments on current programs and critical needs by fielding surveys; they share updates about policy processes and programs through regular emails and newsletters; and they ensure that stakeholders have a voice at various stages of the policy process by meeting regularly with the leaders of advocacy groups and professional associations.

As chapter 4 demonstrated, however, fragmentation influences more than simply the dynamics of state policy processes. Though there are some notable exceptions, school district boundaries have been mostly static for much of the last thirty years. Large numbers of school districts with fixed boundaries amplify the influence of residential segregation within educational systems, especially in terms of racial and socioeconomic status. As fragmented state school systems have interacted with high-stakes accountability policies and public reporting of test scores, parents with means have used these data to sort themselves into better-performing districts, a process that becomes less costly for families when districts are numerous and small, and which deepens preexisting segregation, concentrating resources and social capital in already privileged communities. In other words, this aspect of state governance contributes to the maintenance of one of the most stubborn problems driving racial and socioeconomic gaps in opportunity, achievement, and attainment.

In highly fragmented systems where segregation arises mostly between districts as opposed to within them, the policy tools available to challenge harmful socioeconomic and racial segregation require politically difficult interdistrict cooperation or intervention from a higher state or federal authority. Though there are compelling cases in which districts have voluntarily developed and maintained interdistrict programs in pursuit of integration, there is another trend that offers a troubling counterweight. A small but prominent number of communities have sought to separate from larger districts, and in many cases permissive state laws that ease the process of separation have allowed segregation to grow. In less fragmented systems where segregation exists largely within districts, as in many southern and western states, district leaders have substantial power to act on their own by revising student assignment or adopting magnet school programs that promote integrated schools.[30]

Political Exceptionalism and Integration

Though school district boundaries have remained relatively stable in the last several decades, the political infrastructure and norms of state education governance have shifted, and show signs they will continue to transform. Understanding this aspect of states' education governance requires one to discern who local and state educational leaders are, whether they are treated as traditional partisan or nonpartisan actors, what powers they hold, and whether they are subordinate to or separate from leaders in general government.

At the local level, the majority of states operate systems in which school districts are led by elected school boards whose members are selected in nonpartisan, off-cycle electoral contests, separating education governance from general governance. In very few states are local school boards consistently elected in partisan contests or during on-cycle elections. More than 90 percent of local districts also operate independently from county, municipal, and state governments, meaning they can make determinations about their budgets and levy taxes. Two strands of reform are, however, challenging aspects of this status quo. First, legislatures have enacted or considered bills that would convert local board elections from nonpartisan to partisan, or alter their schedules so that the contests are held on-cycle, along with other major state and national partisan contests. Proponents of these electoral reforms are primarily Republican lawmakers, who have suggested that altering electoral systems will more effectively ally school board members with other local public leaders, thereby facilitating collaboration among them and helping the public more easily draw conclusions about the priorities of candidates and sitting members. Opponents argue that efforts to shift the timing of local education elections and to explicitly insert partisanship into local contests are aimed more at weakening teacher unions than at strengthening democratic governance. Second, in several states, rather than focus on indirectly aligning educational politics with general politics through campaigns and elections, legislators have placed school systems directly under the authority of executives or other agencies of municipal, county, or state government. In a number of prominent cases, mayors, typically with the support of state legislatures, have assumed control over major urban school systems.

At the state level, there is variation in terms of whether or not leaders of the states' educational system—including the state superintendent or the state commissioner of education (the chief state school officer, or CSSO) and the members of a state board of education (SBE)—are elected or appointed, partisan or nonpartisan. In the last few decades, close linkages between these educational leaders and governors have become more common. Governors have pursued expanded authority and influence over schools, politicizing education leadership in some instances when they have failed to secure the formal power to appoint and dismiss CSSOs and SBEs. Under models of state-level governance in which the governor holds this power over one or both bodies (and does not face competition for influence from an elected state-level education leader), the CSSO and the SBE are likely to share the governor's party affiliation, and strong gubernatorial leadership creates the potential for school governance to be more centralized, less separate from other critical state institutions, and in some cases more innovative—or disruptive.

At both levels of government, debates over educational funding and policy are being wrested out of single-issue arenas into more general arenas where the scope of debate is likely to be broader, more overtly partisan, and more decidedly ideological. The spread of the electoral reforms that effect this change is driven partially by historically high levels of partisan polarization and gridlock in many states; in this battle, control of school systems is partly a prize to be won, given the power of schools to shape young minds and cultivate future political leaders. Precisely how education governance will be changed by this closer relationship to partisan debates will depend on the extent to which education governance is integrated or exceptional in that state, and whether control of state governments is divided between the parties or held by a single party.

Local and State Control

If school district boundaries in most states have changed little over the last several decades, and the mechanisms that promote exceptionalism have been challenged but remain formally present in most states, local control is where transformation appears to be most widespread and dramatic. Local self-determination has long been a cherished aspect of education governance in many states, and it is also one of the commonly proffered explanations for why educational outcomes have been unequal and progress has been slow throughout the US. Particularly when localism intersects with fragmented districts and exceptional politics, it can militate against the adoption of new educational reforms, compromise the implementation of educational policies that might otherwise achieve success, and serve to reinforce inequality between communities.[31] Given dramatic resource differences between districts, local control has historically helped to exacerbate inequalities between districts.[32] The reality is that states have always differed in the extent to which they have attempted to lead their school systems, but it is undeniable that just several decades ago, local districts in most states operated within a more open policy space across most states. Today, that space appears considerably denser. While there remains variation in the aggressiveness with which states have led reform efforts, every state has adopted content standards, administers annual assessments in key subjects, operates a system of accountability, gathers and disseminates data, and regulates teacher credentialing. Only a handful of states can make a strong claim to have preserved substantial local autonomy for districts. In most states, state-level policy makers must navigate terrain that has become crowded by preexisting policies and programs, and local districts find themselves with more narrowly circumscribed decision-making power.

There can be little question that, on the whole, clearer content standards as well as growing protections and targeted resources for historically marginalized and vulnerable groups of students have wrought broadly positive changes for students throughout the United States. In fact, evidence suggests that achievement and attainment gaps closed more quickly in response to the most intense state policy efforts. However, some caution is warranted in drawing conclusions beyond the particular historical moment during which state policy density grew and local control diminished. Academic progress was most dramatic in southern states, where disparities were most pronounced at the onset of this movement and where state efforts to increase academic rigor were augmented by federally supervised integration programs, which have since been largely curtailed. Moreover, while much of state policy activity benefited students, researchers have gathered considerable evidence that some requirements of state programs, such as high school exit exams, did real harm to the most vulnerable students, increasing the likelihoods they would drop out of high school and become entangled with the criminal justice system.[33] For other high-profile state efforts, including the takeover of local school districts, evidence of benefit is decidedly unclear, and claims of harm done to communities are manifold.[34]

Advancements in academic achievement and attainment have slowed, have been overstated in some cases by creative reporting, and have often come at the expense of untested but vital subjects. Meanwhile, substantial academic disparities between children from different racial and ethnic backgrounds remain intact, and economic disparities appear to have grown. In light of this, the constraints imposed by those policies have become increasingly salient to parents, schools, and local districts. Today, many report that they feel hemmed in by dense policy environments, unable to adapt or respond to the needs of increasingly diverse student populations, and burdened by the time devoted to compliance paperwork. In the same way that states pushed back against prescriptive federal policies to win concessions and flexibility in the Every Student Succeeds Act (ESSA), diverse districts, parents, and local leaders have begun to push back against state policies and to demand greater local control. As many states give way to this pressure, eliminating textbook commissions, loosening requirements for teacher credentialing, rescinding high school exit exams, and declaring an end to state takeovers, they will face the challenge of determining how to support more expansive local control for districts with vastly unequal resources and capacity.

Interactions

As calls for greater local autonomy proliferate, it is striking to consider how these three dimensions of governance interact with one another. In part, they suggest several common approaches to state education governance. These include both the archetypal system, characterized by high levels of fragmentation, persistent exceptionalism, and high levels of local autonomy (e.g., Wisconsin), and its inverse, consisting of consolidated districts, integrated political structures, and high levels of state control (e.g., North Carolina). Most states do not fit neatly into these two coherent categories. For instance, some maintain highly fragmented systems where education governance is nonetheless integrated with partisan politics and state control over policy is strong (Texas). Close attention to state systems reveals kaleidoscopic variation in terms of the number of local school systems, the degree and type of autonomy they are granted, the level of state prescriptiveness with regards to academics and school choice, and the extent to which traditional partisan politics and education are tied together. Nonetheless, it is the archetypal approach to education governance that looms largest in our discourse, as reformers and advocates often call upon the ideals of local control and democratic participatory governance to advance and legitimate specific policy goals rather than to promote a specific model of governance. Further, if this archetypal model is accepted as a starting point, present conflicts appear to be rooted in reforms of the last several decades that have largely left intact some aspects of the traditional approach to school governance while challenging others. On the one hand, many states continue to operate fragmented systems of school districts that reinforce narrowly defined local identities, formalize divisions between communities with different levels of wealth and social capital, and raise political and administrative barriers to balancing student demographics within schools. On the other hand, while these community boundaries remain relatively fixed, and in many cases become increasingly salient, exposure to partisan political battles has increased and actual local authority has vastly diminished. Fragmentation encourages a certain parochialism, but the increasing integration of education politics and the stronger stance taken by states inevitably frustrates strong local identities. In essence, backlash against education reform is partly framed by changes in state governance.

ESSA: IMPLICATIONS FOR WORKING TOWARD SUSTAINABLE REFORM

These formal and informal features of state school systems affect how politicized education reform is, how many stakeholders have effective veto power in the policy process, which policies are feasible, how long they will take to implement, and whether they will be perceived as legitimate, and therefore maintained or quickly dismantled. As is often the case, it is easier to identify how these institutions have contributed to policy failures than to point with the same certainty to what will work better.

Yet the importance of states' divergent challenges, needs, and traditions has carried the day in federal policy, making it increasingly urgent that reformers strive to make sense of the differences that structure states' school systems—and respond to them. Partly in recognition of the failures of the monolithic approach to education reform, and partly in response to pressure from citizens, governors, and CSSOs, Congress voted to replace NCLB with ESSA, a law that rolls back many of NCLB's narrow prescriptions and offers states greater latitude in the design of their testing and accountability systems. Navigating education reform in this environment presents a challenge, but also an opportunity.

Specifically, ESSA presents an opening for states to leverage their expanded capacity in service of better outcomes for children, better working environments for teachers, and greater transparency for parents. States' singular constitutional authority over schools, combined with the specific knowledge of state leaders and agencies regarding their states' unique challenges and strengths, make them best positioned them to enact policy changes that simultaneously fit the needs of their children and stand a chance of lasting. For those reasons, reformers and federal policy makers need to more consistently attempt to understand the differences in states' education governance and policy regimes.

So, while it is true that education governance is complex, and that this has often stymied policy change, it is also true that citizens, advocates, and scholars can choose to interact with those institutions differently, diagnosing the specific barriers and resources that limit or shape educational opportunities in a local district or state, identifying the local and state leaders and networks who have the authority to act decisively, and going *to* them before going *beyond* them. Governance is a collaborative endeavor, and if stakeholders choose to act from a different paradigm than the one that has recently predominated in education, they may yet effect a different outcome. State differences help make sense of how and why outcomes differ between the states, but are also critical in determining the next steps toward reform. While prescribing a specific model of reform would be antithetical to the premise offered in this book, there are some guidelines that will be important to bear in mind moving forward.

First, in complex systems of education governance where there are many decision makers and many constituencies, effective collaboration requires systems that foster continuous communication, coordination, and transparency in order to ensure that policy processes are informed by high-quality information, but also to shore up a flagging sense of democratic legitimacy. Such an endeavor seems most critical in fragmented states where there are hundreds or even a thousand school districts. Communication needs to flow up to inform policy priorities and safeguard legitimacy. Communication needs to flow down not just at the end of the policy process but throughout; policies fail and resentments build when stakeholders are brought in after decisions have been made. Opportunities to participate and contribute must be many. This is critical not only for legitimacy, but also for efficacy—averting implementation failures that arise as a result of poor communication that yields mismatch or exclusion. A critical element of such systems, particularly in fragmented states, is predictability. Many of the strategies currently employed by state-level education leaders to learn from and speak to school and district leaders rely on personalized ad hoc relationships that may be difficult for district leaders to anticipate and navigate.

Second, because education governance is complex, leaders must choose to invest in and develop civic capacity, regardless of state. Recent reform efforts have nominally included "community engagement" initiatives that have failed to provide citizens and local leaders with real opportunities to weigh in on the direction of or priorities for reform. State strategies for taking over and turning around struggling schools have largely focused on what Mary Mason and Sarah Reckhow call "rootless" reforms, those that have little connection to the community in which schools are situated and therefore have little likelihood of effecting sustainable change over the long term.[35] Instead, the old civil rights adage of "Nothing about us without us" should guide deliberate investments in civic capacity. Employing such a strategy may enable states to both fulfill their constitutional obligation to provide educational opportunities to their children and simultaneously respond to the legitimate desire for local self-determination. Deliberately investing in local civic capacity may also serve as a critical way to ensure that local control is granted within the context of an equitable framework. Grants of local control should not be synonymous with abandonment and withdrawal. Historically marginalized students will continue to need advocates and supporters.

Support for civic capacity may focus on developing local leaders' expertise, but also on subsidizing local participation in governance by considering and addressing barriers to participation including childcare, transportation, and lost wages. This type of investment and development is currently being undertaken by states around the country (for instance, the local control funding formula in California) as well as by nonprofit advocates and via philanthropic initiatives. Local districts, advocates, and researchers have formed the Equity-Centered Capacity Building Network, which seeks to develop equitable and sustainable change in school systems. And districts around the country have joined the Strive Together Network, which recently received a substantial grant from the Chan-Zuckerberg Initiative and aims to support children from "cradle to career" by knitting together the resources of local businesses, civic organizations, and nonprofits, as well as families and teachers, to work toward better health, educational, and career outcomes for the children of that community.

Of course, similar efforts have gained momentum before and then been abandoned or maligned when they slow down the pace of reforms. For instance, in 1988, parents and community advocates from Chicago lobbied for a change to the Illinois school code, and in 1989 more than three hundred thousand of the city's residents voted for the first local school councils.[36] These small councils worked with principals to determine budget priorities, set goals, develop plans, and facilitate community engagement with schools. Around the same time, similar councils were being established in Kentucky as part of its major education reform. In both places, initial participation among parents and community members was enthusiastic, additional resources were forthcoming from the states and eager philanthropic foundations, and the local school councils were credited with helping to ensure the successful implementation of sustained and much-needed improvements in both systems. However, as the novelty of each initiative wore off, participation fell, critical resources diminished, and many became disillusioned with the endeavor. On the one hand, those who served on the local councils often felt their allowed scope of influence was overly narrow; on the other hand, the councils have come under fire, earning criticism and provoking calls for their dissolution from reformers who see them as impediments rather than assets to be leveraged.[37] Efforts to develop civic capacity must be understood as ongoing and evolving.

On a related note, many of the most recent and troubling episodes of reform have emanated from policy processes that were closed in the hopes of avoiding conflict and speeding along policy change. Conflict avoidance on this scale, around issues that are so significant, is just as problematic as waiting for universal consensus to act. These wins risk being short-lived and undermine the endeavor of educational reform and improvement over the long term. At a time when bitter polarization characterizes government, and the era of bipartisanship in education seems to have drawn to a close, those who hope to change schools will need to grapple with real value differences. They may or may not achieve compromise, but legitimate victories stand a greater chance of lasting than those that circumvent deliberative political processes.

Finally, though I largely eschew specific proposals, there is one battle that has long been avoided and which I would argue ought to be considered in most states. As disparities grow between the wealthiest and the poorest families, and as the ethnoracial composition of the US population transitions to become majority minority, confronting racial and socioeconomic segregation should be an imperative for states. Though it may be politically difficult, researchers consistently find that well-implemented desegregation efforts have positive effects on both majority and minority students.[38] These efforts will look different from state to state, but there are some broadly applicable principles. Proposals to split school districts should be regarded with skepticism and scrutinized closely for their potential to impact racial and socioeconomic segregation. Recent proposals to separate school systems in North Carolina purport to advance efficiency, but they threaten the dramatic progress toward racial equity made in city/county consolidated school districts.[39] States in which localities are able to independently secede may want to reconsider policies that allow this process to unfold without state approval or consent from those being left behind. Leaders of larger districts that serve diverse populations should reexamine their systems of school assignment and prioritize diverse schools. Studies have demonstrated that most student assignment plans either leave intact or exacerbate patterns of residential segregation.[40] Therefore, many districts have the power to confront segregation by simply redrawing their school attendance zones. A study focused on North Carolina found that districts with Democratic school board leaders had more often used this authority to achieve those ends.[41] State leaders who wish to support local leaders in making these choices may require districts to maintain racial balance, as in the case of Connecticut.[42] In many cases, it is possible to redraw attendance zones and achieve greater racial balance with minimal effects on travel time. Community leaders in segregated schools systems may also pursue interdistrict consolidation, or establishing two-way interdistrict transfer systems between districts.

In 1996, Elinor Ostrom wrote a brief article in which she declared that "reified abstractions . . . do not provide citizens with the kind of knowledge and tools they need to continue the process of reconstituting a democratic way of life in the everyday life they face."[43] She went on to tell a story, recalled from the radio, about a well-intentioned teacher who had led her students in writing letters to President Clinton about industrial pollution in their town. Ostrom lamented that the teacher and the students had not written to their mayor, county council, or governor—elected leaders nearer to them, who held more immediate power in their communities, and whom they could have pressured and spoken with more directly. She suspected that one of the reasons for this teacher's decision was a decline in the attention paid to local and state governments by scholars, textbooks, and teachers, the results of which were a widespread lesser knowledge of those diverse systems and a reduced inclination to engage with them.

I believe something similar has occurred among educational advocates and scholars, and my hope is that this book will help refocus attention on local and state governments and the ways in which the differences between them impact education reform efforts. This understanding is especially important now as ESSA shifts the locus of control over education back to state capitols. The nuances of state policy and capacity, how each state leverages the authority granted by ESSA, will largely determine how the law unfolds. Ideally, those who better understand these systems will also feel more empowered to engage them. ESSA has created a deliberate path for diverse state and local constituencies to participate in decision-making and implementation and therefore to ensure that policies and programs are adapted to their unique contexts. The success or failure of these efforts will depend on whether activists, leaders, and policy makers take advantage of the opportunity the law presents to learn from the mistakes of the past and negotiate sustainable, effective reform that delivers equitable outcomes for all children, regardless of the state they call home.

Appendix: Notes on Data Sources and Modeling

D ata on education governance systems, policies, and politics for this book are gathered from a multitude of sources; their collection was a significant undertaking, supported in part by my fellowship during graduate training, internal grants, and a semester research leave from Wake Forest University.

The National Center for Education Statistics' *Common Core of Data*, which runs from the 1981–82 school year up to the present, and its precursor, the *Elementary and Secondary Education General Information Survey*, which ran from 1967–68 until 1979–80, are important sources of data on the fragmentation of state school systems as well as on school finance, district independence or dependence, and student characteristics. These data are supplemented further by historical reports including the *Biennial Survey of Education in the United States*, published between 1917–18 and 1957–58, and *Education in the States: Historical Development and Outlook*, a 1,455-page tome recounting the historical development of every state school system, published in 1969 by the Council of the Chief State Schools Officers and the National Education Association. Data on other state and school district characteristics, poverty in particular, are obtained from the US Census's *Small Area Income and Poverty Estimates* for the years available.

The adoption or repeal of specific policies is tracked through reports published and archived by the Education Commission of the States, the National Council of State Legislatures, State Constitutions, and legal codes; local news reports are used to fill in gaps in these series whenever possible. For some policies, a longitudinal series documenting state adoption of a high school exit exam requirement had already been constructed by previous scholars and was graciously shared for use in this analysis. These data are further supplemented by close, qualitative study of a subset of states that represent variable approaches to education governance, and semistructured interviews conducted with a small, purposive sample of elites, educational policy makers and stakeholders who work both in single-issue education-focused agencies and in general-purpose governance.

MODELING RACE TO THE TOP SUCCESS AS A FUNCTION OF FRAGMENTATION (CHAPTER 4)

The linear regression analysis in table A.1 indicates that as the number of districts increased, the expected score for a state declined. The relationship remained statistically significant even when other, related factors, including the number of students enrolled in the state, were accounted for.

State LEA Participation Rates for RTTT During Application and Implementation

Figure A.1 demonstrates that the participation rate for LEAs in less fragmented states was near universal, over 90 percent on average. This was true in each round of application and during the subsequent four years of implementation. However, in more fragmented states, represented by

TABLE A.1   Linear regression of best RTTT application score of phases 1 and 2

	Coeff.	**(SE)**
Per-pupil revenue (log)	110.257**	(39.557)
Enrolled students (log)	34.286**	10.901
Operational LEAs (log)	**−21.421****	**6.853**
Early Gates awardee	56.889**	17.100
Later Gates support	39.107*	17.752
Republican presidential vote	−0.015	1.015
Pct. enrolled in charter schools	10.232***	2.968
Pct. black	0.596	0.601
Constant	−1060.978**	451.267
N	46	
R^2	0.692	
Adj. R^2	**0.625**	

*** $p < .001$, ** $p < .01$, * $p < .05$, † $p < .1$

points located farther to the right on the figure, the average rate of participation among districts was far lower. With each year of implementation,
the disparity in participation rates between more and less fragmented states
appeared to become more pronounced. This suggests that more fragmented
states struggled more to hold their reform coalitions together than states
with fewer school districts.

MODELING THE RELATIONSHIP BETWEEN FRAGMENTATION AND SEGREGATION (CHAPTER 4)

To evaluate the relationship between the fragmentation of a state's school
system and the extent of segregation in that particular state, I matched up the
data on the number of school districts in each state for those years, described
in chapter 2, with indicators of segregation from UCLA's Civil Rights Project/
Proyecto Derechos Civiles. I then estimated simple, cross-sectional regres-
sions to evaluate the extent to which higher levels of fragmentation are associated with higher levels of segregation, after controlling for region and the

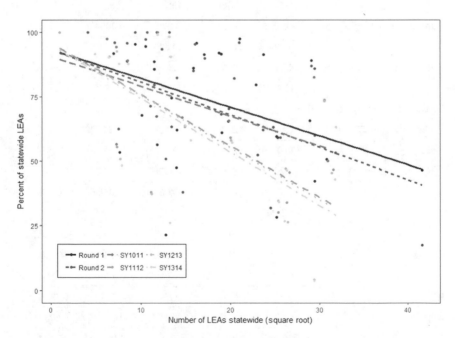

FIGURE A.1   LEA participation rates from application to implementation, by
number of LEAs

demographics of the student population in the state. Across several measures of segregation, fragmentation and segregation were associated.

In the exemplary models reported in table A.2, across the states, the mean percentage of black students who attended schools where 90–100 percent of their peers were members of underrepresented minority (URM) groups was 20.1 in 1981, 21.9 in 1991, 22.3 in 2001, 21.2 in 2006, and 21.9 in 2009. The maximum across the states was approximately 60 percent, and the minimum was 0. The number of regular school districts present in a state ranged from seventeen to a little over one thousand in most years. States in which the population of black students in a state is too small were excluded from the analysis. Fragmentation is consistently, statistically significantly associated with segregation across years. In other words, all else being equal, the

TABLE A.2   Cross-sectional regression models by year: percent black in a 90–100 URM school

	1980 SY	1991 SY	2001 SY	2006 SY	2009 SY
	Coeff. (SE)	Coeff. (SE)	Coeff. (SE)	Coeff. (SE)	Coeff. (SE)
Number of regular districts	0.0003***	0.0002**	0.0003***	0.0004***	0.0003***
	(0.0001)	(0.0001)	(0.0001)	(0.0001)	(0.0001)
Pct. student population black	1.2405***	1.1279***	1.3032***	1.3255***	1.2440***
	(0.2375)	(0.2890)	(0.1993)	(0.1930)	(0.2087)
Census region (ref. to South)					
Midwest (*dummy*)	0.1678*	0.1163	0.1529*	0.1314*	0.1193*
	(0.0709)	(0.0769)	(0.0588)	(0.0549)	(0.0564)
Northeast (*dummy*)	0.2640**	0.2519**	0.1958**	0.1682**	0.1653**
	(0.0735)	(0.0807))	(0.0619)	(0.0586)	(0.0595)
West (*dummy*)	0.1565†	0.08767	0.1337†	0.1297*	0.0895
	(0.0783)	(0.0927)	(0.0679)	(0.0640)	(0.0675)
Constant	−0.2139**	−0.1581	−0.1950**	−0.1954**	−0.1585*
	(0.7339)	(0.1005)	(0.0680)	(0.0648)	(0.0712)
R^2	0.600	0.574	0.700	0.723	0.734
Adj.	0.539	0.497	0.659	0.687	0.698
N	39	34	42	44	42

†$p < .10$, *$p < .05$, **$p < .01$, ***$p < .001$

more school districts that are present in a state, the larger a proportion of the state's black students who will attend schools with other students who also identify as members of an URM group.

MODELING THE END OF SCHOOL DISTRICT CONSOLIDATION (CHAPTER 4)

To evaluate these two potential explanations—the avoidance of integration or the achievement of optimal scale—for the slowing down of school district consolidation, I constructed a panel dataset in which each row comprised a state in a particular year, from 1931 to 2010. I then matched up the data on the number of school districts in each state for those years, described in chapter 2, with a series of other indicators likely to affect whether a state was adding school districts or consolidating them.

These data enabled me to estimate a statistical model in which the outcome (the dependent variable) is the number of school districts in that state, and the contributing factors (the independent variables) are the two suggested explanations for the diminished pace of school district consolidation, as well as other state factors (control variables) that may have contributed to consolidation efforts or hindered them. Next I describe the data and the expected relationship for each indicator with the number of districts in the state, then the model.

Optimal Scale

The panel includes two indicators to assess the hypothesis that optimal scale is associated with the cessation of school district consolidation: a dummy variable that takes on a value of 1 in every state year when average enrollments across its districts are 1,500 or larger, and a measure of population density within the state. A value of 1,500 represents the upper end of where efficiency gains are indicated. Alternately specific models did include dummy variables set at different levels, and the average enrollment measure itself. Other cut points were also statistically significant. While the average enrollment measure did not achieve significance in alternate specifications, it did correlate with other time-dependent variables in the model and so the simpler indicator was included. The enrollment data are drawn from the same government reports and surveys as the number of districts per state. If efficiency concerns and achieving the optimal scale contributed to the end of consolidation, then the relationship to the number of districts in a state for both of these indicators will be positive. In other words, once a state has reached the threshold of 1,500 average enrollment, all else being equal, the number of school districts predicted will be positive, and as population density increases (again, all else being equal), a state will be expected to report a higher number of school districts.

The *Milliken* Decision

To assess the possible effects of *Milliken*, the panel includes a simple trend indicator. In the years prior to 1974, the indicator takes on a value of 0. In 1974 and the following years, the indicator takes on a value of 1, then 2, and so forth. If the *Milliken* decision contributed to the end of school district consolidation, either by hindering consolidation or spurring districts to separate from one another, then the number of school districts predicted will be positive, larger in the period after the decision than before it.

Trends in the Number of Districts

Given that both the *Milliken* decision and increasing population density and enrollment sizes are events that occur at a time period when the average number of districts was decreasing rapidly, a count variable is included to capture the average decline. It begins at 0 in 1931 and increases with each year thereafter. Because the rate of decrease should naturally slow as there are fewer and fewer districts to consolidate, a squared count indicator is included in the panel as well. These indicators ensure that the measures just described will capture *changes* in, or rather *interruptions in*, the larger historical pattern. The count variable should be negatively related to the number of school districts in a state over time, while the squared term should take on a positive value, indicating the slower rate of decline.

Racial Diversity and Economic Inequality

Given that multiple studies have suggested that racial diversity and economic inequality contributed to resistance to consolidation, two measures are included to control for these factors: the percent of a state's population who identify as white, gathered from the US Census, and the Gini index for state pretax income. The percent of a state's population that is white proxies for its level of diversity in the inverse. The Gini index captures the inequality in the distribution of income within the state and is derived from a unique dataset compiled and published by economist Mark W. Frank, reporting state-level inequality metrics from 1913 onward.[1] If diversity hinders consolidation efforts or spurs districts to split from one another, then the relationship between the number of districts and the percent of a state's population that is white should be negative. If rising equality hinders consolidation efforts or provokes fragmentation, then the relationship between the Gini index and the number of districts in a state should be positive.

State Institutional Context

Because school systems are potentially impacted by larger projects to reorganize local and county governments, I also include a count of the number of such governments in the state over time. These data are gathered from the US Census of Governments, collected every five years.[2] If school district consolidation or division is part of a larger state project and less driven by specific concerns about schooling, efficiency, or integration, then these two factors would be related. As the number of general governments increases, so too should the number of school districts, and vice versa.

State Economy

Since school district consolidation is motivated in part by limited resources, I include in the panel a measure of the state's economic well-being, the average per-capita income of its residents in each year. This measure of income for each state is adjusted for inflation to be expressed in terms of 2014 US dollars, rather than the average value at the time. In the models, the per capita is also logged, in keeping with standard practice; income is not related to most things in a consistent way. Growth in income at the lower end of the distribution is typically more impactful than growth in income at the upper end, meaning that the difference between $10,000 and $20,000 is likely to have a greater effect on an individual—or, in the aggregate, on a state—than the difference between $90,000 and $100,000. For that reason, the log of per-capita income is included in the model rather than the actual value of per-capita income.[3]

National Economic Environment

Finally, the Great Depression is widely recognized to have set off state and federal efforts to coerce districts to consolidate with one another, and to have made them more willing to do so given scant resources. Therefore, the panel includes an indicator for whether or not a given year was a recession year. The National Bureau of Economic Research maintains a record of recessions spanning back into the 1850s.[4]

The Model

The model estimated here is specified as follows:

$$Number\ of\ school\ districts\ Yit = \beta 0 + \beta 1Zt + \beta 2Xit + \alpha i + uit$$

The model includes fixed effects for each state, denoted by αi. This means that identification in the models stems from over-time (t) and within-state (i) over-time change. In other words, because there are so many unique characteristics of states for which it would be difficult to control, the estimate of each variable's effect is based on changes in the independent and dependent variables that occur within states. The states are compared to themselves. Z in the model specification represents a set of measures that vary with time but not across states, including an annual count to control for the downward trend in the number of school districts, the squared trend marker to adjust for diminishing rates of decline as systems approach an optimal number and size of districts, and the indicator for economic recessions. This vector also includes the trend indicator that begins in 1974 to test for a period effect of the *Milliken v. Bradley* decision. X represents the vector of indices that vary over time as well as within states including population density (logged), the indicator for average enrollments equaling or exceeding 1,500, racial diversity, per-capita income, income inequality, and the number of general-purpose county and subcounty governments. The error term is denoted by u_{it} and the intercept is denoted by $\beta 0$. Several states are excluded from this model, because there is no variation in the number of school districts in that state, or because the dynamics of district consolidation and fragmentation in that state are too idiosyncratic to include them. The excluded states are Alaska, Hawaii, Maryland, West Virginia, and Florida. The District of Columbia is also excluded. Robust, clustered standard error is employed. The model is estimated in Stata, using the command xtreg.

Results

With regards to efficiency and scale, the indicator for when average enrollments exceed 1,500 was not significant in this model; neither, in additional sensitivity analyses, were other thresholds, nor the numerical value for average enrollment itself. Instead, as population density increases, so does the predicted number of school districts within a state, suggesting that population growth may be a more important factor in slowing down consolidation—or spurring fragmentation—rather than more specific concern about scale. The indicator for national recessions was also significant and negative, suggesting that consolidation is more likely to proceed when resources are limited and concern about efficiency is elevated.

With regards to *Milliken*, the estimated number of school districts in a state increases on average in the aftermath of the decision, or rather the rate of decline diminishes to a statistically significant extent. Though it appears that after *Milliken*, there is an average across-state increase in the number of school districts, this result must be carefully interpreted in connection with the other trend markers. The coefficients for the annual trend and the squared term suggest that for each additional year past 1931 the number of school districts diminishes, but the significance of the squared term makes clear that the decline is not a straight one; rather, the rate of decline tapers off over time. The indicator for *Milliken* does not necessarily mean that the average state has added over eight districts each year since 1974; instead, it means that the rate of decline shifts significantly after that year, on average, in some instances likely leading to an increase in the number of school districts.

Changes in the average income within a state, changes in the number of other local governments, and the economic inequality within a state did not appear to significantly affect the number of school districts within a state. Racial diversity, however, was statistically significant. The higher the percentage of a population that was identified as white during this time period, the more school districts a state is expected to have.

Recall that this is not an estimate based on differences between the states but rather changes within them, meaning that the high numbers of districts and a disproportionately white population in Nebraska should not explain the finding. The coefficient in the model is based on within-state changes. So, as states become less white, fewer districts would be expected. However, a sensitivity analysis is called for, given that rates of demographic change vary across the country, with southern and western states growing more diverse more rapidly than the rest of the country in particular. In estimating this same model, excluding different regions in turn, it does appear that the result is driven largely by the states in the Midwest, which are not becoming as rapidly diverse as the states in the South, West, and throughout much of the Northeast, and which have maintained larger numbers of districts. See table A.3 for the results.

TABLE A.3   Fixed-effects panel regression: results for district reorganization at the state level

	Coeff.	SE
Milliken v. Bradley decision		
(Count of years after Milliken*)*	8.249***	(2.083)
Optimal scale		
(Dummy; average enrollment 1,500 or more)	276.117	(205.527)
(Population density; log of people per square mile)	944.462***	(256.754)
State racial diversity		
(Percent white)	22.197**	(7.526)
State economic inequality		
(Gini coefficient, income, unadjusted)	12.273	(14.053)
State economy		
(Log per-capita income)	455.633	(437.132)
State institutional context		
(County and subcounty general governments)	0.409	(1.378)
Trend		
(Years 1931–2010)	−130.446***	(32.081)
(Years squared)	0.813***	(0.179)
National economic conditions		
(Dummy for recession years)	−58.380**	(19.729)
Constant		
	−7218.939	(4120.899)
Total *N*	2216	
Within R^2	.391	
Group *N*	45	
Minimum obs.	46	
Average obs.	49.2	
Maximum obs.	56	

$^{\dagger}p < .10, {}^{*}p < .05, {}^{**}p < .01, {}^{***}p < .001$

Note: Models include fixed effects for each state. Alaska, Hawaii, Washington, DC, Florida, West Virginia, and Maryland are excluded from the analysis.

POLICY DENSITY AND STATE CHARACTERISTICS (CHAPTER 6)

Policy density is a function of a variety of underlying factors, ranging from the academic performance and needs of a state's students to its political culture. Table A.4 displays the correlation coefficients between policy density

TABLE A.4   Correlation between measure of policy density and state characteristics, selected years

	1980	1990	2000	2010
Political characteristics				
Pct. conservative[1]	0.26[†]	0.29[*]	0.03	0.16
Pct. Republican[1]	−0.32[*]	−0.08	−0.18	0.11
Pct. liberal[1]	−0.40[**]	−0.36[*]	−0.10	−0.18
Pct. Democrat[1]	**0.63[***]**	**0.54[***]**	**0.58[***]**	0.25
Total pct. union members[2]	−0.39[**]	−0.34[*]	−0.20	−0.22
State size				
Land area (log)[3]	0.21	0.10	−0.02	0.07
Total enrolled (log)[4]	0.15	0.26[†]	0.42[**]	0.33[*]
Fragmentation				
Number of districts (log)[4]	−0.30[*]	−0.24[†]	−0.12	−0.13
State economy				
Pct. in poverty[3]	**0.63[***]**	0.40[**]	**0.55[***]**	**0.64[***]**
Per-capita income (log)[3]	−0.39[**]	−0.25	−0.20	−0.35[**]
Racial composition				
Pct. population black[3]	**0.55[***]**	0.41[**]	**0.61[***]**	**0.48[***]**
Pct. population white[3]	**−0.48[***]**	**−0.47[***]**	**−0.54[***]**	**−0.51[***]**
Academic outcomes				
Pct. 18–25 with HS diploma[3]	**−0.49[***]**	**−0.54[***]**	**−0.79[***]**	**−0.75[***]**
N	50	50	50	50

[†]$p < .10,$[*]$p < .05,$[**]$p < .01,$[***]$p < .001$

[1] As measured by Peter K. Enns and Julianna Koch, "Public Opinion in the U.S. States: 1956 to 2010," *State Politics and Policy Quarterly* 132, no. 3 (2013): 349–72.

[2] Private and public sector employees, as compiled by Barry T. Hirsch and David A. Macpherson, "Union Membership and Coverage Database from the Current Population Survey: Note," *ILR Review* 56, no. 2 (2003): 349–54.

[3] United States Census Bureau.

[4] National Center for Education Statistics, Public Elementary and Secondary School Universe Survey, https://nces.ed.gov/ccd/pubschuniv.asp.

[5] Bold indicates significance at 0.05 and robustness to Bonferroni and Sidak corrections.

and a number of these state characteristics for selected years. Because these are for specific years, they indicate whether or not policy density was associated with that characteristics *at that time*, not whether or not that characteristic was associated with *changes* in policy density. For each year and set of correlation coefficients, statistical significance is indicated. Coefficients displayed in bold are robustly significant.

POLICY DENSITY AND VARIATION OVER TIME (CHAPTER 6)

In 1975, at the beginning of the time period captured in chapter 6, the standard deviation for the index of policy density was .89, meaning that roughly 68 percent of the states could be found less than a point in either direction of the mean. By 1985, the standard deviation had grown to 1.47, suggesting a growing variation among the states. That number continued to increase, reaching 1.54 in 1990, climbing to 1.6 in 1995, and peaking at 1.8 in 2000 just before NCLB was enacted. Since 2002 that variation has steadily declined. Challenges like this have presented themselves before to those who would measure and evaluate aspects of state political culture. When all states are swept by a set of policy reforms, these differences diminish and lose their obvious explanatory power. See Catherine Marshall, Douglas E. Mitchell, and Frederick M. Wirt, *Culture and Education Policy in the American States* (Bristol, PA: Falmer Press, 1989).

POLICY DENSITY AND OTHER MEASURES OF LOCAL CONTROL (CHAPTER 6)

Wirt's measure of state and local control correlates with this measure of policy density at a level between .2 and .4, depending on the year. This suggests anywhere between 20 percent and 40 percent of the variation in one measure can be accounted for by the other. As noted earlier, the measure of policy density is most sensitive to state differences before there was convergence on teacher certification examinations and accountability practices, and this is the point at which Wirt's measure and the policy density measure most consistently and strongly correlate. Zeehandelaar and Griffith's measure of local- and state-centric policy authority also correlates with this measure of policy density between .3 and .6, depending on the year. The strongest correlation (.6) occurs between 1998 and 2002, when policy density was more apt to capture states' independent choices as opposed to compliance with NCLB. This suggests that an advantage of Zeehandelaar and Griffiths' measure is that it draws on policies that were less apt to be influenced by NCLB. For that reason, it may more accurately capture a state's underlying tendency toward state or local authority, but underestimate the real level of authority the state assumed in the context of federal pressure.

Notes

Introduction

1. "Table 208.40. Public Elementary and Secondary Teachers, Enrollment, and Pupil/Teacher Ratios, by State or Jurisdiction: Selected Years, Fall 2000 Through Fall 2014," National Center for Education Statistics, https://bit.ly/2z61xMa.
2. Unadjusted dollars; see "Table 236.65. Current Expenditure Per Pupil in Fall Enrollment in Public Elementary and Secondary Schools, by State or Jurisdiction: Selected Years, 1969–70 Through 2013–14," National Center for Education Statistics, https://bit.ly/2ysmlR9.
3. Matthew M. Chingos, *Breaking the Curve: Promises and Pitfalls of Using NAEP Data to Assess the State Role in Student Achievement* (Washington, DC: Urban Institute, 2015).
4. Mark Walsh, "Utah Teachers Stage 1-Day Strike to Protest Tax Cut," *Education Week*, October 4, 1989, https://bit.ly/2ysmqUX.
5. Amber M. Winkler, Janie Scull, and Dara Zeehandelaar, *How Strong Are U.S. Teacher Unions? A State-By-State Comparison* (Washington, DC: Thomas B. Fordham Institute, 2012).
6. Larry Cuban, "The Open Classroom," *Education Next* 4, no. 2 (2004): 69–71.
7. Jack Walker, "The Diffusion of Innovations Among the American States," *American Political Science Review* 63, no. 3 (1969): 880–99; Michael K. McLendon and Lora Cohen-Vogel, "Understanding Education Policy Change in the American States: Lessons from Political Science," in *Handbook of Education Politics and Policy*, ed. Bruce S. Cooper, James G. Cibulka, and Lance D. Fusarelli (New York: Routledge, 2008), 30–51.
8. Though it was committed to local autonomy, the state was also an early adopter of academic standards, and starting in 1990 required students in grades 5, 8, and 11 to take the norm-referenced Stanford Achievement Test. See Jal Mehta, *The Allure of Order: High Hopes, Dashed Expectations, and the Troubled Quest to Remake American Schooling* (New York: Oxford University Press, 2013), 84–117.
9. Devin G. Pope and Justin R. Sydnor, "Geographic Variation in the Gender Differences in Test Scores," *Journal of Economic Perspectives* 24, no. 2 (June 2010): 95–108, https://doi.org/10.1257/jep.24.2.95.
10. Spurred by the *A Nation at Risk* report, the Utah State Board of Education commissioned the drafting of what would eventually be known as its Core Curriculum in 1984. But the state has at the same time been consistently protective of local autonomy.
11. Utah is now one of a growing number of states that administers the ACT or the SAT for free to public high school students, removing at least one hurdle for lower-income college hopefuls, but I was applying to college toward the beginning of a broader shift in the process of college application processes. See Caralee J. Adams, "State Initiatives Widen Reach of ACT, SAT Tests," *Education Week*, October 29, 2014, https://bit.ly/2I7pFRx.

12. Mary E. M. McKilip, Anita Rawls, and Carol Barry, "Improving College Access: A Review of Research on the Role of High School Counselors," *Professional School Counseling* 16, no. 1 (2012): 49–58; James S. Murphy, "The Undervaluing of School Counselors," *The Atlantic*, September 16, 2016, https://theatln.tc/2ndReBQ.

13. "The Role of the School Counselor," American School Counselor Association, https://bit .ly/2M6kiV4.

14. "State Nonfiscal Public Elementary/Secondary Education Survey: School Year 2013–14," National Center for Education Statistics, http://nces.ed.gov/ccd/stnfis.asp.

15. Courtney Boswell, "State Education Finance and Governance Profile: Texas," *Peabody Journal of Education* 85, no. 1 (2010): 101–3, https://doi.org/10.1080/01619560903524001.

16. Abigail Becker, "Wisconsin's Black-White Achievement Gap Worst in Nation Despite Decades of Efforts," WisconsinWatch.org, December 16, 2015, https://bit.ly/1NTkmVA.

17. Edward B. Fiske and Helen F. Ladd, "What's Up with Education Policy in North Carolina?" Public Schools First NC, March 2, 2014, https://bit.ly/2I8SHQG.

18. Joanne Weiss and Frederick Hess, "What Did Race to the Top Accomplish?" *Education Next* 15, no. 4 (2015): 50–6.

19. Alia Wong, "In 2014, One Size Didn't Fit All," *The Atlantic*, December 23, 2014, https://theatln. tc/1B2kCbv; Frederick M. Hess, "The Problem with One-Size-Fits-All Approaches to Teacher Quality," *Education Week*, *Rick Hess Straight Up* blog, March 9, 2012, https://bit.ly/2MbgTED; Jim Inhofe, "Education Is Not One Size Fits All," *Tulsa Today* blog, August 19, 2015, https://bit .ly/1EFhjsc.

20. David B. Grusky, Marybeth J. Mattingly, and Charles Varner, eds., "State of the States: The Poverty and Inequality Report," *Pathways: A Magazine on Poverty, Inequality, and Social Policy* (Special Issue 2015), http://inequality.stanford.edu/sotu/SOTU_2015.pdf.

21. Paul Manna, "State Education Governance and Policy: Dynamic Challenges, Diverse Approaches, and New Frontiers," *Peabody Journal of Education* 87, no. 5 (2012): 627–43, https://doi.org/10.1080/0161956X.2012.723508.

22. David B. Tyack, *The One Best System: A History of American Urban Education* (Cambridge, MA: Harvard University Press, 1974).

23. Carl Kaestle and Marshall Smith, "The Federal Role in Elementary and Secondary Education, 1940–1980," *Harvard Educational Review* 52, no. 4 (1982): 384–408.

24. Michael Mintrom, *Policy Entrepreneurs and School Choice* (Washington, DC: Georgetown University Press, 2000).

25. Gary Orfield, "Tenth Annual Brown Lecture in Education Research: A New Civil Rights Agenda for American Education," *Educational Researcher* 43, no. 6 (2014): 273–92, https://doi .org/10.3102/0013189X14547874.

26. Michael Kirst, "Turning Points: A History of American School Governance," in *Who's in Charge Here? The Tangled Web of School Governance Policy*, ed. Noel Epstein (Washington DC: Brookings Institution Press, 2004), 16–18.

27. Ian Haney López, *Dog Whistle Politics: How Coded Racial Appeals Have Reinvented Racism and Wrecked the Middle Class* (New York: Oxford University Press, 2015).

28. Mark Johnson, "Racial Context, Public Attitudes, and Welfare Effort in the American States," in *Race and the Politics of Welfare Reform*, ed. Sanford F. Schram, Joe Brian Soss, and Richard Carl Fording (Ann Arbor: University of Michigan Press, 2010), 151–68; William D. Hicks, Seth C. McKee, and Daniel A. Smith, "The Determinants of State Legislator Support for Restrictive Voter ID Laws," *State Politics & Policy Quarterly* 16, no. 4 (2016): 411–31, https:// doi.org/10.1177/1532440016630752.

29. Karl Kurtz, *Who We Elect* (Denver: National Conference of State Legislatures, 2015).

30. Sara Dahill-Brown and Lesley Lavery, "Implementing Federal Policy: Confronting State Capacity and Will," *Politics and Policy* 40, no. 4 (2012); Paul Manna, *Collision Course: Federal Education Policy Meets State and Local Realities* (Washington, DC: CQ Press, 2010).

31. Abigail Potts, Rolf K. Blank, and Andra Williams, *Key State Education Policies on PK–12 Education: 2002* (Washington, DC: Council of Chief State School Officers, 2002).

32. Manna, *Collision Course*, 115–18.

33. The federal government does operate a small number of schools, via the Departments of Defense and Interior. Defense schools primarily serve the children of active-duty military officers; those operated by Interior serve Native American children living on reservations. The percentage of K–12 funding that comes from the federal government also varies across the states and school districts. Higher poverty and lower levels of state and local funding, for example, mean that Louisiana and Mississippi rely on the federal government for closer to 15 percent of their funding in a given year, while higher levels of state and local funding combined with lower levels of poverty in Massachusetts and New Jersey mean that federal funding comprises closer to 5 percent of K–12 revenues in most years.

34. There can be little debate that schools increased the time devoted to the most tested subjects under NCLB, reading and math, crowding out other subjects like art, physical education, and civics. There is also evidence that within those core subjects, teachers taught in a way that focused narrowly on the skills they believed were emphasized on state assessments. Some of this may have been under way in states where high-stakes testing had already been implemented. See Jennifer L. Jennings and Jonathan Marc Bearak, "'Teaching to the Test' in the NCLB Era: How Test Predictability Affects Our Understanding of Student Performance," *Educational Researcher* 43, no. 8 (2014): 381–9, https://doi.org/10.3102/0013189X14554449.

35. Sean F. Reardon et al., *Left Behind? The Effect of No Child Left Behind on Academic Achievement Gaps* (Stanford, CA: Stanford Center for Education Policy Analysis, 2013), https://stanford.io/2y7L2Rp.

36. Lyndsey Layton, "How Bill Gates Pulled Off the Swift Common Core Revolution," *Washington Post*, June 7, 2014, https://wapo.st/21Cft98; Tim Murphy, "Inside the Mammoth Backlash to Common Core," *Mother Jones* (September/October 2014), https://bit.ly/1rwh2nE; Frederick M. Hess and Jeffrey R. Henig, eds., *The New Education Philanthropy: Politics, Policy, and Reform* (Cambridge, MA: Harvard Education Press, 2015); Robin Rogers, "Making Public Policy: The New Philanthropists and American Education," *American Journal of Economics and Sociology* 74, no. 4 (2015): 743–4, https://doi.org/10.1111/ajes.12113.

37. Alaska, Nebraska, Texas, and Virginia never adopted the Common Core State Standards. Minnesota adopted the standards only in part. As of August 2016, Indiana, Louisiana, Michigan, Missouri, New Jersey, Oklahoma, South Carolina, and Tennessee had adopted and then repealed the standards. A number of other states have paused or modified their implementation of the standards. See Ashley Jochim and Lesley Lavery, "The Evolving Politics of the Common Core: Policy Implementation and Conflict Expansion," *Publius: The Journal of Federalism* 45, no. 3 (2015): 380–404, https://doi.org/10.1093/publius/pjv015.

38. Catherine Gewertz, "State Lawmakers Assert Influence Over Standards," *Education Week*, July 9, 2014, https://bit.ly/1l3ATDq.

39. Michael B. Henderson, Paul E. Peterson, and Martin R. West, "The 2015 EdNext Poll on School Reform: Public Thinking on Testing, Opt Out, Common Core, Unions, and More," *Education Next* 16, no. 1 (2016), https://bit.ly/1MvZv9r.

40. Elaine Weiss, *Mismatches in Race to the Top Limit Educational Improvement: Lack of Time, Resources, and Tools to Address Opportunity Gaps Puts Lofty State Goals Out of Reach* (Washington, DC: Economic Policy Institute and Broader, Bolder Approach to Education,

2013), https://bit.ly/2I7qCcz; Elaine Weiss and Thomas W. Payzant, "Race to the Top: Good for Mass, but a Mismatch Overall," *Boston Globe*, October 15, 2013, https://bit.ly/2JTPOZV.

41. The states that did not apply for flexibility from NCLB, or withdrew their requests for waivers, included California, Montana, Nebraska, North Dakota, and Vermont. Disputes between states in the process of applying for a waiver and the federal government often revolved around whether or not the state would employ student test scores in the evaluation of teachers.

42. Turbulent educational policy is not unique to this age. Whenever there has been political, social, or economic upheaval, that turbulence has visited itself on the public schools. Yet there are periods of relative stability and relative turbulence. Most would agree that the twenty-first century has been a period of relatively volatile educational policy. The rise of policy churn, and the role of the federal government in encouraging it, is something that both conservative and liberal critics of education reform have observed. See Robert L. Crowson, "The Turbulent Policy Environment in Education: Implications for School Administration and Accountability," *Peabody Journal of Education* 78, no. 4 (2003): 29–43, https://doi.org/10.1207 /S15327930PJE7804_03; Mitchell Robinson, "If You Can't Beat 'Em, Destabilize 'Em!" August 17, 2015, https://bit.ly/2ysKp6G; Michael Q. McShane, "'Reform Fatigue' and the Virtue of Going Small," *Education Week, Rick Hess Straight Up* blog, May 4, 2016, https://bit.ly /2K5jW0q; Robert E. Slavin, "Stop the Churn: How Federal Policy Adds Chaos to Schools," *Huffington Post*, June 23, 2013, https://bit.ly/2K5jYFA.

43. Some of the most compelling evidence of this mounting frustration is qualitative. Matt Collette described the past decade of reform from the perspective of one New York City school, where school staff and faculty grappled with a significant number of successive reforms, some of which were never properly implemented before they were abandoned for the next program. Teachers and school staff became progressively disenchanted with leaders, demoralized, and skeptical toward reform efforts. See Matt Collette, "A Painful Decade of School Reform," *Slate, Schooled* blog, March 5, 2015, https://slate.me/2lmuXPV.

44. The concept of policy churn was developed by Rick Hess in a 1999 study that included fifty-seven big-city school districts. On average, districts introduced an average of twelve major initiatives over the course of three years, translating into a major new project for school leaders and educators to adapt to every three months. Outside of education, researchers have also identified negative consequences of volatile policy environments. A 2013 analysis of volatility across countries, for example, found that higher levels of volatility—after adjustment for exogenous causes of policy change—were associated with slower economic growth. See Frederick M. Hess, *Spinning Wheels: The Politics of Urban School Reform* (Washington, DC: Brookings Institution Press, 1999); Antonio Fatás and Ilian Mihov, "Policy Volatility, Institutions, and Economic Growth," *Review of Economics and Statistics* 95, no. 2 (2012): 362–76, https://doi .org/10.1162/REST_a_00265.

45. Surveys indicate that teachers feel as though their professional autonomy has diminished and that they are fatigued with, anxious about, and skeptical of reform efforts. In 2012, the MetLife Survey of the American Teacher found the highest level of dissatisfaction among teachers since 1989. A 2015 report from the National Center for Education Statistics (NCES) reported that between the 2003–04 and 2011–12 school years, the percentage of teachers reporting low levels of autonomy increased from 18 to 26 percent, while the percentage of those reporting high levels of autonomy fell from 17 to 12. In a 2016 survey from the Center on Education Policy, 38 percent of teachers named constantly changing demands on teachers as the greatest challenge they faced, while 34 percent named constantly changing demands on students as the greatest challenge. Half of teachers in that survey also reported that they would leave the profession if they could find a higher-paying job. See Fernanda Santos, "Teacher Morale

Sinks, Survey Results Show," *New York Times*, March 7, 2012, https://nyti.ms/2tpqEqW; Dinah Sparks and Nat Malkus, *Public School Teacher Autonomy in the Classroom Across School Years 2003–04, 2007–08, and 2011–12* (Washington, DC: National Center for Education Statistics, 2015), http://nces.ed.gov/pubs2015/2015089.pdf; Diane Stark Rentner, Nancy Kober, and Matthew Frizzel, *Listen to Us: Teacher Views and Voices* (Washington, DC: Center on Education Policy, 2016).

46. This kind of reform fatigue has been described in other national contexts where frequent education reform has taken root, and school staff and faculty have found themselves overwhelmed with changing and competing demands. See Jessica Lyle, Christine Cunningham, and Jan Gray, "The New Australian Curriculum, Teachers and Change Fatigue," *Australian Journal of Teacher Education* 39, no. 11 (2014): 45–64; Jon Coles, "Stability Will Raise Standards in Schools, Not Constant Reform," *The Guardian*, February 12, 2013, https://bit.ly/2K7ABn6.

47. Adam Kernan-Schloss and Joshua P. Starr, "Testing Doesn't Measure Up for Americans: The 47th Annual PDK/Gallup Poll of the Public's Attitudes Toward the Public Schools," *Phi Delta Kappan* 97, no. 1 (2015): K1–31, https://bit.ly/2MCZQjp.

48. Results nonetheless show sizeable support for each of these initiatives, but statistically significantly diminished from the previous year. See Henderson, Peterson, and West, "The 2015 EdNext Poll on School Reform."

49. Charles M. Payne, *So Much Reform, So Little Change: The Persistence of Failure in Urban Schools* (Cambridge, MA: Harvard Education Press, 2008).

50. Sarah Reckhow, *Follow the Money: How Foundation Dollars Change Public School Politics* (New York: Oxford University Press, 2013).

51. Dale Russakoff, *The Prize: Who's in Charge of America's Schools?* (New York: Houghton Mifflin Harcourt, 2015).

52. Mehta, *The Allure of Order.*

53. The decline in applications appears due only in part to a rebounding economy. The increasing profile of Teach for America has also meant that criticism of and resistance to the organization's efforts have also increased. See Emma Brown, "Teach for America Applications Fall Again, Diving 35 Percent in Three Years," *Washington Post*, April 12, 2016, https://wapo.st/1YrtmDG.

54. Kimberly Quick, "Why Black Lives Matter in Education, Too," *The Century Foundation* blog, June 21, 2016, https://bit.ly/2fZrO4F; Frederick M. Hess, "Making Sense of the Left-Right School Reform Divide," *Education Week*, *Rick Hess Straight Up* blog, June 1, 2016, https://bit.ly/1Zdd7uD; Derrell Bradford, "Social Justice, Education Reform and How This Whole Left-Right Feud Is Missing the Point," *The 74* blog, May 31, 2016, https://bit.ly/1TPcjxS; Robert Pondiscio, "The Left's Drive to Push Conservatives Out of Education Reform," *Thomas B. Fordham Institute*, *Flypaper* blog, May 25, 2016, https://bit.ly/2tfgkSS.

55. See, for example, David Kirp, *Improbable Scholars: The Rebirth of a Great American School System and a Strategy for America's Schools* (New York: Oxford University Press, 2015), in which he praises tortoises over hares.

56. Weiss and Payzant, "Race to the Top." This is a point also emphasized by Massachusetts Commissioner of Education Mitchell Chester in a 2014 report on the next steps in the state's plan to improve its schools: "The Education Reform Act [of 1993] has enjoyed stable and generous support from leaders from both political parties . . . The basic framework established by the Education Reform Act continues to define and lend coherence to the Commonwealth's approach to improving public education. The stability of that framework has been critical to the success that Massachusetts has experienced and will continue to be critical in the future." See Mitchell D. Chester, *Building on 20 Years of Massachusetts Education Reform* (Malden:

Massachusetts Department of Elementary and Secondary Education, 2014), https://bit.ly/2PHGyax.

57. Thomas W. Payzant, *Continuous Improvement: Sustaining Education Reform Long Enough to Make a Difference* (Providence, RI: Brown University, Annenberg Institute for School Reform, 2005).

58. Eric A. Hanushek, Paul E. Peterson, and Ludger Woessmann, *Achievement Growth: International and U.S. State Trends in Student Performance* (Cambridge, MA: Harvard University's Program on Education Policy and Governance and Education Next, 2012), https://bit.ly/2K6H55U.

59. In his analysis of states' NAEP scores, Matt Chingos of the Urban Institute accounts for a wide range of students' demographic characteristics including gender, race, and ethnicity; eligibility for free or reduced-price lunch; limited proficiency with English; special needs status; age; and family structure. See Chingos, *Breaking the Curve.*

60. Joanna Hornig Fox, Erin S. Ingram, and Jennifer Deapoli, *For All Kids: How Kentucky Is Closing the High School Graduation Gap for Low-Income Students* (Baltimore: Civic Enterprises and the Everyone Graduates Center at the School of Education at Johns Hopkins University, 2016), https://bit.ly/2P5DWlm.

61. The interviews conducted to support this manuscript brought me into contact with legislators, employees in state education agencies, gubernatorial advisors, and past and present leaders of state school systems. With very few exceptions, I do not identify these individuals, given the political nature of their work and the preferences they expressed in the context of our conversations. Because I was able to speak with only a small sample of individuals across several states, and because the community of stakeholders who actively participate in the project of education governance is small, not identifying my interview subjects typically means that I must avoid naming even the state in which they work or the specific policies to which they refer. Instead, I reference qualities of the state that shaped their responses or constrained their actions, as they expressed them to me, and themes that emerged from my meeting notes and/or coding of interview transcripts. Most interviews were recorded and professionally transcribed, though some interviewees requested that I not employ a tape recorder during our conversations. The interviews themselves were semistructured; I brought to each meeting an outline of questions, but allowed the interviewees to steer the conversation in another direction, drawing out their perceptions and beliefs about what was important or salient in their state. To code the interview transcripts, I used an inductive, bottom-up, methodology—not a deductive one designed to test hypotheses or establish causal relationships. By this I mean that I read and reread, highlighted, and sorted transcripts in an effort to identify themes and patterns that emerged from these conversations. Given the inductive nature of my coding process, the evidence drawn from these interviews should be regarded primarily as empirically derived theory, conclusions subject to future testing and closer study, and qualitative context for quantitative analysis.

62. "Local Education Agencies (School District) Universe Survey Data," National Center for Education Statistics, https://nces.ed.gov/ccd/pubagency.asp.

63. Henig, *The End of Exceptionalism*; Arnold F. Shober, "Governors Make the Grade: Growing Gubernatorial Influence in State Education Policy," *Peabody Journal of Education* 87, no. 5 (2012): 559–75, https://doi.org/10.1080/0161956X.2012.723494.

64. Some of the exceptions to this rule: Tyll Van Geel, *Authority to Control the School Program* (Lexington, MA: Lexington Books, 1976); Kenneth K. Wong et al., *The Education Mayor: Improving America's Schools* (Washington, DC: Georgetown University Press, 2007); Frederick M. Hess and Andrew P. Kelly, *Carrots, Sticks, and the Bully Pulpit: Lessons from*

a Half-Century of Federal Efforts to Improve America's Schools (Cambridge, MA: Harvard Education Press, 2011); Paul Manna, "Centralized Governance and Student Outcomes: Excellence, Equity, and Academic Achievement in the U.S. States," *Policy Studies Journal* 41, no. 4 (2013): 682–705, https://doi.org/10.1111/psj.12037.

65. Howard Blume and Seema Mehta, "Public Education in U.S. Falls Short, Obama Says," *Los Angeles Times*, March 11, 2009, https://lat.ms/2terzv4.

66. Lauren Camera, "Legislative Adventure Game: See Why It's Difficult for a Bill to Become Law," *Education Week*, *Politics K–12* blog, May 13, 2015, https://bit.ly/1QM5ojJ.

67. Andrew Saultz, Andrew McEachin, and Lance D. Fusarelli, "Waivering as Governance Federalism During the Obama Administration," *Educational Researcher* 45, no. 6 (2016): 358–66, https://doi.org/10.3102/0013189X16663495.

68. In January 2015 the Council of Chief State School Officers released a letter outlining priorities for the reauthorization of ESEA. Flexibility and autonomy to make determinations about how to hold schools accountable and what assessments to use were core demands. In February 2015, the National Governors' Association (NGA) and the National Conference of State Legislatures released a joint letter articulating their priorities for ESEA. They overlapped in considerable degree, particularly in the extent to which they demanded increased flexibility for states and local districts. See CCSSO, *CCSSO's ESEA Key Priorities* (Washington, DC: Council of Chief State School Officers, 2015), https://bit.ly/2BQgRRY; "Governors' and State Legislators' Plan to Reauthorize the Elementary and Secondary Education Act," National Governors Association and National Conference of State Legislators, February 10, 2015, www.ncsl.org/documents/statefed/NGA_NCSL_ESEAPlan_final.pdf.

69. Patrick McGuinn, "From No Child Left Behind to the Every Student Succeeds Act: Federalism and the Education Legacy of the Obama Administration," *Publius: The Journal of Federalism* 46, no. 3 (2016): 392–415, https://doi.org/10.1093/publius/pjw014.

Chapter 1

1. Albert Shanker, National Press Club speech, March 31, 1988, Washington, DC, https://reuther.wayne.edu/files/64.43.pdf.

2. Alex Medler, "Charter School Movement: Complementing or Competing with Public Education," in *The Emancipatory Promise of Charter Schools: Toward a Progressive Politics of School Choice*, ed. Eric Rofes and Lisa M. Stulberg (Albany: State University of New York Press, 2004), 189–217.

3. National Commission on Excellence in Education, *A Nation at Risk: The Imperative for Educational Reform* (Washington, DC: US Department of Education, Government Printing Office, 1983).

4. Kenneth K. Wong, James W. Guthrie, and Douglas N. Harris, eds., "A Nation at Risk: A 20-Year Reappraisal," *Peabody Journal of Education* 79, no. 1 (2014).

5. At least he agreed publicly; it is difficult to know for certain given the precarious situation for unions and their leadership after President Reagan successfully broke the air traffic controller strike in 1981. Shanker may have viewed these statements as necessary in order to preserve a seat at the table.

6. David T. Conley, *Who Governs Our Schools? Changing Roles and Responsibilities* (New York: Teachers College Press, 2003).

7. Michael W. Kirst, "Recent State Education Reform in the United States: Looking Backward and Forward," *Educational Administration Quarterly* 24, no. 3 (1988): 319–28, https://doi.org/10.1177/0013161X88024003010.

8. Michael W. Kirst, "The Changing Balance in State and Local Power to Control Education," *Phi Delta Kappan* 66, no. 3 (1984): 189–91.

9. Jeffrey R. Henig, *The End of Exceptionalism in American Education: The Changing Politics of School Reform* (Cambridge, MA: Harvard Education Press, 2013).

10. Frank R. Baumgartner and Bryan D. Jones, *Agendas and Instability in American Politics*, 2nd ed. (Chicago: University of Chicago Press, 2010).

11. Christopher Hood, "A Public Management for All Seasons?" *Public Administration* 69, no. 1 (1991): 3–19, https://doi.org/10.1111/j.1467-9299.1991.tb00779.x; Christopher Hood, "The 'New Public Management' in the 1980s: Variations on a Theme," *Accounting, Organizations and Society* 20, no. 2 (1995): 93–109, https://doi.org/10.1016/0361-3682(93)E0001-W.

12. Ray Budde, *Education by Charter: Restructuring School Districts* (Andover, MA: Regional Laboratory for Educational Improvement of the Northeast & Islands, 1988).

13. Ember Reichgott Junge, *Zero Chance of Passage: The Pioneering Charter School Story* (Edina, MN: Beaver's Pond Press, 2012); Rachel Cohen, "The Untold History of Charter Schools," *Democracy Journal*, April 27, 2017, https://bit.ly/2pxh82I.

14. Andy Czajkowski, *Cooperatively Managed Schools: Teachers as Partners* (Minneapolis: Citizens League, 1987), https://bit.ly/2lxMpkE.

15. Mississippi is the one state where there has been some back and forth. The state passed a law in 1997 that did not result in the establishment of any charter schools, and the law expired in 2009. The state legislatures subsequently passed another law in 2010, which proved similarly untenable and was subsequently repealed. A functional charter school law was finally adopted in 2013.

16. "Table 216.30. Number and Percentage Distribution of Public Elementary and Secondary Students and Schools, by Traditional or Charter School Status and Selected Characteristics: Selected Years, 1999–2000 Through 2013–14," National Center for Education Statistics, https://bit.ly/2KjEtlg.

17. Edward Cremata et al., *National Charter School Study* (Stanford, CA: Center for Research on Education Outcomes, 2013), 52–3, https://stanford.io/1hN73Iv.

18. Erica Frankenberg, Genevieve Siegel-Hawley, and Jia Wang, *Choice Without Equity: Charter School Segregation and the Need for Civil Rights Standards* (Los Angeles: The Civil Rights Project/Proyecto Derechos Civiles at UCLA, 2010), https://bit.ly/2tAHumM.

19. Shelby Dawkins-Law and Azaria Verdin, *Public Charter Schools with Transportation: Increasing Access to Learning Opportunities for All* (Raleigh: North Carolina State Board of Education, Department of Public Instruction, 2013), https://bit.ly/2MWqBvu.

20. Matthew M. Chingos and Martin R. West, "The Uneven Performance of Arizona's Charter Schools," *Educational Evaluation and Policy Analysis* 37, no. 1_suppl (2015): 120S–134S, https://doi.org/10.3102/0162373715576077.

21. "Defining Governance," Institute on Governance, http://iog.ca/defining-governance/.

22. Jennifer L. Hochschild and Nathan Scovronick, *The American Dream and the Public Schools* (New York: Oxford University Press, 2004), 9–27.

23. Laurence E. Lynn, Carolyn J. Heinrich, and Carolyn J. Hill, *Improving Governance: A New Logic for Empirical Research* (Washington, DC: Georgetown University Press, 2001), 29.

24. H. K. Colebatch, "Making Sense of Governance," *Policy and Society* 33, no. 4 (2014): 307–16, https://doi.org/10.1016/j.polsoc.2014.10.001; Mark Bevir, *Governance: A Very Short Introduction* (Oxford, UK: Oxford University Press, 2012); Oliver Treib, Holger Bähr, and Gerda Falkner, "Modes of Governance: Towards a Conceptual Clarification," *Journal of European Public Policy* 14, no. 1 (2007): 1–20, https://doi.org/10.1080/135017606061071406; Anne Mette Kjaer, *Governance* (Malden, MA and Cambridge, UK: Polity, 2004).

25. R. A. W. Rhodes, "The New Governance: Governing Without Government," *Political Studies* 44, no. 4 (1996): 652–67, https://doi.org/10.1111/j.1467-9248.1996.tb01747.x.

26. Kenneth J. Meier and Laurence J. O'Toole, *Bureaucracy in a Democratic State: A Governance Perspective* (Baltimore: Johns Hopkins University Press, 2006).

27. Sara Dahill-Brown and Lesley Lavery, "Implementing Federal Policy: Confronting State Capacity and Will," *Politics and Policy* 40, no. 4 (2012): 557–92, https://doi.org/10.1111/j.1747-1346.2012.00368.x.

28. Heather Vogell and Hannah Fresques, "'Alternative' Education: Using Charter Schools to Hide Dropouts and Game the System," *ProPublica/USA Today*, February 21, 2017, https://bit.ly/2kI11QI.

29. Elinor Ostrom, *Governing the Commons: The Evolution of Institutions for Collective Action* (Cambridge, UK: Cambridge University Press, 1990).

30. Jacob S. Hacker and Paul Pierson, "Winner-Take-All Politics: Public Policy, Political Organization, and the Precipitous Rise of Top Incomes in the United States," *Politics & Society* 38, no. 2 (2010): 152–204, https://doi.org/10.1177/0032329210365042.

31. Andy Smarick and Juliet Squire, *The State Education Agency: At the Helm, Not the Oar* (Washington, DC: Thomas B. Fordham Institute and Bellwether Education Partners, 2014), https://bit.ly/2KjSM65.

32. Mark Bevir, *A Theory of Governance* (Berkeley: University of California Press, 2013).

33. Bevir, *A Theory of Governance*.

34. Thomas G. Weiss, "Governance, Good Governance and Global Governance: Conceptual and Actual Challenges," *Third World Quarterly* 21, no. 5 (2000): 795–814, https://doi.org/10.1080/713701075.

35. Wolfgang Michalski, Riel Miller, and Barry Stevens, "Governance in the 21st Century: Power in the Global Knowledge Economy and Society," in *Governance in the 21st Century* (Paris: Organisation for Economic Cooperation and Development, 2001), 7–26.

36. Megan E. Tompkins-Stange, *Policy Patrons: Philanthropy, Education Reform, and the Politics of Influence* (Cambridge, MA: Harvard Education Press, 2016); Sarah Reckhow, *Follow the Money: How Foundation Dollars Change Public School Politics* (New York: Oxford University Press, 2013).

37. Dominic Brewer and Joanna Smith, *Evaluating the "Crazy Quilt": Educational Governance in California* (Los Angeles: Center on Educational Governance, Rossier School of Education, University of Southern California, 2006), 1–203, https://stanford.io/2KmsyD0. Brewer and Smith write: "Broadly interpreted, 'governance' includes the institutions that are part of the educational decision making and delivery system, as well as the constituencies that interact with these institutions, and the ways the parts of the system interact with one another. Policies, laws, regulations, and informal practices are part of this framework and are reflected, one way or another, in the behaviors of all those who are involved."

38. "2012 Census of Governments," United States Census Bureau, https://www.census.gov/govs/cog/.

39. Lynn, Heinrich, and Hill, *Improving Governance*; James D. Thompson, *Organizations in Action: Social Science Bases of Administrative Theory* (Piscataway, NJ: Transaction Publishers, 1967); Talcott Parsons, *Structure and Process in Modern Societies* (Glencoe, IL: Free Press, 1960); Charles Wright Mills, *The Power Elite* (New York: Oxford University Press, 1959).

40. Meier and O'Toole, *Bureaucracy in a Democratic State*, 15.

41. Education for All, *Overcoming Inequality: Why Governance Matters* (Paris: United Nations Educational, Scientific and Cultural Organization, and Oxford, UK: Oxford University Press, 2009), https://bit.ly/1QHvHbd.

42. Tracey Burns and Florian Koster, eds., *Governing Education in a Complex World* (Paris: Organisation for Economic Cooperation and Development, 2016), http://dx.doi.org/10.1787/9789264255364-en.

43. "State Education Governance Matrix," National Association of State Boards of Education, https://bit.ly/2igdQfN; Terry Moe, "Collective Bargaining and the Performance of the Public Schools," *American Journal of Political Science* 53, no. 1 (2009): 156–74, https://doi.org/10.1111/j.1540-5907.2008.00363.x.

44. Jacob Torfing et al., *Interactive Governance: Advancing the Paradigm* (Oxford, UK: Oxford University Press, 2012), 48–70.

45. Patrick J. McGuinn and Paul Manna, "Education Governance in America: Who Leads When Everyone Is in Charge?" in *Education Governance for the Twenty-First Century: Overcoming the Structural Barriers to School Reform*, ed. Paul Manna and Patrick McGuinn (Washington, DC: Brookings Institution, 2013), 9.

46. Meier and O'Toole, *Bureaucracy in a Democratic State*, 16.

47. There are different levels of difficulty associated with changing institutional arrangements. The constitutionally established separation of powers between the three branches of the federal government would be more difficult to alter than relationships established by law or regulation.

48. Jerome T. Murphy, "Progress and Problems: The Paradox of State Reforms," in *Policy Making in Education*, ed. Ann Lieberman and Milbrey Wallin McLaughlin (Chicago: University of Chicago Press, 1982); Kirst, "Recent State Education Reform in the United States"; Susan H. Fuhrman and Richard F. Elmore, "Understanding Local Control in the Wake of State Education Reform," *Educational Evaluation and Policy Analysis* 12, no. 1 (1990): 82–96, https://doi.org/10.3102/01623737012001082; Paul Manna, *School's In: Federalism and the National Education Agenda* (Washington, DC: Georgetown University Press, 2006).

49. Moon-Kie Jung, João Costa Vargas, and Eduardo Bonilla-Silva, *State of White Supremacy: Racism, Governance, and the United States* (Stanford, CA: Stanford University Press, 2011); Joe Soss, Richard C. Fording, and Sanford F. Schram, *Disciplining the Poor: Neoliberal Paternalism and the Persistent Power of Race* (Chicago: University of Chicago Press, 2011).

50. Lynn, Heinrich, and Hill, *Improving Governance*, 6–7.

51. Henig, *End of Exceptionalism*, 3.

52. Oran Young, "Choosing Governance Systems: A Plea for Comparative Research," in *The Oxford Handbook of Public Policy*, ed. Michael Moran, Martin Rein, and Robert E. Goodin (New York: Oxford University Press, 2006), 845. In a plea for more extensive, comparative work in governance, Young asserts that the variation in levels and domains of activity among governance is an underexploited source of variation among researchers.

53. Elinor Ostrom, *Understanding Institutional Diversity* (Princeton, NJ: Princeton University Press, 2009), 12–13.

54. Arthur Koestler, "The Tree and the Candle," in *Unity Through Diversity: A Festschrift for Ludwig Von Bertalanffy*, ed. Nicholas D. Rizzo and William Gray, vol. I (New York: Gordon and Breach, 1973), 287–314.

55. Gedeon M. Mudacumura, "Multiple Dimensions of Governance," in *Challenges to Democratic Governance in Developing Countries, Public Administration, Governance and Globalization* vol. 11, ed. Gedeon Mudacumura and Göktuğ Morçöl (Basel, Switzerland: Springer International Publishing, 2014), 1–16, https://doi.org/10.1007/978-3-319-03143-9_1; Bo Rothstein, "Good Governance," in *The Oxford Handbook of Governance*, ed. David Levi-Faur (New York: Oxford University Press, 2012).

56. Mudacumura, "Multiple Dimensions of Governance"; Rothstein, "Good Governance."

57. Maureen Magee, "Inside the Fight Against California's Charter Schools," *Los Angeles Times*, February 18, 2016, https://lat.ms/24bRQ8S; Claudia Rowe, "More Charter Schools to Open in Washington State, Encouraging New Network," *Seattle Times*, July 10, 2017, https://bit.ly/2tzxjA8.

58. Kristen L. Buras and Members Urban South Grassroots Research Collective, "New Orleans Education Reform: A Guide for Cities or a Warning for Communities? (Grassroots Lessons Learned, 2005–2012)," *Berkeley Review of Education* 4, no. 1 (2013), https://doi.org/10.5070/B84110023.

59. Jane Arnold Lincove, Nathan Barrett, and Katherine O. Strunk, *Did the Teachers Dismissed After Hurricane Katrina Return to Public Education?* (New Orleans: Education Research Alliance for New Orleans, Tulane University, 2017), https://bit.ly/2Io5Jde.

60. Corey Mitchell, "What Happened to New Orleans' Veteran Black Teachers?" *Education Week*, August 19, 2015, https://bit.ly/2tDecUz; Andre M. Perry, "The Education-Reform Movement Is Too White to Do Any Good," *Washington Post*, June 2, 2014, https://wapo.st/1L5QO1a.

61. Kate Babineau, Dave Hand, and Vincent Rossmeier, *What Happens Next? Voters' Perceptions of K–12 Public Education in New Orleans* (New Orleans: Cowen Institute, Tulane University, 2016).

62. Manning Marable and Kristen Clarke, *Seeking Higher Ground: The Hurricane Katrina Crisis, Race, and Public Policy Reader* (New York: Palgrave Macmillan, 2008).

63. Jon Valant, "Charter Schools and Local Control in New Orleans," *Brown Center Chalkboard* blog, May 18, 2016, https://brook.gs/2MYMB9l.

64. "Public Trust in Government: 1958–2017," Pew Research Center, May 3, 2017, https://pewrsr.ch/2qSKokQ; "Trust in Government," Gallup.com, https://bit.ly/2lw2B61.

65. Clare Malone, "Americans Don't Trust Their Institutions Anymore," *FiveThirtyEight*, November 16, 2016, https://53eig.ht/2jjvtjc; Jeffrey M. Jones, "Confidence in U.S. Public Schools at New Low," Gallup.com, June 20, 2012, https://bit.ly/2K6nAuW.

66. Eric Westervelt, "Political Rivals Find Common Ground Over Common Core," *Morning Edition*, National Public Radio, January 28, 2014, https://n.pr/1ncCEmi.

67. Lance Izumi, "Trump's Right—The System Is Rigged. Look at Common Core," *Washington Examiner*, August 3, 2016, https://washex.am/2lycKzd.

68. Stan Karp, "The Problems with the Common Core," *Rethinking Schools* 28, no. 2 (Winter 2013/2014), https://bit.ly/2ttyyQU.

69. Justin McCarthy, "Americans Still More Trusting in Local Over State Government," Gallup.com, September 19, 2016, https://bit.ly/2fW6Fv8.

70. Francis Fukuyama, "What Is Governance?" *Governance* 26, no. 3 (2013): 347–68, https://doi.org/10.1111/gove.12035; Merilee S. Grindle, "Good Governance: The Inflation of an Idea," in *Planning Ideas That Matter: Livability, Territoriality, Governance, and Reflective Practice*, ed. Bishwapriya Sanyal, Lawrence J. Vale, and Christina D. Rosan (Cambridge, MA: MIT Press, 2012), 259–82.

71. R. Douglas Arnold, *The Logic of Congressional Action* (New Haven, CT: Yale University Press, 1992).

72. Joshua Bleiberg and Darrell M. West, *In Defense of the Common Core Standards* (Washington, DC: Center for Technology Innovation at Brookings, 2014); Joy Resmovits, "Bill Gates Comes to the Defense of the Common Core," *Huffington Post*, March 14, 2014, https://bit.ly/1kZtnfC.

73. The *Times* Editorial Board, "In Defense of Common Core," *Los Angeles Times*, March 13, 2014, https://lat.ms/2KmAUKS.

74. Douglas N. Harris, "Good News for New Orleans," *Education Next* 15, no. 4 (2015): 8–15, https://bit.ly/1VZ8N2c.

75. Mary L. Landrieu, "Public Charter Schools a Big Success in New Orleans," *The Advocate*, August 15, 2016, https://bit.ly/2Irw3D3.

76. Danielle Dreilinger, "New Orleans' Katrina School Takeover to End, Legislature Decides," *Times-Picayune*, May 5, 2016, https://bit.ly/1OgaUIK.

Chapter 2

1. "Table 214.10. Number of Public School Districts and Public and Private Elementary and Secondary Schools: Selected Years, 1869–70 through 2013–14," National Center for Education Statistics, https://bit.ly/2Kia9bc.

2. Paul Pierson, *Politics in Time: History, Institutions, and Social Analysis* (Princeton, NJ: Princeton University Press, 2004).

3. Wayne J. Urban and Jennings L. Wagoner, *American Education: A History* (Abingdon, UK: Routledge, 2009), 15–70.

4. Andy Green, *Education and State Formation: The Rise of Education Systems in England, France and the USA* (London: Palgrave Macmillan, 1990), 172.

5. Urban and Wagoner, *American Education*, 45.

6. Green, *Education and State Formation*.

7. Joel H. Spring, *The American School, 1642–2004* (New York: McGraw-Hill, 2004); Carl F. Kaestle, *Pillars of the Republic: Common Schools and American Society 1780–1860* (New York: Hill and Wang, 1983).

8. Urban and Wagoner, *American Education*, 54.

9. Urban and Wagoner, *American Education*, 36.

10. Green, *Education and State Formation*, 178.

11. Urban and Wagoner, *American Education*, 15–70.

12. Ellwood Patterson Cubberley, *Public Education in the United States: A Study and Interpretation of American Educational History; an Introductory Textbook Dealing with the Larger Problems of Present-Day Education in the Light of Their Historical Development* (Boston: Houghton Mifflin, 1919), 219.

13. Raymond E. Callahan, "The American Board of Education 1789–1960," in *Understanding School Boards: Problems and Prospects*, ed. Peter J. Cistone (Lexington, MA: Lexington Books, 1975).

14. Jacqueline P. Danzberger, "School Boards: A Troubled American Institution," in Danzberger, *Facing the Challenge: The Report of the Twentieth Century Fund Task Force on School Governance* (New York: Twentieth Century Fund Press, 1992).

15. Kaestle, *Pillars of the Republic*, 56.

16. Green, *Education and State Formation*, 183.

17. Kaestle, *Pillars of the Republic*, 24; Albert Fishlow, "The American Common School Revival: Fact or Fancy?" in *Industrialization in Two Systems: Essays in Honor of Alexander Gerschenkron* (New York: John Wiley & Sons, 1966), 40–67.

18. Green, *Education and State Formation*, 183–4.

19. David Tyack and Thomas James, "State Government and American Public Education: Exploring the 'Primeval Forest,'" *History of Education Quarterly* 26, no. 1 (1986): 64, https://doi.org/10.2307/368876.

20. Article 3 of the law specified "religion, morality, and knowledge being necessary to good government and the happiness of mankind, schools and the means of education shall forever be encouraged." Tyack and James, "State Government and American Public Education," 57.

21. Daniel Feller, *The Public Lands in Jacksonian Politics* (Madison: University of Wisconsin Press, 1984).

22. Donald S. Lutz, *The Origins of American Constitutionalism* (Baton Rouge: Louisiana State University Press, 1988).

23. Tyack and James, "State Government and American Public Education."

24. Green, *Education and State Formation*, 186.

25. Arnold F. Shober, *Splintered Accountability: State Governance and Education Reform* (Albany: State University of New York Press, 2010), 58–59.

26. Thomas B. Timar, "The Institutional Role of State Education Departments: A Historical Perspective," *American Journal of Education* 105, no. 3 (1997): 231–60.

27. Michael Kirst, "Turning Points: A History of American School Governance," in *Who's in Charge Here? The Tangled Web of School Governance Policy*, ed. Noel Epstein (Washington DC: Brookings Institution Press, 2004), 18.

28. Kaestle, *Pillars of the Republic*; Sol Cohen, *Education in the United States: A Documentary History* (New York: Random House, 1973).

29. Urban and Wagoner, *American Education*, 107–40.

30. Judith R. Blau, *Race in the Schools: Perpetuating White Dominance?* (Boulder, CO: Lynne Rienner Publishers, 2004), 47–48.

31. Michael B. Katz, *Reconstructing American Education* (Cambridge, MA: Harvard University Press, 1987).

32. Ronald G. Walters and Eric Foner, *American Reformers, 1815–1860*, rev. ed. (New York: Hill and Wang, 1997), 216.

33. Green, *Education and State Formation*, 193; Cohen, *Education in the United States*, 1050–70.

34. Urban and Wagoner, *American Education*, 113.

35. Urban and Wagoner, *American Education*, 145–47.

36. Kaestle, *Pillars of the Republic*, 152.

37. Cubberley, *Public Education in the United States*, 163.

38. Carl F. Kaestle and Maris Vinovskis, *Education and Social Change in Nineteenth-Century Massachusetts* (Cambridge, UK: Cambridge University Press, 1980).

39. Kaestle, *Pillars of the Republic*, 182–217.

40. Kaestle, *Pillars of the Republic*, 182–217; Urban and Wagoner, *American Education*, 141–84.

41. Edgar Wallace Knight, *A Documentary History of Education in the South Before 1860: Private and Denominational Efforts*, vol. 4 (Chapel Hill: University of North Carolina Press, 1953); Dale Glenwood Robinson, *The Academies of Virginia, 1776–1861* (Richmond, VA: Dietz Press, 1977), 55–56.

42. Virginius Dabney, *Virginia, the New Dominion: A History from 1607 to the Present* (Charlottesville: University Press of Virginia, 1971).

43. Urban and Wagoner, *American Education*, 145.

44. Edward E. Baptist, *The Half Has Never Been Told: Slavery and the Making of American Capitalism* (New York: Basic Books, 2016).

45. Urban and Wagoner, *American Education*, 148.

46. Cohen, *Education in the United States*, 1621.

47. Green, *Education and State Formation*, 200.

48. James D. Anderson, *The Education of Blacks in the South, 1860–1935* (Chapel Hill: University of North Carolina Press, 2010).

49. Eric Foner, *Reconstruction: America's Unfinished Revolution* (New York: Harper & Row, 1988).

50. Alfred H. Kelly, "The Congressional Controversy Over School Segregation, 1867–1875," *American Historical Review* 64, no. 3 (1959): 166, https://doi.org/10.2307/1905178; Urban and Wagoner, *American Education*.

51. Tyack and James, "State Government and American Public Education," 60.

52. Michael Perman, *Struggle for Mastery: Disfranchisement in the South, 1888–1908* (Chapel Hill: University of North Carolina Press, 2003).

53. While some who voted against the referenda did so out of racial animus, others worried the right to an education in the state could only be located in that section of the document. Campbell Robertson, "Alabama Simmers Before Vote on Its Constitution's Racist Language," *New York Times*, October 31, 2012, https://nyti.ms/2lH5Wz8.

54. Urban and Wagoner, *American Education*, 187.

55. Urban and Wagoner, *American Education*.

56. "Table 4: Population: 1790 to 1990," 1990 US Census, https://bit.ly/2IF95sj.

57. Lawrence A. Cremin, *The Transformation of the School: Progressivism in American Education, 1876–1957* (New York: Knopf, 1961); David B. Tyack, *The One Best System: A History of American Urban Education* (Cambridge, MA: Harvard University Press, 1974).

58. Cremin, *The Transformation of the School*; Tyack, *The One Best System*.

59. Ellwood Patterson Cubberley, *A Brief History of Education: A History of the Practice and Progress and Organization of Education* (Boston: Houghton Mifflin, 1922).

60. Deborah Land, "Local School Boards Under Review: Their Role and Effectiveness in Relation to Students' Academic Achievement," *Review of Educational Research* 72, no. 2 (2002): 229–78, https://doi.org/10.3102/00346543072002229.

61. David B. Tyack and Elisabeth Hansot, *Managers of Virtue: Public School Leadership in America, 1820–1980* (Boulder, CO: Westview Press, 1986).

62. Callahan, "The American Board of Education 1789–1960."

63. George Counts, *The Social Composition of Boards of Education* (New York: Arno Press, 1929).

64. Arthur Stanley Link, *The Progressive Movement in the South, 1870–1914* (Indianapolis: Bobbs-Merrill, 1946).

65. David N. Plank, Richard K. Scotch, and Janet L. Gamble, "Rethinking Progressive School Reform: Organizational Dynamics and Educational Change," *American Journal of Education* 104, no. 2 (1996): 79–102.

66. Spring, *The American School, 1642–2004*, 291.

67. Michael S. Katz, *A History of Compulsory Education Laws. Fastback Series, No. 75. Bicentennial Series* (Bloomington, IN: Phi Delta Kappa, 1976).

68. Jeremy Felt, *Hostages of Fortune: Child Labor Reform in New York State* (Syracuse, NY: Syracuse University Press, 1965); Henry Perkinson, *The Imperfect Panacea: American Faith in Education, 1865–1965* (New York: Random House, 1968); Ira Katznelson and Margaret Weir, *Schooling for All: Class, Race, and the Decline of the Democratic Ideal* (New York: Basic Books, 1985).

69. Katz, *A History of Compulsory Education Laws*.

70. Urban and Wagoner, *American Education*, 185.

71. David Strang, "The Administrative Transformation of American Education: School District Consolidation, 1938–1980," *Administrative Science Quarterly* 32, no. 3 (1987): 355, https://doi.org/10.2307/2392909.

72. Urban and Wagoner, *American Education*, 301.

73. Charles S. Benson and Kevin O'Halloran, "The Economic History of School Finance in the United States," *Journal of Education Finance* 12, no. 4 (1987): 495–515.

74. Christopher R. Berry and Martin R. West, "Growing Pains: The School Consolidation Movement and Student Outcomes," *Journal of Law Economics and Organization* 26, no. 1 (2008).

75. Urban and Wagoner, *American Education*, 337.

76. Sean P. Corcoran and William N. Evans, "Equity, Adequacy and the Evolving State Role in Education Finance," in *Handbook of Research in Education Finance and Policy*, ed. Helen F. Ladd and Edward Fiske (New York: Routledge, 2008), 332–56.

77. David R. Reynolds, *There Goes the Neighborhood: Rural School Consolidation at the Grass Roots in Early Twentieth-Century Iowa* (Iowa City: University of Iowa Press, 1999).

78. Alberto Alesina, Reza Baqir, and Caroline Hoxby, "Political Jurisdictions in Heterogeneous Communities," *Journal of Political Economy* 112, no. 2 (2004): 348–96, https://doi.org/10.1086/381474; Lawrence W. Kenny and Amy B. Schmidt, "The Decline in the Number of School Districts in the U.S.: 1950–1980," *Public Choice* 79, no. 1/2 (1994): 1–18.

79. Christopher R. Berry and Martin R. West, "Growing Pains: The School Consolidation Movement and Student Outcomes," *Journal of Law, Economics, and Organization* 26, no. 1 (2010): 1–29, https://doi.org/10.1093/jleo/ewn015.

80. For the 1931–32, 1937–38, 1947–48, 1957–58, 1959–60, 1965–66, 1967–68, 1969–70, and 1971–72 school years, the number of districts in each state was collected from the *Digest of Education Statistics*, published by the US Office of Education; these reports can be accessed at www.eric.ed.gov. District counts for the 1969–70 through 1983–84 school years were extracted from the Elementary and Secondary Education General Information System (ELSEGIS): Public School District Universe Data Surveys, conducted by ED and accessible at http://www.icpsr.umich.edu/icpsrweb/ICPSR/series/101. All subsequent years of data were obtained from the National Center for Education Statistics Common Core of Data, accessible at https://nces.ed.gov/ccd/pubagency.asp.

81. Strang, "The Administrative Transformation of American Education."

82. William Duncombe and John Yinger, "Does School District Consolidation Cut Costs?" *Education Finance and Policy* 2, no. 4 (2007): 341–75.

Chapter 3

1. Mary L. Dudziak, "Brown as a Cold War Case," *Journal of American History* 91, no. 1 (2004): 33, https://doi.org/10.2307/3659611.33.

2. Clayborne Carson, "Two Cheers for Brown v. Board of Education," *Journal of American History* 91, no. 1 (2004): 26, https://doi.org/10.2307/3659610; Michael J. Klarman, "Reply: Brown v. Board of Education: Facts and Political Correctness," *Virginia Law Review* 80, no. 1 (1994): 185–6, https://doi.org/10.2307/1073596; Joy Ann Williams, "A Tale of Two Movements: The Power and Consequences of Misrembering Brown," in *Yearbook of the National Society for the Study of Education* 105, no. 2 (2006): 38.

3. Deirdre Oakley, Jacob Stowell, and John R. Logan, "The Impact of Desegregation on Black Teachers in the Metropolis, 1970–2000," *Ethnic and Racial Studies* 39, no. 9 (2009): 1576–98, https://doi.org/10.1080/01419870902780997; Williams, "A Tale of Two Movements."

4. Adam Fairclough, "The Costs of Brown: Black Teachers and School Integration," *Journal of American History* 91, no. 1 (2004): 43–55, https://doi.org/10.2307/3659612.

5. Michael J. Klarman, "How Brown Changed Race Relations: The Backlash Thesis," *Journal of American History* 81, no. 1 (1994): 81–118, https://doi.org/10.2307/2080994; Charles M. Payne, "'The Whole United States Is Southern!': Brown v. Board and the Mystification of Race," *Journal of American History* 91, no. 1 (2004): 83–91, https://doi.org/10.2307/3659615.

6. Klarman, "How Brown Changed Race Relations."

7. Klarman, "How Brown Changed Race Relations"; David B. Tyack and Elisabeth Hansot, *Managers of Virtue: Public School Leadership in America, 1820–1980* (Boulder, CO: Westview Press, 1986).

8. Julie A. Reuben, "Beyond Politics: Community Civics and the Redefinition of Citizenship in the Progressive Era," *History of Education Quarterly* 37, no. 4 (1997): 399–420, https://doi.org/10.2307/369872; Marshall E. Dimock, "Appendix B: Report of the Committee on Citizenship Education," *American Political Science Review* 38, no. 1 (1944): 150–51; Richard J. Altenbaugh, *The American People and Their Education: A Social History* (Upper Saddle River, NJ: Merrill/Prentice Hall, 2003).

9. John L. Rury, *Education and Social Change: Themes in the History of American Schooling* (Mahwah, NJ: Lawrence Erlbaum Associates, 2005).

10. Victor R. Durrance, "Public Textbook Selection in Forty-Eight States," *Phi Delta Kappan* 33, no. 5 (1952): 262–7.

11. James Bryant Conant, *General Education in a Free Society: Report of the Harvard Committee; with an Introduction by James Bryant Conant* (Cambridge, MA: Harvard University Press, 1955); Benjamin Fine, *Our Children Are Cheated: The Crisis in American Education* (New York: Henry Holt, 1947).

12. Carl F. Kaestle, "Ideology and American Educational History," *History of Education Quarterly* 22, no. 2 (1982): 123–37, https://doi.org/10.2307/367745.

13. James Sundquist, *Politics and Policy: The Eisenhower, Kennedy, and Johnson Years* (Washington, DC: Brookings Institution Press, 2010), 178.

14. Wayne J. Urban, *More Than Science and Sputnik: The National Defense Education Act of 1958* (Tuscaloosa: University of Alabama Press, 2010).

15. Carl F. Kaestle and Marshall S. Smith, "The Federal Role in Elementary and Secondary Education, 1940–1980," *Harvard Educational Review* 52, no. 4 (1982): 384–408.

16. Harvey Kantor, "Education, Social Reform, and the State: ESEA and Federal Education Policy in the 1960s," *American Journal of Education* 100, no. 1 (1991): 47–83.

17. James M. Enelow, "Saving Amendments, Killer Amendments, and an Expected Utility Theory of Sophisticated Voting," *Journal of Politics* 43, no. 4 (1981): 1062–89, https://doi.org/10.2307/2130189.

18. Kantor, "Education, Social Reform, and the State," 56.

19. Hugh D. Graham, *The Uncertain Triumph: Federal Education Policy in the Kennedy and Johnson Years* (Chapel Hill: University of North Carolina Press, 1984); Lorraine McDonnell, "No Child Left Behind and the Federal Role in Education: Evolution or Revolution?" *Peabody Journal of Education* 80, no. 2 (2005): 19–38.

20. Paul Manna, *School's In: Federalism and the National Education Agenda* (Washington, DC: Georgetown University Press, 2006).

21. Jerome T. Murphy, *State Education Agencies and Discretionary Funds: Grease the Squeaky Wheel* (Lexington, MA: Lexington Books, 1974).

22. Alan Rosenthal, "State Legislatures—Where It's At," *Political Science Teacher* 1, no. 4 (1988); Susan Fuhrman and Alan Rosenthal, *Shaping Education Policy in the States* (Washington, DC: Institute for Educational Leadership, 1981); Alan Rosenthal, "The Emerging Legislative Role in Education," *Compact* (Winter 1977).

23. Beryl Radin and Willis D. Hawley, *The Politics of Federal Reorganization: Creating the U.S. Department of Education* (Oxford, UK: Pergamon Press, 1988).

24. Michael W. Kirst, "The State Role in Education Policy Innovation," *Review of Policy Research* 1, no. 2 (1981): 298–308.

25. Eric A. Hanushek and Alfred A. Lindseth, *Schoolhouses, Courthouses, and Statehouses: Solving the Funding-Achievement Puzzle in America's Public Schools* (Princeton, NJ: Princeton University Press, 2009).

26. Douglas S. Reed, *On Equal Terms: The Constitutional Politics of Educational Opportunity* (Princeton, NJ: Princeton University Press, 2003).

27. William E. Thro, "Third Wave: The Impact of the Montana, Kentucky, and Texas Decisions on the Future of Public School Finance Reform Litigation," *Journal of Law & Education* 19 (1990): 219; Michael Heise, "State Constitutions, School Finance Litigation, and the 'Third Wave': From Equity to Adequacy," *Temple Law Review* 68, no. 3 (1995).

28. Education finance cases are tracked by the National Council of State Legislatures. A spreadsheet and summative information about the cases can be found at https://bit.ly/2msFqwy.

29. Martin R. West and Paul E. Peterson, *School Money Trials: The Legal Pursuit of Educational Adequacy* (Washington, DC: Brookings Institution Press, 2007).

30. Kathryn M. Borman and Sherman Dorn, *Education Reform in Florida: Diversity and Equity in Public Policy* (Albany: State University of New York Press, 2007); William E. Thro, "To Render Them Safe: The Analysis of State Constitutional Provisions in Public School Finance Reform Litigation," *Virginia Law Review* 75, no. 8 (1989): 1639–79, https://doi.org/10.2307/1073248.

31. Hanushek and Lindseth, *Schoolhouses, Courthouses, and Statehouses*, 107.

32. Jon Sonstelie, Eric J. Brunner, and Kenneth Ardon, *For Better or for Worse? School Finance Reform in California* (San Francisco: Public Policy Institute of California, 2000), https://bit.ly/2NjyWtw.

33. West and Peterson, *School Money Trials*.

34. Amy M. Hightower, Hajime Mitani, and Christopher B. Swanson, *State Policies That Count: A Survey of School Finance Policies and Outcomes* (Bethesda, MD: Editorial Project in Education, 2010).

35. Joanna Smith et al., *Categorical Funds: The Intersection of School Finance and Governance* (Washington, DC: Center for American Progress, 2013), https://ampr.gs/2Kn8xNs.

36. Eric A Hanushek, "The Failure of Input-Based Schooling Policies," *Economic Journal* 113, no. 485 (2003): F64–98.

37. C. Kirabo Jackson, Rucker C. Johnson, and Claudia Persico, "The Effects of School Spending on Educational and Economic Outcomes: Evidence from School Finance Reforms," *Quarterly Journal of Economics* 131, no. 1 (2016): 157–218, https://doi.org/10.1093/qje/qjv036; Bruce D. Baker, *Does Money Matter in Education?* (Washington, DC: Albert Shanker Institute, 2016), https://bit.ly/2dOScl5.

38. Bruce D. Baker et al., *Is School Funding Fair? A National Report Card* (Newark, NJ: Education Law Center at Rutgers University, 2016), www.schoolfundingfairness.org.

39. Walt Haney and George Madaus, "Making Sense of the Competency Testing Movement," *Harvard Educational Review* 48, no. 4 (1978): 462–84; Jal Mehta, *The Allure of Order: High Hopes, Dashed Expectations, and the Troubled Quest to Remake American Schooling* (New York: Oxford University Press, 2013), 64–83.

40. Scott Baker, "Desegregation, Minimum Competency Testing, and the Origins of Accountability: North Carolina and the Nation," *History of Education Quarterly* 55, no. 1 (2015): 33–57, https://doi.org/10.1111/hoeq.12091.

41. The states at the time were thought to be under intense political pressure to redirect at least some aid to suburban districts where voter turnout and tax revenues were higher. See Milbrey Wallin McLaughlin, "States and the New Federalism," *Harvard Educational Review* 52, no. 4 (1982): 564–83, https://doi.org/10.17763/haer.52.4.h68670435w6p1291.

42. Joseph P. Viteritti, "From Excellence to Equity: Observations on Politics, History, and Policy," *Peabody Journal of Education* 79, no. 1 (2004): 64–86, https://doi.org/10.1207/s15327930pje7901_4.

43. National Commission on Excellence in Education, *A Nation at Risk: The Imperative for Educational Reform* (Washington, DC: US Department of Education, Government Printing Office, 1983).

44. Susan H. Fuhrman and Richard F. Elmore, "Understanding Local Control in the Wake of State Education Reform," *Educational Evaluation and Policy Analysis* 12, no. 1 (1990): 82–96, https://doi.org/10.3102/01623737012001082; Harry A. Passow, "How It Happened, Wave by Wave," in *Education Reform: Making Sense of It All*, ed. Samuel B. Bacharach (Boston: Allyn & Bacon, 1990), 10–19.

45. Mehta, *The Allure of Order*, 194–95. Previous researchers have disagreed over whether or not the Charlottesville summit constituted a collaboratively determined agenda or one handed down by Bush. However, as Mehta has observed, the idea of the goals seems to have come from the governors.

46. "National Education Goals Report: Building a Nation of Learners," National Education Goals Panel, https://bit.ly/2tZZ0ko.

47. "America 2000: An Education Strategy," US Department of Education, May 1991, http://eric.ed.gov/?id=ED327985.

48. Marshall S. Smith and Jennifer O'Day, "Systemic School Reform," *Journal of Education Policy* 5, no. 5 (1990): 233–67, https://doi.org/10.1080/02680939008549074.

49. Mehta, *The Allure of Order*, 225.

50. Robert B. Schwartz and Marian A. Robinson, "Goals 2000 and the Standards Movement," *Brookings Papers on Education Policy* 2000, no. 1 (2000): 173–206.

51. Jon F. Hale, "The Making of the New Democrats," *Political Science Quarterly* 110, no. 2 (1995): 207–32, https://doi.org/10.2307/2152360.

52. Mehta, *The Allure of Order*, 230.

53. Elizabeth Debray, *Politics, Ideology, and Education: Federal Policy During the Clinton and Bush Administrations* (New York: Teachers College Press, 2006).

54. David Hurst et al., *Overview and Inventory of State Education Reforms: 1990 to 2000* (Washington, DC: US Department of Education, National Center for Education Statistics, Common Core of Data, 2003), https://bit.ly/2NrzEUV.

55. Martin Carnoy and Susan Loeb, "Does External Accountability Affect Student Outcomes? A Cross-State Analysis," *Educational Evaluation and Policy Analysis* 24, no. 4 (2002): 305–31; Thomas Dee and Brian A. Jacob, "Evaluating NCLB," *Education Next* 10, no. 3 (Summer 2010), http://educationnext.org/evaluating-nclb/.

56. John F. Jennings, "Title I: Its Legislative History and Its Promise," *Phi Delta Kappan* 81, no. 7 (2000): 516–22; McDonnell, "No Child Left Behind"; Geoffrey Borman and Jerome D'Agostino, "Title I and Student Achievement: A Meta-Analysis of Federal Evaluation Results," *Educational Evaluation and Policy Analysis* 18, no. 4 (1996): 309–26; Michael Puma et al., *Prospects: Final Report on Student Outcomes* (Washington, DC: US Department of Education, 1997).

57. Victor Bandeira de Mello et al., *With Fanfare, Bush Signs Education Bill; President, Lawmakers Hit 3 States in 12 Hours to Tout Biggest Schools Change Since '65* (Boston: Institute of Education Sciences, National Center for Education Statistics, 2002).

58. Paul Manna, *Collision Course: Federal Education Policy Meets State and Local Realities* (Washington, DC: CQ Press, 2010).

59. Victor Bandeira de Mello et al., *Mapping State Proficiency Standards Onto NAEP Scales: 2005–2007* (Boston: Institute of Education Sciences, National Center for Education Statistics, 2009); Sara Dahill-Brown and Lesley Lavery, "Implementing Federal Policy: Confronting State Capacity and Will," *Politics and Policy* 40, no. 4 (2012).

60. US Department of Education, "Part III: Department of Education, 34 CFR Subtitle B, Chapter II [Docket ID ED-2009-OESE-0006] RIN 1810-AB07, Race to the Top Fund, Final Rule," *Federal Register* 74, no. 221, https://bit.ly/2Kzk2AT.

61. Sam Dillon, "Education Grant Effort Faces Late Opposition," *New York Times*, January 18, 2010, https://nyti.ms/2KDw0Jx.

62. Jeffrey R. Henig, David M. Houston, and Melissa Arnold Lyon, "From NCLB to ESSA: Lessons Learned or Politics Reaffirmed," in *The Every Student Succeeds Act: What It Means for Schools, Systems, and States*, ed. Frederick M. Hess and Max Eden (Cambridge, MA: Harvard Education Press, 2017), 29–42.

63. Andrew Saultz, Andrew McEachin, and Lance D. Fusarelli, "Waivering as Governance: Federalism During the Obama Administration," *Educational Researcher* 45, no. 6 (2016), https://doi.org/10.3102/0013189X16663495.

64. Ben Casselman, "No Child Left Behind Worked," *FiveThirtyEight*, December 22, 2015, https://53eig.ht/2MHiF0i.

65. Thomas Dee and Brian Jacob, "The Impact of No Child Left Behind on Student Achievement," *Journal of Policy Analysis and Management* 30, no. 3 (2011): 418–46.

66. Douglas N. Harris, "Educational Outcomes of Disadvantaged Students: From Desegregation to Accountability," in *Handbook of Research in Education Finance and Policy*, ed. Helen F. Ladd and Edward B. Fiske (Abingdon, UK: Routledge, 2008), 551–70.

67. "NAEP—Achievement Gaps," National Center for Education Statistics, https://bit.ly/1Fv6jnd.

68. Sean F. Reardon, "The Widening Income Achievement Gap," *Educational Leadership* 70, no. 8 (2013): 10–16.

69. Sean F. Reardon et al., *Left Behind? The Effect of No Child Left Behind on Academic Achievement Gaps* (Stanford, CA: Stanford Center for Education Policy Analysis, 2013), https://stanford.io/2y7L2Rp.

70. Alyson Klein, "How ESSA Passed," in Hess and Eden, *The Every Student Succeeds Act*.

71. Lyndsey Layton, "To Get Support for Education Bill, Senators Conjure Lost Art: Compromise," *Washington Post*, July 28, 2015, https://wapo.st/2KsxQOn.

72. Patrick J. Egan, *Partisan Priorities: How Issue Ownership Drives and Distorts American Politics* (New York: Cambridge University Press, 2013).

73. Frederick M. Hess and Kelsey Hamilton, *Republicans, Democrats, and Schooling: What the Public Thinks* (Washington, DC: American Enterprise Institute, 2017).

74. Lauren Camera, "House Passes ESEA Rewrite 218-213; Senate Debate Continues," *Education Week, Politics K–12* blog, July 8, 2015, https://bit.ly/1NQPySk.

75. Lauren Camera, "Senate Passes ESEA Rewrite with Big Bipartisan Backing, 81–17," *Education Week, Politics K–12* blog, July 16, 2015, https://bit.ly/1CJLdA0.

76. Lauren Camera, "No Child Left Behind Has Finally Been Left Behind," *US News & World Report*, December 9, 2015, https://www.usnews.com/news/articles/2015/12/09/congress-replaces-no-child-left-behind-shifts-power-to-states https://bit.ly/2MEF7Hy.

77. Alyson Klein, "President Signs ESEA Rewrite, Giving States, Districts Bigger Say on Policy," *Education Week, Politics K–12* blog, December 10, 2015, https://bit.ly/2z376yr.

78. Andrew Ujifusa, "Praise from Governors, State Chiefs Highlight Reactions to ESEA Bill," *Education Week, Politics K–12* blog, November 30, 2015, https://bit.ly/1LLtTrX.

79. Andrew Ujifusa, "Civil Rights, Disability, Education Groups Give Lukewarm Nod to ESEA Rewrite," *Education Week, Politics K–12* blog, December 1, 2015, https://bit.ly/1YL6HDt.

80. Arnold F. Shober, "ESEA Reauthorization Continues a Long Federal Retreat from American Classrooms," *Brookings, Brown Center Chalkboard* blog, December 8, 2015, https://brook.gs/2ME9XzQ.

81. Several outlets have produced excellent and reliable guides on ESSA—Education Trust, Education Commission for the States, the Council of Chief State School Officers, and *Education Week*, for example. See also Charles Barone, "What ESSA Says," in Hess and Eden, *The Every Student Succeeds Act*, 59–73.

82. Christopher P. Loss and Patrick J. McGuinn, eds., *The Convergence of K–12 and Higher Education: Policies and Programs in a Changing Era* (Cambridge, MA: Harvard Education Press, 2016).

83. Secretary of Education John King, "Letter on Every Student Succeeds Act Implementation," Dear Colleague Letter, June 23, 2016, https://bit.ly/2u4YT7t.

84. Lamar Alexander, "Every Student Succeeds Act," Pub. L. No. 114–95 (2015), https://bit.ly/2lMTEp5.

85. Jennifer Lin Russell et al., "Designing Inter-Organizational Networks to Implement Education Reform: An Analysis of State Race to the Top Applications," *Educational Evaluation and Policy Analysis* 37, no. 1 (2015): 92–112, https://doi.org/10.3102/0162373714527341.

Chapter 4

1. While 37.5 percent of parents of school-age children reported that public school choice of some kind was available to them, only 13 percent of children attending public schools during 2012 were attending a chosen school rather than an assigned school. National Center for Education Statistics, "Elementary and Secondary Education," in NCES 2016-014, *Digest of Education Statistics: 2015* (Washington, DC: US Department of Education, 2016), https://bit.ly/2PJ2HVI.

2. Unless otherwise noted, interviewees wished to remain anonymous and interviews were conducted in 2014 or 2015.

3. Joe Burris, "In Light of Declining Test Scores, Lowery Looks to Tackle Reforms," *Baltimore Sun*, July 25, 2013, https://bsun.md/2DdgUDI.

4. Liz Bowie, "Maryland Schools Superintendent Lowery Resigns for New Job," *Baltimore Sun*, August 28, 2015, https://bsun.md/2zbBerx.

5. Tim Tooten, "New State School Superintendent Talks Education," WBAL, August 23, 2016, https://bit.ly/2z9rduV.

6. Winnie Hu, "N.J. Superintendents Call State Agency Ineffective," *New York Times*, August 15, 2011, https://nyti.ms/2IRwLdl.

7. Daniel E. Bergan and Richard T. Cole, "Call Your Legislator: A Field Experimental Study of the Impact of a Constituency Mobilization Campaign on Legislative Voting," *Political Behavior* 37, no. 1 (2015): 27–42, https://doi.org/10.1007/s11109-014-9277-1.

8. Thirty-three is a minimum; RESAs may be present in as many as forty-five states. The varying legal status of the agencies from state to state leads to different counts. See E. Robert Stephens and William G. Keane, *The Educational Service Agency: American Education's Invisible Partner* (Lanham, MD: University Press of America, 2005).

9. Paul Cairney, *Understanding Public Policy: Theories and Issues* (Basingstoke, UK: Palgrave Macmillan, 2011), 175–99.

10. Hugh Heclo, "Issue Networks and the Executive Establishment," *Public Adm. Concepts Cases* 413 (1978): 46–57.

11. Tamara Young, Catherine DiMartino, and Brian Boggs, "Interest Groups Revisited," in *Handbook of Education Politics and Policy*, ed. Bruce S. Cooper, James G. Cibulka, and Lance D. Fusarelli (Abingdon, UK: Routledge, 2014), 411–23.

12. James G. Cibulka, "The Changing Role of Interest Groups in Education: Nationalization and the New Politics of Education Productivity," *Educational Policy* 15, no. 1 (2001): 12–40, https://doi.org/10.1177/0895904801015001002; Christopher Lubienski, Janelle Scott, and Elizabeth DeBray, "The Rise of Intermediary Organizations in Knowledge Production, Advocacy, and Educational Policy," *Teachers College Record*, July 22, 2011.

13. Kay Lehman Schlozman, Sidney Verba, and Henry E. Brady, The Unheavenly Chorus: Unequal Political Voice and the Broken Promise of American Democracy (Princeton, NJ: Princeton University Press, 2012).

14. Priscilla Wohlstetter, Darius R. Brown, and Megan Duff, "Which States Are Ready for ESSA?" *Education Week*, March 8, 2017, https://bit.ly/2MIZ3MX.

15. "Lobbying Database," Center for Responsive Politics, https://www.opensecrets.org/lobby/.

16. Adrian Jania, "17 School Districts Pay Statehouse Lobbyists, Report Finds," *Hastings Tribune*, April 7, 2017, https://bit.ly/2KxrmOg.

17. "Dividing Lines: Gated School Districts, EdBuild's Second Annual Report on Student Poverty," EdBuild, https://bit.ly/29ooD3Y.

18. Paul Jargowsky and Mary Jo Bane, "Ghetto Poverty in the United States," in *The Urban Underclass*, ed. Christopher Jencks and Paul E. Peterson (Washington, DC: Brookings Institution Press, 1991), 235–73.

19. "History of Piedmont," City of Piedmont, CA, https://bit.ly/2MJWR4b; Carolyn Jones, "Oakland, Piedmont Borders at Issue," *SFGate*, November 23, 2012, https://bit.ly/2KRTMPa.

20. Bruce D. Baker et al., *Is School Funding Fair? A National Report Card* (Newark, NJ: Education Law Center at Rutgers University, 2016), www.schoolfundingfairness.org; Danielle Farrie and David G. Sciarra, "California Must Stay the Course on Path to Achieving Fair School Funding," *EdSource* blog, May 23, 2016, https://bit.ly/2IR9qII.

21. For many reasons, class size reductions may not be the most cost-efficient means of improving academic outcomes for disadvantaged students, but there is a growing consensus that it matters, particularly when the magnitude of the reduction is sizeable. Grover J. "Russ" Whitehurst and Matthew M. Chingos, *Class Size: What Research Says and What It Means for State Policy* (Washington, DC: Brookings Institution, 2011).

22. "Table 1. Public High School 4-Year Adjusted Cohort Graduation Rate (ACGR), By Race/Ethnicity and Selected Demographics for the United States, the 50 States, and the District of Columbia: School Year 2013–14," National Center for Education Statistics, https://bit.ly/1P4YtU1.

23. "Annual Fund & Endowment," *Piedmont Education Foundation* (blog), https://bit.ly/2lVbWok; Ashlyn Aiko Nelson and Beth Gazley, "The Rise of School-Supporting Nonprofits," *Education Finance and Policy* 9, no. 4 (2014): 541–66, https://doi.org/10.1162/EDFP_a_00146.

24. Stephen J. Caldas and Carl Bankston, "Effect of School Population Socioeconomic Status on Individual Academic Achievement," *Journal of Educational Research* 90, no. 5 (1997): 269–77.

25. Barbara Pepe, *Freehold: A Hometown History* (Mount Pleasant, SC: Arcadia Publishing, 2003), 132–5.

26. The EdBuild report noted the presence of approximately 180 island school districts. However, 16 of those were located in Alaska and were therefore not visible on the main map, which focused on the contiguous 48 states.

27. "Fault Lines: America's Most Segregating School District Borders," EdBuild, August 23, 2016, https://bit.ly/2bNSgNg.

28. Caroline Ratcliffe, *Child Poverty and Adult Success* (Washington, DC: Urban Institute, 2015).

29. Sean F. Reardon, "School Segregation and Racial Academic Achievement Gaps," *Educational*

Leadership 70, no. 8 (2013): 10–16; Dennis J. Condron et al., "Racial Segregation and the Black/White Achievement Gap, 1992 to 2009," *Sociological Quarterly* 54, no. 1 (2013): 130–57.

30. Amy Stuart Wells, Lauren Fox, and Diana Cordova-Cobo, *How Racially Diverse Schools and Classrooms Can Benefit All Students* (Washington, DC: The Century Foundation, 2016).

31. Jeremy Fiel, "Decomposing School Resegregation Social Closure, Racial Imbalance, and Racial Isolation," *American Sociological Review* 78, no. 5 (2013): 834, https://doi.org/10.1177/0003122413496252.

32. Genevieve Siegel-Hawley and Erica Frankenberg, *Reviving Magnet Schools: Strengthening a Successful Choice Option. A Research Brief* (Los Angeles: Civil Rights Project/Proyecto Derechos Civiles at UCLA, 2012), http://eric.ed.gov/?id=ED529163.

33. Siegel-Hawley and Frankenberg, *Reviving Magnet Schools.*

34. Institute on Metropolitan Opportunity, *Open Enrollment and Racial Segregation in the Twin Cities: 2000–2010* (Minneapolis: University of Minnesota Law School, 2013), https://bit.ly/2KOSgNq; Lesley Lavery and Deven Carlson, "Dynamic Participation in Interdistrict Open Enrollment," *Educational Policy* 29, no. 5 (2015): 746–79, https://doi.org/10.1177/0895904813518103.

35. Ann Owens, Sean F. Reardon, and Christopher Jencks, "Income Segregation Between Schools and School Districts," *American Educational Research Journal* 53, no. 4 (2016), https://doi.org/10.3102/0002831216652722.

36. Fiel, "Decomposing School Resegregation."

37. In fact, in several places in the Every Student Succeeds Act of 2015, the language of the law refers specifically to school districts, rather than to states or schools. See Andy Smarick, "States v. Districts in the Every Student Succeeds Act," *Flypaper* blog, December 4, 2015, https://bit.ly/2tU1K3L.

38. The average percentage point gap in child poverty across school district borders for each state with county districts, as measured in the EdBuild report "Fault Lines," is also lower than the national average states aside from Florida. None of the school district borders in any of these four states ranked among the top fifty most economically segregating.

39. "Fault Lines."

40. William A. Fischel, *The Congruence of American School Districts with Other Local Government Boundaries: A Google-Earth Exploration* (working paper, Dartmouth College Economics Department, Hanover, NH, 2007), https://bit.ly/2MKl76j.

41. See also Kelli Young, "Shaping School Districts: How They Got That Way," *Canton Repository*, August 31, 2014, https://bit.ly/2KuV8Db.

42. Kendra Bischoff, "School District Fragmentation and Racial Residential Segregation: How Do Boundaries Matter?" *Urban Affairs Review* 44, no. 2 (2008): 182–217, https://doi.org/10.1177/1078087408320651.

43. Bischoff, "School District Fragmentation," 185.

44. Erica Frankenberg, "Splintering School Districts: Understanding the Link Between Segregation and Fragmentation," *Law & Social Inquiry* 34, no. 4 (2009): 869–909, https://doi.org/10.1111/j.1747-4469.2009.01166.x.

45. Gary Orfield, John Kucsera, and Genevieve Siegel-Hawley, *E Pluribus . . . Separation: Deepening Double Segregation for More Students* (Los Angeles: The Civil Rights Project/Proyecto Derechos Civiles at UCLA, 2012), https://bit.ly/2KGzivF.

46. This assertion is based on analyses using data from UCLA's Civil Rights Project/Proyecto Derechos Civiles, available in the appendix.

47. Alberto Alesina, Reza Baqir, and Caroline Hoxby, "Political Jurisdictions in Heterogeneous Communities," *Journal of Political Economy* 112, no. 2 (2004): 348–96, https://doi.org/10.1086/381474.

48. Roslyn Arlin Mickelson, Stephen Samuel Smith, and Amy Hawn Nelson, *Yesterday, Today, and Tomorrow: School Desegregation and Resegregation in Charlotte* (Cambridge, MA: Harvard Education Press, 2015).

49. Davison M. Douglas, *Reading, Writing and Race: The Desegregation of the Charlotte Schools* (Chapel Hill: University of North Carolina Press, 2012).

50. Charles T. Clotfelter, *After "Brown": The Rise and Retreat of School Desegregation* (Princeton, NJ: Princeton University Press, 2004).

51. Christopher R. Berry and Martin R. West, "Growing Pains: The School Consolidation Movement and Student Outcomes," *Journal of Law Economics and Organization* 26, no. 1 (2008); William D. Duncombe and John M. Yinger, "School District Consolidation: The Benefits and Costs," *School Administrator* 67, no. 5 (2010): 10–7.

52. Berry and West, "Growing Pains"; Jonathan N. Mills, Josh B. McGee, and Jay P. Greene, *An Analysis of the Effect of Consolidation on Student Achievement: Evidence from Arkansas* (Fayetteville: University of Arkansas EDRE Working Paper No. 2013-02, 2013), https://bit .ly/2NnlEfs.

53. Matthew Andrews, William Duncombe, and John Yinger, "Revisiting Economies of Size in American Education: Are We Any Closer to a Consensus?" *Economics of Education Review* 21, no. 3 (2002): 245–62, https://doi.org/10.1016/S0272-7757(01)00006-1.

54. Daniel Kiel, "Memphis Dilemma: A Half-Century of Public Education Reform in Memphis and Shelby County from Desegregation to Consolidation," *University of Memphis Law Review* 41 (2011): 787.

55. Kiel, "Memphis Dilemma"; Wanda Rushing, "School Segregation and Its Discontents: Chaos and Community in Post–Civil Rights Memphis," *Urban Education* 52, no. 1 (2015): 3–31, https://doi.org/10.1177/0042085915574520.

56. Linda Wesson, *Statutory Options for School District Mergers: Report Addressing House Resolution 30, 2011* (Nashville: Offices of Research and Education Accountability, 2012), https://bit.ly/2KOv1mL.

57. Wesson, *Statutory Options.*

58. Kiel, "Memphis Dilemma."

59. Campbell Robertson, "Memphis to Vote on Transferring Its School System to County," *New York Times*, January 27, 2011, https://nyti.ms/2lVNxyU; Christina A. Samuels, "Memphis Voters to Weigh In on Merger Proposal," *Education Week*, March 7, 2011, https://bit.ly/2zax1Er.

60. Sam Dillon, "Merger of Memphis and County School Districts Revives Race and Class Challenges," *New York Times*, November 5, 2011, https://nyti.ms/2Kvsgup; Samuels, "Memphis School Board."

61. Christina Samuels, "Memphis Residents Vote to Merge City, County Schools," *Education Week, District Dossier* blog, March 9, 2011, https://bit.ly/2NnQFQp; Dillon, "Merger."

62. Dillon, "Merger."

63. Denisa R. Superville, "Memphis-Area School Year Starts with Opening of Six Breakaway Districts," *Education Week, District Dossier* blog, August 5, 2014, https://bit.ly/2KJaQKm.

64. Christine Campbell and Libuse Binder, *In-Depth Portfolio Assessment: Shelby County Schools, Memphis, TN* (Washington, DC: Center on Reinventing Public Education, 2014), https://bit .ly/2NqaSVR.

65. Erica Frankenberg, Genevieve Siegal-Hawley, and Sara Diem, "Segregation by District Boundary Line: The Fragmentation of Memphis Area Schools," *Educational Researcher* 46, no. 8 (2017): 449–63.

66. Data are from the National Center for Education Statistics Common Core of Data for the 2014–2015 school year https://bit.ly/2leykqu.

67. Craig B. Howley, Jerry Johnson, and Jennifer Petrie, *Consolidation of Schools and Districts: What the Research Says and What It Means* (Boulder, CO: National Education Policy Center, 2011), https://bit.ly/2KN6nTv; Ulrich Boser, *Size Matters: A Look at School-District Consolidation* (Washington, DC: Center for American Progress, 2013), https://ampr. gs/2KNX5Xq.

68. Susan Eaton, "How a 'New Secessionist' Movement Is Threatening to Worsen School Segregation and Widen Inequalities," *The Nation*, May 15, 2014, https://bit.ly/2u1lHFZ.

Chapter 5

1. Jeffrey Henig defines exceptionalism in this manner, but highlights the challenges to it along somewhat broader dimensions, from decentralized governance to centralized governance, from purely public institutions to increasingly privatized and hybrid systems, and from single purpose to general purpose. Similarly, the concept of integrated governance is developed by Kenneth Wong but originally focused on mayoral governance in city districts. I use the term here in a modified sense to reference connections between education and general governance broadly, beyond urban district settings. Jeffrey R. Henig, *The End of Exceptionalism in American Education: The Changing Politics of School Reform* (Cambridge, MA: Harvard Education Press, 2013); Kenneth K. Wong et al., *The Education Mayor: Improving America's Schools* (Washington, DC: Georgetown University Press, 2007).

2. Governor Doug Ducey, State of the State address, January 11, 2016, Tucson, Arizona.

3. Governor Larry Hogan, State of the State address, February 3, 2016, Annapolis, Maryland.

4. Governor Earl Tomblin, State of the State address, January 13, 2016, Charleston, West Virginia.

5. Governor Mark Dayton, State of the State address, March 9, 2016, St. Paul, Minnesota.

6. Earl Taylor et al., "Keep Partisan Politics Out of School Board Elections," *Daily News* (Jacksonville, NC), April 17, 2017, https://bit.ly/2N53DSq.

7. Julie McMahon, "Mayoral Candidate Laura Lavine Explains Controversial Idea to Take Over Schools," *Post-Standard* (Syracuse, NY), October 16, 2017, https://bit.ly/2KVVzG8; Robert E. DiFlorio, "Mayoral Candidate Should Keep Politics Out of Syracuse Schools," *Post-Standard* (Syracuse, NY), October 19, 2017, https://bit.ly/2uhUtdu.

8. Kathryn A. McDermott, *Controlling Public Education: Localism Versus Equity* (Lawrence: University Press of Kansas, 1999), 80–99.

9. Nicholas A. Masters, Robert H. Salisbury, and Thomas H. Eliot, *State Politics and the Public Schools: An Exploratory Analysis* (New York: Knopf, 1964), 3.

10. Michael R. Ford and Douglas M. Ihrke, "Board Conflict and Public Performance on Urban and Non-Urban Boards: Evidence from a National Sample of School Board Members," *Journal of Urban Affairs* 39, no. 1 (2017): 108–21, https://doi.org/10.1111/juaf.12315.

11. Christina Wolbrecht and Michael T. Hartney, "'Ideas about Interests': Explaining the Changing Partisan Politics of Education," *Perspectives on Politics; Cambridge* 12, no. 3 (2014): 603–30, http://dx.doi.org.go.libproxy.wakehealth.edu/10.1017/S1537592714001613.

12. Evan Crawford, "How Nonpartisan Ballot Design Conceals Partisanship: A Survey Experiment of School Board Members in Two States," *Political Research Quarterly* 71, no. 1 (2017): 143–56, https://doi.org/10.1177/1065912917725405.

13. David B. Tyack, *Seeking Common Ground: Public Schools in a Diverse Society* (Cambridge, MA: Harvard University Press, 2003).

14. Tom Loveless, *Conflicting Missions?: Teachers Unions and Educational Reform* (Washington, DC: Brookings Institution Press, 2000).

15. Joel H. Spring, *The American School, 1642–2004* (New York: McGraw-Hill, 2004); Sarah F. Anzia, *Timing and Turnout: How Off-Cycle Elections Favor Organized Groups* (Chicago: University of Chicago Press, 2013). See also chapter 2 of this volume.

16. Chester E. Finn Jr., "Beyond the School District," *National Affairs* 9 (Fall 2011), https://bit.ly/2N1zQcZ.

17. Anzia, *Timing and Turnout*.

18. Jeffrey R. Henig and Wilbur C. Rich, *Mayors in the Middle: Politics, Race, and Mayoral Control of Urban Schools* (Princeton, NJ: Princeton University Press, 2004).

19. Ferrel Guillory, *Education Governors for the 21st Century* (Durham, NC: James B. Hunt, Jr. Institute for Educational Leadership and Policy and the Wallace Foundation, November 2005), https://bit.ly/2u6myF8.

20. Anzia, *Timing and Turnout*.

21. Kent Willis, "Why We Have—and Should Have—Elected School Boards in Virginia," *American Civil Liberties Union of Virginia* blog, October 15, 2009, https://bit.ly/2L23wq0.

22. Patte Barth, *Toward Collaboration, Not a Coup: What Research Says About Mayoral Involvement in Urban Schools* (Alexandria, VA: National School Boards Association, Center for Public Education, 2014), https://bit.ly/2ukzOFB.

23. Kara Hildreth, "School Board Elections Move to Even-Year Cycle," *Jordan Independent*, November 22, 2016, https://bit.ly/2J9Jkke.

24. Mandy Gillip, "More Than 12 Percentage Point Spike in Contested November School Board Elections Compared to 2016," Ballotpedia, November 10, 2017, https://bit.ly/2KMmEfm.

25. Anzia, *Timing and Turnout*.

26. "School Board Elections, 2016," Ballotpedia, https://bit.ly/2zvEr5g.

27. Daarel Burnette II, "Partisan School Board Elections a Source of Anxiety for North Carolina," *Education Week*, December 12, 2017, https://bit.ly/2u6sRst; Jess Clark, "Power Grab or Reality: Lawmakers Move to Make More School Board Elections Partisan," *WRAL*, April 20, 2017, https://bit.ly/2zo3YNN.

28. Benjamin Wood, "Utah Judge Rules Against Partisan Elections for State School Board," *Salt Lake Tribune*, December 11, 2017, https://bit.ly/2iUszyP.

29. Luther Harmon Zeigler, M. Kent Jennings, and G. Wayne Peak, *Governing American Schools: Political Interaction in Local School Districts* (North Scituate, MA: Duxbury Press, 1974).

30. Frederick M. Hess, *School Boards at the Dawn of the 21st Century: Conditions and Challenges of District Governance* (Alexandria, VA: National School Boards Association, 2002).

31. Edwin Darden, "Should School Board Elections Be Moved to November?" On Board Online, October 11, 2010, https://bit.ly/2N2uFgO. State association reports are typically based on surveys of membership or of superintendents, as most states have not regularly collected data on school board elections.

32. Frederick M. Hess and Olivia Meeks, *School Boards Circa 2010: Governance in the Accountability Era* (Alexandria, VA, Washington, DC, and Des Moines: National School Boards Association, Thomas B. Fordham Foundation, and Iowa School Boards Foundation, 2010), https://bit.ly/2NDn7OX.

33. "School Board Incumbency Analysis: 2016 in Brief," Ballotpedia, https://bit.ly/2L0DkMd.

34. Julia A. Payson, "When Are Local Incumbents Held Accountable for Government Performance? Evidence from US School Districts," *Legislative Studies Quarterly* 42, no. 3 (2016): 421–48, https://doi.org/10.1111/lsq.12159.

35. Anzia, *Timing and Turnout*.

36. Naomi Nix, "Welcome to New Jersey, Where More Than Half of All School Board Races Have One—or No—Candidate," *The 74 Million* blog, March 20, 2016, https://bit.ly/2KVjcyu.

37. This last, dramatic surge may be attributable in part to the rescheduling of many of the school board contests in California, though the upward trend in previous years suggests that competition for school board seats may be on the increase. Gillip, "12 Percentage Point Spike."

38. Nic Garcia, "Spending on Colorado School Board Races by Outside Groups Surpasses $1.5 Million," *Chalkbeat* blog, October 31, 2017, https://bit.ly/2udqPG6.

39. US Census Bureau, *Public Education Finances 2008* (Washington, DC: US Census Bureau, 2008), https://bit.ly/2m4LCYT.

40. Christopher David Johnston, "Superintendents and Fiscally Dependent School Districts" (PhD diss., Virginia Polytechnic Institute and State University, Falls Church, VA, 2017), https://bit.ly/2u4L1uK.

41. Barth, *Toward Collaboration*.

42. Sam P. Harris, *State Departments of Education, State Boards of Education, and Chief State School Officers* (Washington, DC: US Bureau of Elementary and Secondary Education, 1973); Paul Manna, "State Education Governance and Policy: Dynamic Challenges, Diverse Approaches, and New Frontiers," *Peabody Journal of Education* 87, no. 5 (2012): 627–43, https://doi.org/10.1080/0161956X.2012.723508.

43. Paul Manna and Jack Cooper, "Education Policy, Performance, and Democratic Accountability: State and Local Voting Behavior in Elections for State Education Chief" (paper presented at the Annual Meeting of the Midwest Political Science Association, Chicago, Illinois, April 3–6, 2014), https://bit.ly/2L2hJqk.

44. Jennifer Dounay Zinth, *Governors: Seeking Greater Control Over Education, Governance* (Denver: Education Commission of the States, 2011).

45. Paul Manna and Timothy Harwood, "Governance and Educational Expectations in the U.S. States," *State Politics & Policy Quarterly* 11, no. 4 (2011): 483–509, https://doi.org/10.1177/1532440011421302.

46. National Council of State Legislatures, "State Partisan Composition," November 8, 2017, https://bit.ly/2eOIFWP.

47. "Election and Voting Statistics," Wisconsin Elections Commission, https://bit.ly/2L37KO4.

48. Patrick Marley, "State Supreme Court Upholds Education Chief's Independence," *Milwaukee Journal Sentinel*, May 18, 2016, https://bit.ly/2m3DzLG.

49. Jared E. Knowles, "School Boards and the Democratic Promise" (PhD diss., University of Wisconsin–Madison, 2015), https://bit.ly/2m6MmfO.

50. Fenit Nirappil, "Poll: Democrat Northam Leads in Va. Governor Race; Education Tops Voter Concerns," *Washington Post*, September 25, 2017, https://wapo.st/2xutMn3.

51. Carolyn Phenicie, "In Virginia Governor's Race, Education Issues Take Center Stage Mainly Through Trump and DeVos," *The 74 Million* blog, October 27, 2017, https://bit.ly/2J9OcWy.

52. Even in 1972, Virginia was the only state in which general government leaders appointed school board members consistently across all of its county and municipal districts.

53. Johnston, "Superintendents and Fiscally Dependent School Districts."

54. Nicole Steenburgh, "Amherst Votes 'Yes' to Referendum for Elected School Board," *Amherst New Era Progress*, November 8, 2016, https://bit.ly/2fDAcpO; Kristin Smith, "Hanover Parents Pushing for Elected—Not Appointed—School Board," *ABC News WRIC*, May 30, 2017, https://bit.ly/2KJPDRa.

55. Larry A. Massie, "Perceptions of Superintendents and School Board Members Who Experienced the Transition from Appointed to Elected School Boards" (PhD diss., Virginia Polytechnic Institute and State University, Blacksburg, VA, 2010), https://bit.ly/2L3S8K4.

56. Graham Moomaw, "McAuliffe Breaks All-Time Veto Record for Virginia Governors by

Striking 'Religious Freedom' Legislation; Bill on Sexually Explicit Material Also Vetoed," *Richmond Times-Dispatch*, March 23, 2017, https://bit.ly/2o9WJ2r.

57. Carroll Doherty, Jocelyn Kiley, and Bridget Jameson, "Partisanship and Political Animosity in 2016," Pew Research Center, June 22, 2016, https://pewrsr.ch/28WYkmr.

58. Boris Shor and Nolan McCarty, "The Ideological Mapping of American Legislatures," *American Political Science Review* 105, no. 3 (2011): 530–51, https://doi.org/10.1017/S0003055411000153.

59. Nolan McCarty, "What We Know and Don't Know About Our Polarized Politics," *Washington Post*, January 8, 2014, https://wapo.st/2l5nPt8.

60. Alan I. Abramowitz and Steven Webster, "The Rise of Negative Partisanship and the Nationalization of U.S. Elections in the 21st Century," *Electoral Studies* 41, suppl. C (2016): 12–22, https://doi.org/10.1016/j.electstud.2015.11.001.

61. Katherine J. Cramer, *The Politics of Resentment: Rural Consciousness in Wisconsin and the Rise of Scott Walker* (Chicago: University of Chicago Press, 2016).

62. Soren Jordan and Cynthia J. Bowling, "Introduction: The State of Polarization in the States," *State and Local Government Review* 48, no. 4 (2016): 220–26, https://doi.org/10.1177/0160323X17699527.

63. Sarah F. Anzia and Terry M. Moe, "Polarization and Policy: The Politics of Public-Sector Pensions," *Legislative Studies Quarterly* 42, no. 1 (2017): 33–62, https://doi.org/10.1111/lsq.12145.

64. Nathaniel A. Birkhead, "State Budgetary Delays in an Era of Party Polarization," *State and Local Government Review* 48, no. 4 (2016): 259–69, https://doi.org/10.1177/0160323X16687813.

65. Laura Vozzella and Jenna Portnoy, "Va. Lawmakers Finalize State Budget, Avert Government Shutdown, Block Gov. Terry McAuliffe on Medicaid," *Washington Post*, June 23, 2014, https://wapo.st/2N2Rmhe.

Chapter 6

1. Michael J. Feuer, "Moderation: A Radical Approach to Education Policy," *Education Week*, June 14, 2006, https://bit.ly/2Ji2sfX.

2. Brenda Flanagan, "Newark Regains Local Control of Public Schools," *NJTV News* blog, September 13, 2017, https://bit.ly/2ufYyzF.

3. Neil Macfarquhar, "Judge Orders a State Takeover of the Newark School District," *New York Times*, April 14, 1995, https://nyti.ms/2ueHYzR.

4. Ras J. Baraka, "A New Start for Newark Schools," *New York Times*, October 19, 2014, https://nyti.ms/2LduYRQ.

5. Mark J. Chin et al., "School District Reform in Newark: Within- and Between-School Changes in Achievement Growth" (NBER Working Paper No. 23922, National Bureau of Economic Research, October 2017), https://doi.org/10.3386/w23922; Dale Russakoff, *The Prize: Who's in Charge of America's Schools?* (New York: Houghton Mifflin Harcourt, 2015).

6. Baraka, "A New Start."

7. "Newark's High School Graduation Rate Increases Four Percentage Points in the 2015–16 School Year," Newark Public Schools (press release), January 17, 2017, https://bit.ly/2umvkhE.

8. Ang Santos, "State Board of Ed Approves, Newark Will Regain Control of Schools," WBGO, September 14, 2017, https://bit.ly/2maQ2gF.

9. Susan H. Fuhrman and Richard F. Elmore, "Understanding Local Control in the Wake of State Education Reform," *Educational Evaluation and Policy Analysis* 12, no. 1 (1990): 82–96, https://doi.org/10.3102/01623737012001082.

10. Alan Greenblatt, "Tougher Than Wall Street," *Governing*, December 2007, https://bit. ly/2mdKemN; Alan J. Karcher, *New Jersey's Multiple Municipal Madness* (New Brunswick, NJ: Rutgers University Press, 1998), 75.

11. Robert Hanley, "New Jersey Seizes School District in Jersey City, Citing Total Failure," *New York Times*, October 5, 1989, https://nyti.ms/2N9nGPn.

12. A focus on policy suggests that in New Jersey, the contradiction between the reality of strong state control and the rhetoric of adherence to local control is long-standing. Two studies of state and local control during the 1970s classified the state's approach to education governance as "moderately centralized" and characterized by a "high" level of state control. More than forty years ago, before the state had launched its first district takeover, empirical assessments of New Jersey's approach to education governance and its formally endorsed policies indicated that local control was not as sacrosanct as it might have seemed. See Tyll van Geel, *Authority to Control the School Program* (Lexington, MA: Lexington Books, 1976); Frederick M. Wirt, "What State Laws Say About Local Control," *Phi Delta Kappan* 59, no. 8 (1978): 517–20.

13. "Having a Problem with Your School or District?" Ohio Department of Education, November 29, 2017, https://bit.ly/2JiEb9A.

14. Hannah Sparling, "Superintendent: State Making It 'Nearly Impossible' to Teach," *Cincinnati Enquirer*, August 3, 2015, https://cin.ci/2Jhug3W.

15. *Address School Assessments and Curricula and Teacher Evaluations*, House Bill 176, Ohio General Assembly session 132, https://bit.ly/2JhSI5m.

16. J. Brian Charles, "In School Funding Fight, Connecticut Weighs Uncertain Next Steps," *Governing*, February 7, 2018, https://bit.ly/2nIYfKf.

17. van Geel, *Authority*; Frederick M. Wirt, "School Policy Culture and State Decentralization," in *The Politics of Education: The Seventy-Sixth Yearbook of the National Society for the Study of Education, Part II*, ed. Jay D. Scribner (Chicago: University of Chicago Press, 1977); Wirt, "State Laws."

18. Dara Zeehandelaar and David Griffith, *Schools of Thought: A Taxonomy of American Education Governance* (Washington, DC: Thomas B. Fordham Institute, 2015), https://bit. ly/2NMh3DJ.

19. van Geel, *Authority*, 74–83.

20. Lawyers' Committee for Civil Rights Under Law, *State Legal Standards for the Provision of Public Education* (Washington, DC: National Institute of Education, Department of Health, Education, and Welfare, 1978), https://bit.ly/2ugjeHu.

21. Wirt, "State Laws," 518.

22. Zeehandelaar and Griffith, *Schools of Thought*.

23. David T. Conley, *Who Governs Our Schools? Changing Roles and Responsibilities* (New York: Teachers College Press, 2003).

24. Bonnie C. Fusarelli and Bruce Cooper, eds., *The Rising State: How State Power Is Transforming Our Nation's Schools* (Albany: SUNY Press, 2009).

25. Clyde Jesse Tidwell, *State Control of Textbooks: With Special Reference to Florida* (New York: Teachers College, Columbia University, 1928).

26. Michael G. Watt, "Research on the Textbook Selection Process in the United States of America," *IARTEM E-Journal* 2, no. 1 (2009): 1–24.

27. Chester E. Finn and Diane Ravitch, *The Mad, Mad World of Textbook Adoption* (Washington, DC: Thomas B. Fordham Institute, 2004). Michelle Phillips also suggests that state regulation of textbook adoption was driven by religious fundamentalism, and was less likely in states where education levels were high and school districts were small and numerous. See "State

Involvement in Limiting Textbook Choice by School Districts," *Public Choice* 160, no. 1–2 (2013): 181–203, https://doi.org/10.1007/s11127-013-0075-9.

28. Julia H. Kaufman, Lindsey E. Thompson, and V. Darleen Opfer, *Creating a Coherent System to Support Instruction Aligned with State Standards: Promising Practices of the Louisiana Department of Education* (Santa Monica, CA: RAND Corporation, 2016), https://bit .ly/2zzUAH4.

29. David L. Angus, *Professionalism and the Public Good: A Brief History of Teacher Certification* (Washington, DC: Thomas B. Fordham Foundation, 2001), https://bit.ly/2ugqDqy.

30. Benjamin W. Frazier, *Development of State Programs for the Certification of Teachers*, US Office of Education, Circular No. 12 (Washington, DC: US Government Printing Office, 1938).

31. Adam Fairclough, "The Costs of Brown: Black Teachers and School Integration," *Journal of American History* 91, no. 1 (2004): 43–55, https://doi.org/10.2307/3659612.

32. Dana Goldstein, *The Teacher Wars: A History of America's Most Embattled Profession* (New York: Knopf Doubleday, 2014), 111; Michael Fultz, "The Displacement of Black Educators Post-Brown: An Overview and Analysis," *History of Education Quarterly* 44, no. 1 (2004): 11–45.

33. Kerri Tobin, "Control of Teacher Certification in the United States," *Peabody Journal of Education* 87, no. 4 (2012): 485–99, https://doi.org/10.1080/0161956X.2012.705150.

34. "Table 3.1. Test Requirements for Initial Certification of Elementary and Secondary Teachers, by Type of Test and State: 2016 and 2017," National Center for Education Statistics, 2017, https://bit.ly/2KQGqqg.

35. Walt Haney and George Madaus, "Making Sense of the Competency Testing Movement," *Harvard Educational Review* 48, no. 4 (1978): 462–84.

36. Grace S. Wright, "Trends in High-School Graduation Requirements at the State Level," *School Review* 64, no. 4 (1956): 178–80.

37. Task Force on Graduation Requirements, *Graduation Requirements: An NASSP Special Task Force Report* (Reston, VA: National Association of Secondary School Principals, 1975).

38. Bradford Chaney, Kenneth Burgdorf, and Nadir Atash, "Influencing Achievement Through High School Graduation Requirements," *Educational Evaluation and Policy Analysis* 19, no. 3 (1997): 229–44, https://doi.org/10.2307/1164464.

39. Jal Mehta, *The Allure of Order: High Hopes, Dashed Expectations, and the Troubled Quest to Remake American Schooling* (New York: Oxford University Press, 2013); Alyson Klein, "Historic Summit Fueled Push for K–12 Standards," *Education Week*, September 24, 2014, https://bit.ly/2NIh9fI.

40. Thomas Dee and Brian Jacob, "The Impact of No Child Left Behind on Student Achievement" (NBER Working Paper no. 15531, National Bureau of Economic Research, November 2009), http://doi.org/10.3386/w15531.

41. "N.J. First to Attempt Complete Takeover," *Education Week*, June 1, 1988, https://bit. ly/2urbu4Y.

42. Todd Ziebarth, *State Takeovers and Reconstitutions* (Denver: Education Commission of the States, 2002).

43. David W. Chen, "After More Than 20 Years, Newark to Regain Control of Its Schools," *New York Times*, September 12, 2017, https://nyti.ms/2w5lty2.

44. Another reason for reducing these policies to a simple indicator is to ensure that they are scored on the same scale and can be readily combined into a summative index. Among the seven indicators included in this analysis, the scale reliability for the index of policy density indicates that there is high enough internal consistency for the analysis to proceed; Cronbach's alpha is .74 for the seven indicators.

45. Fusarelli and Cooper, *The Rising State*.

46. Anne Schneider and Helen Ingram, "Social Construction of Target Populations: Implications for Politics and Policy," *American Political Science Review* 87, no. 2 (1993): 334–47, https://doi.org/10.2307/2939044.

47. Joe Soss, Richard C. Fording, and Sanford F. Schram, *Disciplining the Poor: Neoliberal Paternalism and the Persistent Power of Race* (Chicago: University of Chicago Press, 2011).

48. Gubernatorial strength, as measured by the governor's ability to appoint both the CSSO and the SBE, does not appear to contribute to a substantially higher level of state authority, in any year. Many education governors have emerged in states where they lack institutional authority, so this absence is not especially surprising.

49. Amy M. Hightower, Hajime Mitani, and Christopher B. Swanson, *State Policies That Count: A Survey of School Finance Policies and Outcomes* (Bethesda, MD: Editorial Project in Education, 2010); Joanna Smith et al., *Categorical Funds: The Intersection of School Finance and Governance* (Washington, DC: Center for American Progress, 2013), https://ampr.gs/2NMi2nI.

50. Hightower et al., *State Policies*.

51. Smith et al., *Categorical Funds*.

52. George H. Gallup, "The 12th Annual PDK/Gallup Poll of the Public's Attitudes Toward the Public Schools," *Phi Delta Kappan* 62, no. 1 (1980): 33–46, https://bit.ly/2uh6Sir.

53. William Bushaw and Valerie Calderon, "Try It Again, Uncle Sam: The 46th Annual PDK/Gallup Poll of the Public's Attitudes Toward the Public Schools," *Phi Delta Kappan* 96, no. 1 (2014): 9–20, https://bit.ly/2Ld7JqX.

54. Michael Stratford, "3 Takeaways from DeVos' Major Policy Address," Politico, January 1, 2018, http://politi.co/2Dr7CHO.

55. Chester E. Finn, "Re-Imagining Local Control," *Education Next*, December 6, 2010, https://bit.ly/2zuEI8A.

56. Hart Research Associates, Public School Parents on the Value of Public Education: Findings from a National Survey of Public School Parents Conducted for the AFT (Washington, DC: American Federation of Teachers, 2017), https://bit.ly/2uuD9So.

57. Frederick M. Hess and Andy Smarick, "In Defense of Local Schools," *National Review*, March 1, 2018, https://bit.ly/2L75WXq.

58. Denisa R. Superville, "Chicago's Local School Councils 'Experiment' Endures 25 Years of Change," *Education Week*, October 8, 2014, https://bit.ly/2KRHA4H.

59. Rebecca Jacobsen, "The Voice of the People in Education," in *Handbook of Education Policy Research*, ed. Gary Sykes, Barbara Schneider, and David N. Plank (New York: Routledge, 2014), 307–18.

60. Kathryn A. McDermott, *Controlling Public Education: Localism Versus Equity* (Lawrence: University Press of Kansas, 1999).

61. Campbell F. Scribner, *The Fight for Local Control: Schools, Suburbs, and American Democracy* (Ithaca, NY: Cornell University Press, 2016), 18.

62. Laurence Iannaccone, *Politics in Education* (New York: Center for Applied Research in Education, 1967), 38.

63. Colorado stands out as perhaps the clearest exception to this rule, declaring in Article IX, Section 15, that "control of instruction" is to remain with local school boards and in Section 16 that "neither the general assembly nor the state board of education shall have power to prescribe textbooks to be used in the public schools."

64. Despite all of this, the practical need for some degree of local control has been recognized in both state and federal policy. For instance, ESSA frequently refers to local districts, and in a

number of sections requires states to distribute aid directly to them or to defer to them in the process of school improvement. Many state and federal courts have likewise issued decisions recognizing local control as a concern that warrants at least some legal consideration.

65. Scribner, *The Fight for Local Control*, 15–34.

66. "Fractured: The Breakdown of America's School Districts," EdBuild, June 2016, https://bit .ly/2supET4.

67. Stokely Carmichael, "Free Huey Rally," February 17, 1968, Oakland, CA, https://bit.ly /2urxa0U.

68. Jon N. Hale, *The Freedom Schools: Student Activists in the Mississippi Civil Rights Movement* (New York: Columbia University Press, 2016), 179–80; Goldstein, *The Teacher Wars*, 133–63.

69. "The Time Is NOW for Local Control of Philly's Public Schools," Philadelphia Federation of Teachers, September 29, 2017, https://pft.org/local-control/.

70. James Q. Lynch, "Labor Committee Sends Iowa Collective Bargaining Changes to Full Senate," *The Gazette* (Cedar Rapids, IA), January 10, 2017, https://bit.ly/2NNUU7Y.

71. Claude Lévi-Strauss, *Introduction to the Work of Marcel Mauss*, trans. Felicity Baker (London: Taylor & Francis, 1987), 63–4.

Conclusion

1. Kate Alexander, "Perry Picks Ex–Railroad Commissioner Williams to Be Texas Education Chief," *Austin American-Statesman*, August 28, 2012, https://atxne.ws/2Jrpst4.

2. Sean Cavanagh and Heather Hollingsworth, "Stimulus' End Puts Squeeze on Education Budgets," *Education Week*, April 5, 2011, https://bit.ly/2Lnaea4.

3. Gary Scharrer, "600 Texas School Districts Take Funding Complaints to Court," *Houston Chronicle*, October 21, 2012, https://bit.ly/2uoBlLK.

4. Farzad Mashhood, "TEA to Lay Off 178 Workers," *Austin American-Statesman*, July 12, 2011, https://atxne.ws/2uqln3t.

5. Paul Burka, "The Big Test," *Texas Monthly*, July 31, 2012, https://bit.ly/2L0wI4R; Morgan Smith, "Texas Schools Chief Stepping Down," *Texas Tribune*, May 1, 2012, https://bit.ly /2minRMW.

6. Interview with author, July 24, 2014.

7. Patrick J. Egan and Megan Mullin, "Turning Personal Experience into Political Attitudes: The Effect of Local Weather on Americans' Perceptions about Global Warming," *Journal of Politics* 74, no. 3 (2012): 796–809; Aaron B. Strauss, "Political Ground Truth: How Personal Issue Experience Counters Partisan Biases" (PhD diss., Princeton University, 2009), https:// bit.ly/2LCrGqA.

8. US Department of Education, "The American Recovery and Reinvestment Act of 2009: Saving and Creating Jobs and Reforming Education," March 7, 2009, https://bit.ly/2uCrp0o.

9. The degree to which major political questions become ideological battles that play out in schools has recently made headlines with regards to the rights of transgender citizens. When North Carolina passed HB2, or "the bathroom bill," mandating that transgender individuals use the bathroom corresponding to their biological sex instead of the one matching their gender identity, the state legislature seemingly gave little consideration to the potential impact on the public school system. Though many public school districts sought to preserve transgender students' access to the bathroom of their choosing, the federal government considered withholding the billions of dollars of aid it annually provides to the state's schools as a consequence for discrimination. The loss of this funding would be catastrophic for the state's schools— especially as funding levels have not bounced back to prerecession levels—but also potentially for state leadership. The state's public schools seemed poised either to be instrumental in the

victory against the policy or to become a casualty of the fight. See Matt Apuzzo and Alan Blinder, "North Carolina Law May Risk Federal Aid," *New York Times*, April 1, 2016, https:// nyti.ms/1RSgJDb.

10. "Education," Gallup.com, https://bit.ly/2LkiqYB.

11. PDK/Gallup, "The 47th Annual PDK/Gallup Poll of the Public's Attitudes Towards the Public Schools: Testing Doesn't Measure Up for Americans," *Phi Delta Kappan* 97, no. 1 (2015), https://bit.ly/2NlhRi4.

12. Ira Katznelson and Margaret Weir, *Schooling for All: Class, Race, and the Decline of the Democratic Ideal* (New York: Basic Books, 1985); James T. Patterson, *America's Struggle Against Poverty in the Twentieth Century, Enlarged Edition* (Cambridge, MA: Harvard University Press, 2009).

13. Jack Schneider, "America's Not-So-Broken Education System," *The Atlantic*, June 22, 2016, https://bit.ly/28NSLoF.

14. Richard D. Brown, *The Strength of a People: The Idea of an Informed Citizenry in America, 1650–1870* (Chapel Hill: University of North Carolina Press, 1997), 100.

15. The special role played by schools in American public life, and the inherent conflicts between the many expectations we hold for them, are explained thoroughly in Jennifer L. Hochschild and Nathan Scovronick, *The American Dream and the Public Schools* (New York: Oxford University Press, 2003).

16. Miriam Cohen, "Reconsidering Schools and the American Welfare State," *History of Education Quarterly* 45, no. 4 (2005): 511–37, doi:10.1111/j.1748-5959.2005.tb00052.x; Hochschild and Scovronick, *The American Dream*.

17. David B. Tyack and Larry Cuban, *Tinkering Toward Utopia: A Century of Public School Reform* (Cambridge, MA: Harvard University Press, 1995).

18. This is based on my tabulation of articles and blog posts available in *Education Week*'s online archives. Articles and blogs mentioning crisis have not increased as a proportion of total coverage, but the absolute number of articles mentioning crisis are the salient fact. With more than two hundred articles referencing crisis, in recent years, those who follow education news cannot help but encounter such narratives. Notable also is that, while there are clear spikes in mention of crisis (both in absolute terms and in proportional terms) in 2008 during the financial crisis and 2001 after 9/11, the upward trend was evident and persistent.

19. Education Writers Association, *State of the Education Beat 2016: A Field with a Future* (Washington, DC: Education Writers Association, 2016), https://bit.ly/2LnEfH1.

20. Ethan Hutt, "The Crisis Problem: On the Pervasiveness of Crisis Rhetoric in American Education Research," in *Educational Research: Discourses of Change and Changes of Discourse*, ed. Paul Smeyers and Marc Depaepe (Basel, Switzerland: Springer International, 2016).

21. Diane Stark Rentner, Nancy Kober, and Matthew Frizzell, *Listen to Us: Teacher Views and Voices* (Washington, DC: Center on Education Policy, 2016), https://bit.ly/2uEF8nb; Dana Goldstein, *The Teacher Wars: A History of America's Most Embattled Profession* (New York: Knopf Doubleday, 2014); Kevin K. Kumashiro, *Bad Teacher!: How Blaming Teachers Distorts the Bigger Picture* (New York: Teachers College Press, 2015); Tyack and Cuban, *Tinkering Toward Utopia*.

22. Cited here is a small sample of the work demonstrating the very real power of great schools: David L. Weimer and Michael J. Wolkoff, "School Performance and Housing Values: Using Non-Contiguous District and Incorporation Boundaries to Identify School Effects," *National Tax Journal* 54, no. 2 (2001): 231–53; Lance Lochner and Enrico Moretti, "The Effect of Education on Crime: Evidence from Prison Inmates, Arrests, and Self-Reports," *American Economic Review* 94, no. 1 (2004): 155–89; Lynn Karoly et al., *Investing in Our Children: What*

We Know and Don't Know About the Costs and Benefits of Early Childhood Interventions (Santa Monica, CA: RAND, 1998); Jonathan Gould, "Guardian of Democracy: The Civic Mission of Schools" (Philadelphia: Leonore Annenberg Institute for Civics of the Annenberg Public Policy Center at the University of Pennsylvania and the Campaign for the Civic Mission of Schools, 2011).

23. "Table 202.25. Percentage of 3- and 4-Year-Old Children Enrolled in School, by Race/Ethnicity and State: 2013," National Center for Education Statistics, https://bit.ly/2L0FDmR.

24. NAEP is administered every two years to a sample of fourth-, eighth-, and twelfth-grade students in each state who are carefully selected to be representative of the students in that state. NAEP scores therefore provide an estimate of what students in that state know, and allow researchers and policy makers to make between-state comparisons that could not as easily be made using any other assessment. State assessments cannot serve this function because they are quite different from one another, and even when they are shared or similar, standards for proficiency can be set at different levels. Other assessments, like the SAT and the ACT, are taken by selected groups of students—every high school student in many states and only the more ambitious college-bound students in others—and so again these cannot easily be used to compare student achievement in each state. NAEP itself has been administered to all fifty states only since NCLB was enacted in 2002, meaning that prior to this point NAEP comparison could be leveraged only for the states that volunteered to participate in the testing.

25. "2015 Mathematics & Reading Math Assessments," The Nation's Report Card, https://bit.ly/2pTwnW6.

26. "Table 219.35. Public High School Averaged Freshman Graduation Rate (AFGR), by State or Jurisdiction: Selected Years, 1990–91 Through 2012–13," National Center for Education Statistics, https://bit.ly/2uCEQNS.

27. Jennifer L. Hochschild, "Social Class in Public Schools," *Journal of Social Issues* 59, no. 4 (2003): 821–40, http://dx.doi.org/10.1046/j.0022-4537.2003.00092.x

28. Sheila E. Murray, William N. Evans, and Robert M. Schwab, "Education-Finance Reform and the Distribution of Education Resources," *American Economic Review* 88, no. 4 (1998): 789–812.

29. Kathryn A. McDermott, "The Expansion of State Policy Research," in *The Handbook of Education Policy Research*, ed. Gary Sykes, Barbara Schneider, and David N. Plank (New York: Routledge, 2009), 749–66.

30. At least one state, Connecticut, requires school districts to measure, report, and limit racial imbalance in student assignment to schools. Al Baker, "Law on Racial Diversity Stirs Greenwich Schools," *New York Times*, July 19, 2013, https://nyti.ms/2L2bEL5.

31. Margaret E. Goertz, "Implementing the No Child Left Behind Act: Challenges for the States," *Peabody Journal of Education* 80, no. 2 (2005): 73–89; Paul Manna and Patrick McGuinn, eds., *Education Governance for the Twenty-First Century: Overcoming the Structural Barriers to School Reform* (Washington, DC: Brookings Institution Press, 2013).

32. Bernard Dafflon, "The Assignment of Functions to Decentralized Government: From Theory to Practice," in *Handbook of Fiscal Federalism*, ed. Ehtisham Ahmad and Giorgio Brosio (Cheltenham, UK: Edward Elgar Publishing, 2006); Rémy Prud'homme, "The Dangers of Decentralization," *World Bank Research Observer* 10, no. 2 (1995): 201–20.

33. Anne Hyslop, *The Case Against Exit Exams* (Washington, DC: New America, 2014), https://bit.ly/2JsaqDf.

34. Aditi Sen, "State Takeovers of Low-Performing Schools: A Record of Academic Failure, Financial Mismanagement, and Student Harm" (New York: Center for Popular Democracy, 2016), https://bit.ly/29W2FHf.

35. Mary L. Mason and Sarah Reckhow, "Rootless Reforms? State Takeovers and School Governance in Detroit and Memphis," *Peabody Journal of Education* 92, no. 1 (2017): 64–75, https://doi.org/10.1080/0161956X.2016.1264813.

36. Denisa R. Superville, "Chicago's Local School Councils 'Experiment' Endures 25 Years of Change," *Education Week*, October 8, 2014, https://bit.ly/2KRHA4H.

37. Stuart Luppescu et al., "Trends in Chicago's Schools Across Three Eras of Reform" (Chicago: University of Chicago, Consortium on Chicago School Research, 2011), https://bit.ly/2uE12qW.

38. Amy Stuart Wells, Lauren Fox, and Diana Cordova-Cobo, *How Racially Diverse Schools and Classrooms Can Benefit All Students* (Washington, DC: The Century Foundation, 2016); George Bohrnstedt, *School Composition and the Black–White Achievement Gap* (Washington, DC: National Center for Education Statistics, 2015), https://bit.ly/1kmOeOE.

39. Barry Yeoman, "Why North Carolina Schools Are Talking Secession," CityLab, February 16, 2018, https://bit.ly/2EwS0j3.

40. Hugh Macartney and John D. Singleton, "School Boards and Student Segregation," *Journal of Public Economics* 164 (2018): 165–82, https://doi.org/10.1016/j.jpubeco.2018.05.011; Tomas Monarrez, "Attendance Boundary Policy and the Segregation of Public Schools in the United States" (working paper, Department of Economics, University of California Berkeley, 2018), https://bit.ly/2wqb2p8; Salvatore Saporito and David Van Riper, "Do Irregularly Shaped School Attendance Zones Contribute to Racial Segregation or Integration?" *Social Currents* 3, no. 1 (2016): 64–83, https://doi.org/10.1177/2329496515604637; Meredith P. Richards, "The Gerrymandering of School Attendance Zones and the Segregation of Public Schools: A Geospatial Analysis," *American Educational Research Journal* 51, no. 6 (2014): 1119–57, https://doi.org/10.3102/0002831214553652.

41. Macartney and Singleton, "School Boards and Student Segregation."

42. Baker, "Law on Racial Diversity."

43. Elinor Ostrom, "Civic Education for the Next Century: A Task Force to Initiate Professional Activity," *PS, Political Science & Politics* 29, no. 4 (1996): 755.

Appendix

1. Mark W. Frank, "Inequality and Growth in the United States: Evidence from a New State-Level Panel of Income Inequality Measures," *Economic Inquiry* 47, no. 1 (2009): 55–68.

2. "2012 Census of Governments," United States Census Bureau, 2013, https://www.census.gov/programs-surveys/cog.html.

3. These data are gathered from the US Bureau of Economic Analysis. See FRED (Federal Reserve Bank of St. Louis Economic Research), "Per Capita Personal Income," US Bureau of Economic Analysis, https://fred.stlouisfed.org/.

4. "US Business Cycle Expansions and Contractions," National Bureau of Economic Research, http://www.nber.org/cycles.html.

Acknowledgments

The first glimmer of insight for this project struck me during a planning period while I was working as a middle school special education teacher in South Texas. Schools all over Texas were adjusting to the state's new (NCLB-compliant) accountability system, and in that environment, I grew impatient with paperwork and practice exams that felt excessive. My students were funny and bright, yet as eleven- and twelve-year-olds they struggled with basic reading. They needed intensive emotional and academic support. Every minute of class time was precious, so daylong, grade-level practice exams felt like a cruel joke. As a young teacher, I had little choice but to shrug off my frustration and shake my head at the irony of confronting a dense regulatory environment in Texas. Everything is bigger in Texas, except, proudly, its government: there is no income tax, and the legislature meets only every other year.

I found the luxury of time to contemplate this contradiction when I enrolled in graduate school at the University of Wisconsin–Madison. In the second year of my doctoral studies, I enrolled in a course on educational politics. Speaking to the class, a leader from the Wisconsin Department of Public Instruction described the state education agency's efforts to implement NCLB in a way that protected local districts' autonomy and minimized impact on teachers and classrooms. Wisconsin, at least at the time, was not known as a small-government state, and the contrast between NCLB in Texas and NCLB in Wisconsin gnawed at me.

Mentors and friends at UW-Madison helped me to translate that puzzle into a more concrete research plan and eventually a doctoral thesis. I am especially grateful to the incomparable and indomitable John Witte, and to David Weimer, Kenneth Goldstein, Geoffrey Borman, and Bobbi Wolfe, who all sat on my dissertation committee. They offered sage advice and encouragement, and they each modeled in their own way what it means to be an

Acknowledgments

engaged scholar and teacher. Deb McFarland and Mary Tedeschi provided administrative support and good humor, and schooled me in the ways of the Badger State.

The US Department of Education funded two years of my doctoral training at UW-Madison through the Interdisciplinary Training Program (ITP) for Predoctoral Research in the Education Sciences (award R305B090009). Adam Gamoran built ITP and created a vibrant intellectual community for graduate students. He is a paragon of generous leadership.

Lesley Lavery, Dominique Bradley, Deven Carlson, Jared Knowles, Jess Clayton, Dimitri Kelly, Yujin Kim, Geraldine O'Mahoney, Lacy Ferrell, and Rachel Feldman walked (and sometimes ran) alongside me throughout graduate school. I do not see them as often as I would like, but they contributed in myriad ways to whatever success I can claim. I am grateful to call such people my friends.

The community at Wake Forest University in North Carolina has provided further support, both financial and practical, helping me to make this project something more than a doctoral thesis. My colleagues in Politics and International Affairs have built a dynamic, truly collegial department, and I have been lucky to be a part of it. Helga Welsh, Katy Harriger, Kathy Smith, David Coates, Betina Wilkinson, Michael Pisapia, Melissa Harris-Perry, Rogan Kersh, Will Walldorf, and Elide Vargas have offered me special encouragement at various junctures.

Alan Brown, Sharee Fowler, and many others have helped me navigate Winston-Salem and make sense of politics and policy in North Carolina. Karin Friedrich, Mary Good, Brian Burke, Annalise Glauz-Todrank, and Sarah Fick have become close friends as we've climbed mountains and graded papers together in our new home state. Enthusiastic students in my Politics of Education class have posed insightful questions semester after semester, reliably leading me toward a different set of ideas than the ones with which I began. Maeve Coyle, Anthony Myers, Brittany Vazquez, Elizabeth Busby, Kathryn Norcross, Mankaprr Conteh, Rance Orrell, Anujan Jeevaprakesh, Eugenia Huang, and Amy Weinstock deserve special thanks for going above and beyond as conversation partners or research assistants.

Rick Hess has connected me with engaging practitioners and scholars of all stripes and reminded me how important it is to get to the point with as little jargon as possible. Caroline Chauncey at Harvard Education Press has guided me with warmth, patience, and constructive criticism. I have read many acknowledgments in which authors gush about their editors. I can now say with confidence that I understand the sentiment.

Equal parts apology and thank you to my friends, family, and partner, who certainly deserve more from me than they have gotten in the last few years while my mind has been occupied by the questions of this book: the Looneys, whom I love dearly and who have provided me a home away from home in three different Census regions; Angelina Chan, who sends the best and brightest of care packages; Amy Beth Coggins, who knew she wanted to be a teacher in our freshman year of college; my brilliant sister, Ellen, who has displayed an unwavering faith in me, even when I was quite sure that all of the available evidence undermined her position; and Guy Witzel, who has radically transformed my thinking and my heart.

My grandparents, Mahlon and Dee, passed away as I was working to finish this manuscript, and I regret that they will not get to see a finished product. A long-time professor at Marshall University, my grandfather was a significant reason I thought to enter the academy at all, and I will miss his stories about the joy of teaching—and pranking—university students. He and my grandmother were my steadfast cheerleaders for as long as I can remember.

Finally, whatever good there is to be found in these pages belongs without question or hesitation to my parents, Nancy Dahill and Bill Brown. With each passing year, my extraordinary good fortune becomes more and more undeniable. Errors and omissions are mine alone.

About the Author

Sara E. Dahill-Brown is an associate professor in the politics and international affairs department at Wake Forest University. She is an alumna of Utah's public schools and a recovering Texas middle school teacher. She has worked as a researcher and volunteer in the school systems of Wisconsin, where she earned her doctorate, and North Carolina, where she now lives. Her writing has appeared in the *Russell Sage Journal of the Social Sciences*, *Studies in Educational Evaluation*, and *Politics and Policy*.

Index